Eisenhower and American Public Opinion on China

Mara Oliva

Eisenhower and American Public Opinion on China

palgrave
macmillan

Mara Oliva
Department of History
University of Reading
Reading, UK

ISBN 978-3-319-76194-7   ISBN 978-3-319-76195-4   (eBook)
https://doi.org/10.1007/978-3-319-76195-4

Library of Congress Control Number: 2018935697

Cover credit: Everett Collection Historical / Alamy Stock Photo

Printed on acid-free paper

This Palgrave Macmillan imprint is published by the registered company Springer International
Publishing AG part of Springer Nature.
The registered company address is: Gewerbestrasse 11, 6330 Cham, Switzerland

To Jordi,
my Love, my Life, my Everything

ACKNOWLEDGMENTS

The best thing about completing a book is the opportunity to express my gratitude to the many people who made it possible; to all those who provided support, talked things over, read, offered comments, assisted in the editing, proofreading, and design.

This monograph is the result of my Doctor of Philosophy work, therefore, my first thank you goes to Professor Iwan Morgan. He has been an excellent supervisor, whose careful review and incisive comments sharpened my thinking on every facet of this project. I have greatly benefited from the ideas, suggestions, and support of many at the University of London. I would like to particularly thank Professor Steven Casey, whose advice was crucial during the early stages of this project and Professor Mark J. White, who has been a generous mentor in supporting the development of my academic career.

The American Politics Group family, and particularly Professor Philip Davies, has been so much more than just a learned society. Friends and colleagues have given me precious advice on how to transition from a PhD student to an early career researcher and navigate the world of modern academia. I am forever grateful for their time and support.

Since 2008, I have had the privilege of teaching at many brilliant higher education institutions: Queen Mary, University of London, University of Portsmouth, Canterbury Christ Church University, and University of Reading. The friendly atmosphere at these universities has made the task of completing my book a more enjoyable experience. I would like to thank all my undergraduate and postgraduate students whose enthusiasm for the subject helped to sustain my own interest over the years.

During the course of my research, I have visited many libraries and archives. All the librarians have been extremely helpful, but I would particularly like to thank the staff at the Eisenhower Library in Kansas and at the Tamiment Library at New York University.

My research in the United States was made possible thanks to the financial support of the British Association of American Studies, the University of London Central Research Fund, the Institute for the Study of the America, School of Advanced Study, the Royal Historical Society, the UK Fulbright Commission, the Scouloudi Historical Awards, Institute of Historical Research, and the University of Reading.

Finally, a special thank you to everyone at Palgrave, especially Christine Pardue, for their work and assistance.

There would be no book without the immeasurable support of my family and friends. Their unconditional love is my strength!

CONTENTS

LIST OF ABBREVIATIONS

ACPA	American China Policy Association
ADA	Americans for Democratic Action
AP	Associated Press
BBDO	Batten, Barton, Durstine, and Osborn
CCP	Chinese Communist Party
COOM	Committee for One Million Against the Admission of Communist China in the United Nations
GMD	Guomindag
JCS	Joint Chiefs of Staff
NATO	North Atlantic Treaty Organization
NORC	National Opinion Research Center
NSC	National Security Council
PRC	People's Republic of China
ROC	Republic of China
SDBPA	State Department Bureau of Public Affairs
SEATO	Southeast Asia Treaty Organization
SOS	Save Our Sons Committee
UN	United Nations
UNSC	United Nations Security Council
USIA	United States Information Agency

LIST OF ABBREVIATIONS USED IN THE FOOTNOTES

CT   China Telegram
CUNY   Columbia University, New York
DDE   Dwight D. Eisenhower
DDEL   Dwight D. Eisenhower Presidential Library, Abilene, Kansas
DOS   Department of State
DSB   *Department of State Bulletin*
EPP   Eisenhower Public Papers
FRUS   *Foreign Relations of the United States*
JFD   John Foster Dulles
LoC   Library of Congress, Washington, DC
ML   Seely G. Mudd Library, Princeton, New Jersey
NAII   National Archives II, College Park, Maryland
NYU   New York University, New York

LIST OF FIGURES

LIST OF TABLES

.

CHAPTER 1

Introduction

In November 1943, Columbia University professor and China expert Nathaniel Peffer wrote an article for The *New York Times Magazine* entitled: "Our Distorted View of China," in which he accused missionaries, businessmen, and other Americans who had lived in China of having a sentimental predisposition about everything Chinese. In his view, that had led to the construction of an idealized image of China, as a country willing to embrace American Christianity, medical aid, and political ideas, that in the end, "more harm than good would come out to Sino-American relations."[1]

Peffer's ill-fated prediction came true on October 1, 1949, when the Communists took over mainland China and forced US ally, Nationalist leader Generalissimo Jiang Jieshi (Chiang Kai-shek),[2] to withdraw to the

---

[1] Nathaniel Peffer, "Our Distorted Image of China," The *New York Times Magazine*, November 7, 1943; Christopher Jespersen, *American Images of China, 1931–1949* (Stanford: Stanford University Press, 1996), 74.

[2] Chinese personal names, place names, and sources are given in pinyin with the original version in brackets when mentioned for the first time.

Parts of this chapter were originally published in Mara Oliva, "Beaten at Their Own Game: Eisenhower, Dulles, US Public Opinion and the Sino-American Ambassadorial Talks of 1955–1957," *Journal of Cold War Studies* 20 (2018): forthcoming.

island of Taiwan (Formosa). America's self-centered image of China prevented it from realizing that Chinese politics were far more complex than was imagined. It was absolutely inconceivable to Americans that the Chinese people had voluntarily chosen communism. The only plausible explanation was that Communism had been imposed on them because they had fallen victims to an international conspiracy orchestrated by Moscow. That belief triggered a painful witch-hunt that was famously and shamefully exploited by Wisconsin Republican Senator Joseph McCarthy.[3]

McCarthy's search for culprits for the "loss of China" combined with the Truman administration's negative propaganda campaign against the People's Republic of China (PRC) to rally support for the American effort in the Korean War and the terrible stories of atrocities from the front strengthened the already hostile feelings among the American people toward the Chinese Communists. According to several National Opinion Research Center surveys and Gallup polls conducted in the first half of 1950, 62–12% of the general public opposed diplomatic recognition of the Beijing (Peiping) regime, 78% of the respondents opposed the PRC's admission into the United Nations and 76% opposed trade relations with Communist China.[4]

The vast historiography on the presidency of Dwight D. Eisenhower and China policy in the 1950s has often blamed that hostile public opinion for the tensions and the lack of diplomatic relations between the US and the PRC. For example, political scientist Hans Morgenthau described US policy toward mainland China as "irrational." He believed that Washington officials, including the President, wanted to recognize Beijing's regime, but the administration was prevented "by its fears of public opinion from devising and executing a positive policy of its own." Similarly, political scientist Leonard Kusnitz, in his extensive quantitative study of US public opinion and America's China policy between 1949 and

[3] Amy Kaplan, "Left Alone with America," in *Cultures of United States Imperialism,* ed. Amy Kaplan et al. (Durham: Durham University Press, 1993), 16.

[4] Steven Casey, *Selling the Korean War* (Oxford: Oxford University Press, 2008); China Telegram, January through June 1950, Records of the State Department Bureau of Public Affairs, 1954, AI568P, box 29, National Archives II, College Park, Maryland (hereafter DOS, followed by the file reference, box number, and NAII). The China Telegram was a weekly analysis of Congressional, press and public opinion on foreign policy issues in Asia compiled by the State Department Office of Public Opinion. It was distributed to the White House, the State Department, and was also sent to the US embassies and consulates throughout the world.

1979, has argued that Eisenhower tried to push changes in China policy, particularly during his second term, but popular hostility blocked any openings toward the Chinese Communists.[5]

More recently, David Mayers and Rosemary Foot have contended that conservative opinion in the US, represented by the Republican right wing in Congress, was also very influential in preventing alteration in policy toward the PRC. According to both, the President understood as early as 1953 that a review of China policy was necessary. However, pursuing a policy even remotely hinting of conciliation with Mao Zedong (Mao Tse-tung) would have meant challenging McCarthy's wing of the Republican party, something Eisenhower was not willing to do. Foot further argues that the White House had to wait until the mid-1960s to reassess China policy. It took the Sino-Soviet split combined with Beijing's newly acquired nuclear capability and the perception that the American strategy had become ineffective for Congress to finally launch its own investigation and the Council of Foreign Relations to initiate a series of studies on the PRC.[6]

Historian Nancy Bernkopf Tucker went even further in arguing that China was not a major concern for Eisenhower. The President was first and foremost an Atlanticist and believed that the most serious challenge for the US would come from the Soviet Union, not the PRC. His minor interest in Communist China was reflected in a lack of an adequate under-standing of the American public's views of Beijing. He therefore "pursued policies toward China that he did not believe in wholeheartedly because he thought public opinion wanted a hard line stance against Beijing." This ultimately led to a muddled and disappointing approach to China policy.[7]

The historiography has also put more emphasis on the role played by Secretary of State John Foster Dulles in shaping China policy. Many, including Tucker and Steven Goldstein, argued that Dulles was the major

[5] Hans Morgenthau, "John Foster Dulles" in *An Uncertain Tradition: American Secretaries of State in the Twentieth Century,* ed. Norman A. Graebner (New York: McGraw Hill, 1961), 302; Leonard A. Kusnitz, *Public Opinion and Foreign Policy: America's China Policy 1949–1979* (Westport: Greenwood Press, 1984).

[6] David Mayers, *Cracking the Monolith: US Policy Against the Sino-Soviet Alliance, 1946–1955* (Baton Rouge: Louisiana State University Press, 1986); Rosemary Foot, *The Practice of Power: US Relations with China since 1949* (Oxford: Oxford University Press, 1997); and "The Eisenhower Administration's Fear of Empowering the Chinese," *Political Science Quarterly* 111 (1996): 505–522.

[7] Nancy Bernkopf Tucker, *The China Threat: Memories, Myths and Realities in the 1950s* (New York: Columbia University Press, 2012), 22.

force in formulating China policy. Similar to the President, he was a prisoner of pressure groups, such as the Committee of One Million against the Admission of the PRC in the United Nations, which had replaced the China Lobby in Congress to advocate support for the Nationalist regime on the island of Taiwan since 1953.[8]

The purpose of this book is to show that the role that domestic public opinion played in shaping US-China relations in the 1950s has been greatly understudied and misinterpreted. Contrary to traditional historiography, it argues that the Eisenhower administration's hard line policy toward Beijing had been formulated in line with US national security interests and not as a result of pressure from popular feelings. While public opinion opposed relaxing tensions with the PRC until the middle of 1955, the first Taiwan crisis of 1954–1955 combined with Senator McCarthy's fall from grace marked a turning point in US popular attitudes toward Beijing. The military crisis particularly forced a significant change in public opinion, not so much a change in how Americans saw the Chinese Communists, but a change in how to deal with the enemy. In the summer of 1954, an overwhelming number of the public, 85%, saw Moscow as the main US enemy. In the spring of 1955, immediately after the threat over the Straits ended, the State Department reported that six out of 10 Americans interviewed considered Communist China to be more dangerous than the Soviet Union and thought World War III would "break out" fairly soon because of the PRC. The same survey also found that 73% of Americans interviewed believed that rather than continuing to antagonize Beijing, it would be better to enter into talks "in order to avoid another global conflict." President Eisenhower was fully aware of the changing public opinion. An investigation of his public and private papers clearly shows that he kept a careful eye on public opinion in general and more specifically on its views on China. Had he wanted to implement a more flexible policy toward Beijing, he knew he had enough public support.[9]

Revisionist and post-revisionist scholars such as Fred Greenstein, Stephen Ambrose, and Martin Medhurst have already amply demonstrated how the President intentionally projected an image of warmth and

[8] Tucker, *The China Threat*; Steven Goldstein, "Dialogue of the Deaf? The Sino-American Ambassadorial Level Talks, 1955–1970," in *Re-Examining the Cold War: US-China Diplomacy, 1953–1973*, ed. Robert S. Ross et al. (Cambridge: Harvard University Press, 2001); for more information on the China Lobby see Ross Koen, *The China Lobby in American Politics* (New York: Macmillan, 1960).

[9] China Telegram, August 7 through 14, DOS, AI568P, box 29, NAII.

used garbled syntax to deflect criticism, avoid polarization, and retain flexibility to implement his policies. Likewise, they have also dispelled the myth of a US foreign policy being dominated by John Foster Dulles. As historian Richard Immerman asserts, the two men 'were in a real sense a team,' because they both shared the same fundamental outlook about international relations and the role the US should play in it. While in public, the President might have given the impression that the GOP and popular feelings or Dulles' beliefs shaped his China policy, he was in reality in full control of the foreign policy making process.[10]

Eisenhower believed that the US position in the Far East had considerably weakened since the end of World War II. First, the outcome of the Korean War had elevated Communist China's image within the Soviet sphere and in Southeast Asia, thereby diminishing US prestige. Second, the PRC was an emergent threat to the US in Asia and had widened the divisions among Western allies. This re-evaluation of China's role in international relations meant that the "bipolarity which distinguished the immediate post-hostilities period was losing much of its rationale" and Beijing had become a power to be reckoned with. Although a strong China could also create problems for the Kremlin, ultimately, the President believed that the Chinese Communists, as Communists, would continue to maintain a basic hostility for the West in general, and particularly the US.[11]

Secretary of State Dulles concurred with the President. A Communist China, whether allied with the Soviet Union or not, represented a national security issue for the US in Asia. The US goal was therefore to secure, through a hard line policy, a re-orientation of the Chinese Communist Regime that would not be hostile to the US. That was not possible in the 1950s because China's military capacities made the invasion of its territory

---

[10] Stephen Ambrose, *Eisenhower, The President, 1952–1959* (London: Allen and Unwind, 1984); Fred Greenstein, *The Hidden-Hand Presidency: Eisenhower as a Leader* (New York: Basic Books, 1982); Martin Medhurst, *Dwight D. Eisenhower: Strategic Communicator* (Westport: Greenwood, 1993); Richard Immerman, ed., *John Foster Dulles and the Diplomacy of Cold War* (Princeton: Princeton University Press, 1990).

[11] "Notes on NSC meeting", August 24, 1953, Dwight D. Eisenhower Papers, Subject Series, box 9, Dwight D. Eisenhower Presidential Library, Abilene, Kansas, US (hereafter DDEL); "CIA Special Estimate on Probable Consequences of the Death of Stalin and the Elevation of Melankov to leadership in the USSR", CD Jackson Papers, March 10, 1953, box 1, DDEL; Memorandum of Discussion at 169 meeting of NSC, November 5, 1953, *Foreign Relations of the United States*, XIX, 1952–1954 (Washington, DC: US Government Printing Office, 1985): 347–369 (hereafter *FRUS* followed by volume, date and page number).

costly and required a commitment of forces that the US was not ready to make after the Korean War. In the absence of future Chinese Communist aggression or a basic change in the situation, the two men agreed that the main target of US policy should be to weaken or retard the growth of the PRC, which would also have the added benefit of putting pressure on Beijing's alliance with Moscow and possibly drive a wedge between the two Communist giants.[12]

In practice, that resulted in the decision to reject the establishment of diplomatic relations with Beijing, continue the total trade embargo imposed at the outbreak of the Korean War, and oppose Communist China's admission to the United Nations. It also led to the removal of the Seventh Fleet from patrolling the Taiwan Straits in 1953; a move meant to signal to the communist world the intention of the US to regain the initiative in the Pacific. It negatively influenced the talks at the Geneva conference on Korea and Indochina in 1954, where the US behaved in a consistently obstructionist manner and resisted giving the negotiations the slightest opportunity. Additionally, it finally culminated in the two military crises over the Taiwan Straits in 1955 and in 1958, which brought the world to the brink of nuclear war.

How did the President and the Secretary of State reconcile their hard line policy with the support of public opinion for a relaxation of tensions following the first Taiwan crisis? What attempts did they make to generate public support for their tough stance? In turn, how did popular feeling affect the administration's thinking? And, what impact did the interaction between government officials and domestic public opinion have on Sino-American relations and the broader Cold War in the 1950s? Political scientists Ira Chernus and Chris Tudda have argued that Eisenhower's attempts at maintaining national unity and support for his foreign policy often created a paradox. Although the President's rhetorical diplomacy was directed at creating peace, it instead increased tensions between Washington and Moscow. Eisenhower privately rejected military liberation as impractical and dangerous, but his rhetorical diplomacy involved the use of belligerent words in private meetings with allied and Soviet officials, as well as in public speeches, addresses, and conferences. By constantly emphasizing the threat from the Soviet Union, he tried to persuade the US public and the North Atlantic Treaty Organization allies to maintain an active foreign policy, but at the same time made the Union of

---

[12] Ibid.

Soviet Social Republics more insecure, thus increasing its hostility toward the West. Did his rhetoric on China have the same effect on Beijing?[13]

To better understand the interaction between domestic public opinion and the Eisenhower administration's China policy, we need to briefly look at the persisting debate in American politics and international relations surrounding the public's role in determining foreign policy. Classically, that debate has been divided broadly between liberal democrats, such as philosopher Jeremy Bentham and President Woodrow Wilson, who believed public opinion should always influence foreign policy decision making because of its capacity to act as a brake on an overambitious and adventurous leaders; and realists, such as journalist Walter Lippmann and political scientist Gabriel Almond, who considered public opinion to be ignorant, amorphous, and dominated by emotions and, therefore, a dangerous constraint on policy makers' freedom to reach the right decision.[14]

In the past twenty years, a third approach has emerged to occupy a position between the liberal-democratic tradition and what political scientist Ole Holsti has termed the "Lippmann-Almond Consensus." Its adherents argue that foreign policy makers always take public opinion into consideration but in such a way that narrows their options rather than determines choices. Those scholars believe that public opinion does not lead to a selection of one specific policy, but it sets "the parameters of acceptable alternatives" by eliminating one or more policies. As political scientist Bruce Russett observed, "public opinion sets the broad limits of the constraint, identifying a range of policies in which they must choose, if they are not to face rejection in the voting booths." Similarly, Thomas Graham contends that "public opinion influences presidential decisions primarily about tactics, timing and political communication strategy, rather than determining the ultimate goals of an administration's foreign

[13] Ira Chernus, *Eisenhower's Atoms for Peace* (College Station: Texas A&M University Press, 2002); Chris Tudda, "Re-Enacting the Story of Tantalus: Eisenhower, Dulles and the Failed Rhetoric of Liberation," *Journal of Cold War Studies* 7 (2005): 3–35; and *The Truth Is Our Weapon: The Rhetorical Diplomacy of Dwight D. Eisenhower and John Foster Dulles* (Baton Rouge: Louisiana State University Press, 2006); Mara Oliva, "The Oratory of Dwight D. Eisenhower," in *Republican Orators from Eisenhower to Trump*, ed. Andrew S. Crines et al. (New York: Palgrave Macmillan, 2018):11–39.

[14] Hans Reiss ed., *Kant's Political Writings* (Cambridge: Cambridge University Press, 1990); Nicholas G. Herbert, "Building on the Wilsonian Heritage," in *Woodrow Wilson*, ed. Arthur Link (New York: Hill and Wang, 1968); Walter Lippmann, *Public Opinion* (New York: Macmillan, 1922); *Essays in Public Philosophy* (New York: Macmillan, 1955); Gabriel Almond, *The American People and Foreign Policy* (New York: Praeger, 1950).

policy." That connection is better described as an "interaction": leaders both react to and manipulate public opinion.[15]

What did Eisenhower and Dulles think about the role that public opinion played in foreign policy? To what extent did the public's thinking have an impact on their China policy? Did it influence their entire foreign policy strategy? Did it limit their choice of options? Or, did it only shape the implementation, the timing, and the communication tactics?

One of the challenges of establishing the impact that public opinion had on the Eisenhower administration's China policy is to define public opinion. Social scientist V.O. Key defined public opinion as "those opinions held by private persons which Governments find it prudent to heed." Political scientist Philip Powlick noted that that definition raises more questions than it answers. Which opinion? Which issues? Which private citizens? According to Gabriel Almond and Bernard Cohen, those are the people who are interested in foreign affairs and, more importantly, are highly knowledgeable in foreign affairs. Through social and political circuits, those "elite" have access to foreign policy makers and, therefore, are a source of public opinion and are able to influence policy outcome.[16]

What about the rest of the population? Is the mass public too emotional and too ignorant, as argued by realist Mongethau, to offer informed views on foreign policy? Or is Rousseau correct in claiming that citizens express their foreign policy views by electing officials who act as delegates? For example, in the US, Congress is the true representative of the people's wishes.[17]

---

[15] Ole R. Holsti, "Public Opinion and Foreign Policy: Challenges to the Almond-Lippmann Consensus," Mershon Series: Research Program Debates, *International Studies Quarterly* 36 (1992): 439–466; Bruce Russett, *Controlling the Sword: The Democratic Governance of National Security* (Cambridge: Harvard University Press, 1990): 110; Douglass C. Foyle, *Counting the Public In: Presidents, Public Opinion, and Foreign Policy* (New York: Columbia University Press, 1999); Thomas W. Graham, "Public Opinion and US Foreign Policy Decision Making," in *The New Politics of American Foreign Policy,* ed. David Deese (New York: St Martin's Press, 1994): 201; Steven Casey, *Cautious Crusades: Franklin D. Roosevelt, American Public Opinion, and the War Against Nazi Germany* (Oxford: Oxford University Press, 2001).

[16] V.O. Key, *Public Opinion and American Democracy* (New York: Alfred Kopf, 1964); Philip Powlick, "The Sources of Public Opinion for American Foreign Policy Officials," *International Studies Quarterly* 39 (1995): 427–451; Gabriel Almond, *The American People and Foreign Policy;* Bernard Cohen, *The Public's Impact on Foreign Policy* (Boston: Little, Brown and Company, 1973).

[17] Powlick, "The Sources of Public Opinion for American Foreign Policy Officials," 429.

Media are often considered both a part of public opinion and one of the main influences on popular feelings. The decision to cover a certain foreign policy issue as well as how to cover it can shape the public's reaction to it and propel it to the front page of a newspaper or land it in oblivion. In the specific case of reporting on China in the 1950s, the Eisenhower administration was in a very powerful position to direct the news agenda. First, it was the high point of "objective" journalism whereby reporters based their stories on hard evidence and attributable sources. Accordingly, journalists regularly attended the White House and the State Department's briefings and press conferences. Second, the administration propaganda efforts received plenty of support from a very friendly press led by *Time* and *Life* magazines publisher, Henry R. Luce, a staunch supporter of Nationalist leader Jiang Jieshi who was opposed to Mao's regime. Finally, American correspondents were forbidden to travel to Communist China because Beijing had made foreign press accreditation dependent on the establishment of diplomatic relations with relevant foreign government and because of the US travel ban issued at the outbreak of the Korean War. With no direct access to news sources, US reporters depended on official information put out by the government, thus making them very susceptible to attempts to manipulate the news.[18]

The main purpose of this book, however, is not to make an objective evaluation of popular thinking, but to determine the influence on the administration's policy. Its definition of public opinion, therefore, is limited to whether Eisenhower and Dulles considered it to be. To that end, only public opinion data commissioned or accessed by the President or the Secretary of State has been used to support the argument.

The work of political scientist Douglas Foyle is a useful tool in this instance. Foyle argued that to establish the extent of the influence of popular feelings on a given foreign policy, it is necessary to uncover the normative and practical beliefs of the decision maker. Normative beliefs are "an individual's judgment concerning the desirability of input from public opinion affecting foreign policy." Practical beliefs are a person's "assessment

[18] Powlick, "The Sources of Public Opinion for American Foreign Officials," 429; Iyengar Shanto and Donald Kinder, *News That Matters* (Chicago: University of Chicago Press, 1987); Bernard Cohen, *The Press and Foreign Policy* (Princeton: Princeton University Press, 1963); Douglass Carter, *The Fourth Branch of Government* (Boston: Houghton Mifflin, 1959); Leon Sigal, *Reporters and Officials: The Organizations and the Politics of Newsmaking* (Lexington: Heath, 1973); Chang Tsan-kou, The Press and China Policy: The Illusion of Sino-American Relations, 1950–1984 (Norwood: Ablex Pub. Co., 1983).

of the necessity of public support of a foreign policy issue for it to be successful."[19]

Chapter 2, therefore, begins to look at Eisenhower and Dulles's sensitivity to, and perception of, public opinion during the 1952 presidential campaign. Fully aware of the American people's discontent and frustration over the stalemate in Korea, the Republican Party candidate Eisenhower endorsed the Asia-first foreign policy plank written by aspiring Secretary of State Dulles. Together, they made "the loss of China" the key issue of the campaign and successfully blamed the Truman administration for America's loss of prestige abroad, and communist infiltration at home. But, was the rhetoric a reiteration of their private views? Or did they tailor their message to please the electorate and gain more votes?

Chapter 3 explores the Eisenhower administration's first year in the White House. First, it considers how the views of the President and the Secretary of State regarding the role that public opinion should play in the foreign policy-making process changed once they assumed office. It then examines the opinion-tracking channels they developed, the credence they gave to them, and the information they conveyed. Finally, it looks at the impact that the mass attitudes had on the administration's formulation of foreign policy toward Communist China and the extent to which domestic opinion determined the choices that Eisenhower and Dulles made in 1953.

Chapters 4, 5, 6, and 7 look at the implementation of the administration's China policy, how that was communicated to the public, and how in turn, the reaction of public opinion shaped Washington's strategy and propaganda efforts, and ultimately Sino-American relations. Chapters 4 and 5 focus on the Dienbienphu military crisis of 1954 and the first Taiwan crisis of 1955, respectively. Those crises represented the dilemma that plagued the administration's China policy throughout its eight years. If the US became involved in another limited war, much like the Korean conflict, the White House faced the prospect that a war-weary public would turn against its policy. However, doing nothing and risking losing yet another country to the Communists meant appearing weak in the eyes of domestic public opinion as well as allies and enemies. How did the administration's private and public image of the PRC change during the military crises? How did it present the enemy to the public? What consequences did its rhetoric have on the public and the enemy? How did the

---

[19] Foyle, *Counting the Public In*, 9–10.

public react to the danger of war? To what extent did those crises impinge on the 1954 mid-term elections?

Chapter 6 analyzes the consequences of the nuclear war scare triggered by the first Taiwan crisis. It focuses particularly on the Sino-American Ambassadorial talks held in Geneva between 1955 and 1957. Although they were highly supported by the American public, the negotiations proved to be inconclusive because of Washington's inflexibility and refusal to relax the total trade embargo implemented in 1951 and allow free travel and cultural exchange with Beijing. What attempts did the administration make to rally support or, at least, justify its policy to the public? And, how did the lack of domestic support affect the talks?

The last chapter looks at public discontent with Eisenhower's China policy that plagued the last years of his presidency. The calls for reassessment of Sino-American relations, which began at the end of the first Taiwan crisis, intensified through 1958 and reached a peak when the Chinese Communists began shelling the offshore islands for a second time in the autumn of that year. While support for establishing diplomatic relations with Beijing and its admission to the United Nations never reached an overall national majority, removal of the trade embargo and negotiations to minimize tensions and lower the risk of nuclear conflict were advocated by an overwhelming majority in Congress, the press, as well as the general public. Yet the President and the Secretary of State refused to acquiesce to popular demands. They did, however, begin to make concessions, such as allowing relatives of Americans imprisoned in China to travel to Beijing. What effect did that have on US-China policy? Was that the beginning of the long reconciliation process that occurred in the 1960s and eventually led to reconciliation under President Nixon in 1972?

To assess the opinion-policy link, this intensive historical study will employ a qualitative content analysis to explore the administration's propaganda message and two well-established social science techniques, process-tracing and congruence procedure, to determine the impact US public opinion had on the Eisenhower administration's China policy. As Ole Holsti, a political scientist, writes, "intensive case studies shed more direct light on how, if at all, public opinion influences foreign policy." Whereas large-scale quantitative studies such as Kusnitz's are not enough to determine the views of public opinion on a given foreign policy issue, even if they are consistent with the government's actions. Instead, analyzing one foreign policy issue over a limited time, in this case eight years, allows us to trace the evolution of popular feelings and establish if it had the same influence throughout that time or if it changed according to domestic and international variables.[20]

Designed by political scientist Alexander George and successfully employed in Foyle and Casey's works, among others, process tracing and congruence procedure will support the reliability of the findings. By analyzing the private and public papers of Eisenhower and Dulles, we can gain insight on the importance they placed on public opinion and at what stages of their China policy formulation that was considered. Once that has been established, the congruence procedure will then help in determining if there was a link between policy and opinion. For example, if Eisenhower's and Dulles' China policy was consistently opposed to public preferences, then it is clear that feelings did not have an influence on policy. However, if the administration's actions showed some parallelism with public attitudes, then it can be inferred that public opinion might have exercised some influence at one point or another.[21]

As historian Steven Casey has pointed out, there is a risk to the technique, it might attribute exaggerated weight to public opinion. Indeed, finding a correlation between government actions and popular feelings does not mean that there is a link between policy and opinion. The book therefore will also look at one other variable, the international system, to support its argument. Both Eisenhower and Dulles believed that a close relationship with the allies, particularly the British and the French, was essential in the fight against Communsim. However, they also understood the importance of projecting an image of a strong and loyal US to sway neutral countries and international public opinion. Analyzing how those variables influenced their decision-making process will allow us to determine more accurately the role played by US domestic opinion in shaping Sino-American relations in the 1950s. Ultimately, this will not only fill a gap in the current literature, but it will also provide a new prism to explain one of the most difficult decades in the history of those two countries.

---

[20] Holsti, "Challenges to the Almond-Lippmann Consensus," 453; Kusnitz, *Public Opinion and Foreign Policy: America's China Policy 1949–1979.*

[21] Thomas Knecht, *Paying Attention to Foreign Affairs: How Public Opinion Affects Presidential Decision Making* (University Park: Pennsylvania State University Press, 2011).

REFERENCES

Almond, Gabriel. *The American People and Foreign Policy*. New York: Praeger, 1950.

Ambrose, Stephen. *Eisenhower, the President, 1952–1959*. London: Allen and Unwind, 1984.

Bernkopf Tucker, Nancy. *The China Threat: Memories, Myths and Realities in the 1950s*. New York: Columbia University Press, 2012.

Carter, Douglass. *The Fourth Branch Government*. Boston: Houghton Mifflin, 1959.

Casey, Steven. *Cautious Crusades: Franklin D. Roosevelt, American Public Opinion, and the War Against Nazi Germany*. Oxford: Oxford University Press, 2001.

———. *Selling the Korean War*. Oxford: Oxford University Press, 2008.

Chang, Tsnan-kou. *The Press and China Policy: The Illusion of Sino-American Relations, 1950–1984*. Norwood: Ablex Pub. Co., 1983.

Chernus, Ira. *Eisenhower's Atoms for Peace*. College Station: Texas A&M University Press, 2002.

Cohen, Bernard. *The Press and Foreign Policy*. Princeton: Princeton University Press, 1963.

———. *The Public's Impact on Foreign Policy*. Boston: Little, Brown and Company, 1973.

Foot, Rosemary. *The Practice of Power: US Relations with China since 1949*. Oxford: Oxford University Press, 1987.

———. "The Eisenhower Administration's Fear of Empowering the Chinese." *Political Science Quarterly* III (1996): 505–522.

Foyle, Douglass C. *Counting the Public In: Presidents, Public Opinion, and Foreign Policy*. New York: Columbia University Press, 1999.

Goldstein, Steven. "Dialogue of the Deaf? The Sino-American Ambassadorial Level Talks, 1955–1970." In *Re-Examining the Cold War: US-China Diplomacy, 1953–1973*, edited by Robert Ross and Jiang Changbin, 200–238. Cambridge: Harvard University Press, 2001.

Graham, Thomas W. "Public Opinion and US Foreign Policy Decision Making." In *the New Politics of American Foreign Policy*, edited by David Deese. New York: St Martin's Press, 1994.

Greenstein, Fred. *The Hidden-Hand Presidency: Eisenhower as a Leader*. New York: Basic Books, 1982.

Herbert, Nicholas G. "Building on the Wilsonian Heritage." In Woodrow Wilson, edited by Arthur Link. New York: Hill and Wang, 1968.

Holsti, Ole R. "Public Opinion and Foreign Policy: Challenges to the Almond-Lippmann Consensus." *International Studies Quarterly* 36 (1992): 439–466.

Immerman, Richard, ed. *John Foster Dulles and the Diplomacy of Cold War*. Princeton: Princeton University Press, 1990.

Jespersen, Christopher. *America's Images Of China, 1931–1949*. Stanford: Stanford University Press, 1996.

Kaplan, Amy. "Left Alone with America." In *Cultures of United States Imperialism*, edited by Amy Kaplan and Donald Pease, Durham: Durham University Press, 1993.

Key, V.O. *Public Opinion and American Democracy*. New York: Alfred Knopf, 1964.

Knecht, Thomas. *Paying Attention to Foreign Affairs: How Public Opinion Affects Presidential Decision Making*. University Park: Pennsylvania State University Press, 2011.

Koen, Ross. *The China Lobby in American Politics*. New York: Macmillan, 1960.

Kusnitz, Leonard A. *Public Opinion and Foreign Policy: America's China Policy 1949–1979*. Westport: Greenwood Press, 1984.

Lippmann, Walter. *Public Opinion*. New York: Macmillan, 1922.

———. *Essays in Public Philosophy*. New York: Macmillan, 1955.

Mayers, David. *Cracking the Monolith: US Policy Against the Sino-Soviet Alliance, 1946–1955*. Baton Rouge: Louisiana State University Press, 1986.

Medhurst, Martin. *Dwight D. Eisenhower: Strategic Communicator*. Westport: Greenwood, 1993.

Morgenthau, Hans. "John Foster Dulles." In *An Uncertain Tradition: American Secretaries of State in the Twentieth Century*, edited by Norman A. Graebner, 189–308. New York: McGraw Hill, 1961.

Oliva, Mara. "The Oratory of Dwight D. Eisenhower." in *Republican Orators from Eisenhower to Trump*, edited by Andrew S. Crines and Sophia Hatzisavvidou, 11–39. New York: Palgrave Macmillan, 2017.

———. "Beaten at Their Own Game: Eisenhower, Dulles, US Public Opinion and the Sino-Ambassadorial Talks of 1955–1957." *Journal of Cold War Studies* 20, no. 1 (2018).

Powlick, Philip. "The Sources of Public Opinion for American Foreign Policy Officials." *International Studies Quarterly* 39 (1995): 427–451.

Reiss, Hans. *Kant's Political Writings*. Cambridge: Cambridge University Press, 1990.

Russett, Bruce. *Controlling the Sword: The Democratic Governance of National Security*. Cambridge: Harvard University Press, 1990.

Shanto, Iyengar, and Donald Kinder. *News that Matters*. Chicago: University of Chicago Press, 1987.

Sigal, Leon. *Reporters and Officials: The Organisation and Politics of News making*. Lexington: Heath, 1973.

Tudda, Chris. "Re-Enacting the Story of Tantalus: Eisenhower, Dulles and the Failed Rhetoric of Liberation." *Journal of Cold War Studies* 7 (2005): 3–35.

———. *The Truth Is Our Weapon: The Rhetorical Diplomacy of Dwight D. Eisenhower and John Foster Dulles*. Baton Rouge: Louisiana State University Press, 2006.

CHAPTER 2

America's Distorted Image of China

In his memoir, *Present at Creation*, Secretary of State, Dean G. Acheson, perfectly captured America's fascination with China in the early twentieth century: "Hardly a town in our land was without its society to collect funds and clothing for Chinese missions, to worry about those who labored in distant, dangerous and exotic vineyards of the Lord, and to hear the missionaries' inspiring reports."[1] The purpose of this chapter is two-fold. First, it presents a historiographical review of Sino-American relations prior to the 1952 Presidential election. To understand US public opinion toward China in the 1950s, it is necessary to look at how Americans developed an idealized image of China and how that, in turn, ill-prepared them for the shock of the communist takeover of the mainland in 1949 and the unexpected North Korean attack on South Korea in June 1950. Second, this chapter analyzes how those illusions affected the US domestic political debate and influenced the 1952 Presidential contest. No other aspect of American foreign affairs was more deeply involved in domestic politics than US-China relations.

As historians Michael Hunt and Christopher Jespersen have explained, at the root of the idea that China needed America and that the Chinese people wanted to be like Americans, lay the belief that the United States, as the most advanced nation in the world, had a moral obligation to promote freedom and progress. Acting under the assumption that their

---

[1] Dean Acheson, *Present at Creation: My Years in the State Department* (New York: W.W. Norton & Company, 1987), 8.

© The Author(s) 2018

M. Oliva, *Eisenhower and American Public Opinion on China*,
https://doi.org/10.1007/978-3-319-76195-4_2

national experience was the best model for other countries and that its values were universally applicable, Americans elected China as a perfect target for that mission. China was like a child and America was like a devoted father, offering knowledge and experience to a grateful recipient.[2]

The American image of the Chinese was, in essence, an image of an inferior people who could not achieve real stature in the world until they had abandoned their practices and converted to Christianity. Only through a religious conversion to Christ could they comprehend and enjoy the democratic way of life. From an economic point of view, spreading democracy also had the extra advantage of increasing demand for American agricultural, industrial, and manufactured products. The very phrase "China Market" evoked a picture of 450 million clients who aspired to become just like Americans, and in the process, could also solve the problems of expanding American commerce.[3]

Nationalist leader Jiang Jieshi (Chang Kei-shek) had epitomized this idealized image. In American eyes, he was a far-seeing and enlightened leader, who had converted to Christianity thanks to his US-educated wife, Soong Meiling. He was hailed as a political and military genius who had outmaneuvered the Communist Party in gaining China's leadership, and then had bravely fought back the evil Japanese during World War II. In other words, in symbolizing Chinese acceptance of American ideals, he became the personification of their China image.[4]

Jiang's popularity in the United States, however, did not derive solely from his religious beliefs. Through his wife's powerful family, he had been able to cultivate a huge coterie of supporters: politicians, philanthropists, business leaders, and people active in Hollywood and in the arts. Their common interest was the preservation of the Nationalist regime in China.

---

[2] Michael Hunt, *Ideology and US Foreign Policy* (New Haven: Yale University Press, 1987), 69–71; Christopher Jespersen, *American Images of China* (Stanford: Stanford University Press, 1996), 41–47; Emily Rosenberg, *Spreading the American Dream* (New York: Hill & Wang, 1982), 7–8.

[3] Michael Hunt, "East Asia in Henry Luce's "American Century"," *Diplomatic History* 22 (1999): 321–328; Jespersen, *American Images of China*, 3–10; Rosenberg, *Spreading the American Dream*, 7–8; Michael Schaller, *The United States and China* (New York: Oxford University Press, 2002), 17.

[4] Jonathan Spence, *The Search for Modern China* (New York: Norton, 1999); James Sheridan, *China in Disintegration: The Republican Era in Chinese History, 1912–1949* (New York: Free Press, 1977).

Their reasons were as varied as the membership of the China Lobby, as it came to be known. As historian Ross Koen has proved, some used the China issue as an aid in their fight against the Democratic Party. For others, the prevailing consideration was fear of Communism. Others saw the continuation of their financial and religious activities in China as dependent on the maintenance of the Nationalist regime. All used their influential positions to promote a positive image of Jiang Jieshi with the US public to obtain financial help from the US Government to support the Nationalists.[5]

Among the most influential members of the China Lobby was Henry R. Luce. The owner of the first multimedia empire, Time Inc., which included magazines such as *Time, Life,* and *Fortune,* and radio broadcasting and newsreel production; he considered himself an expert on China because he had grown up there. Luce was the son a Presbyterian missionary. Like his father, he believed God had uniquely appointed the United States to spread Christianity throughout the world because America was a deeply religious and virtuous country. To him, China was the ideal target for that mission: "as the most powerful and vital nation in the world" the US had the moral obligation to redeem the heathen Chinese who hungered for what America had to offer.[6]

Luce transformed Jiang Jieshi into the embodiment of his hopes for the rise of a liberal and American-oriented China. Luce dedicated to him an unprecedented seven *Time* covers. He produced a newsreel entitled "The Far East" to illustrate how Jiang's policies had brought progress to China. The movie showed the Americanization of China: skyscrapers, shopping malls, social life. The overall message was: "China needs Jiang to lead her." Portraying China as the ideal market for American trade, his media outlets praised the integrity of the Nationalist Government, and credited Jiang's Christian convictions, moral courage, and strength for turning the Chinese into honest, hard-working, brave, and religious people. Any negative information about Jiang or his regime was ignored so that a "larger picture of an Americanised China remained viable." Luce's publications did not relate events. They became, instead, a tool to promote a distorted

[5] Ross Koen, *The China Lobby in American Politics* (New York: Octagon Books, 1974), 28–39; Stanley Bachrack, *The Committee of One Million, "China Lobby" Politics* (New York: Columbia University Press, 1976), 36–39.

[6] William Swanberg, *Luce and His Empire* (New York: Scribner, 1972), 257–261; Jespersen, *American Images of China*, 23; Henry Luce, "The American Century," *Life* magazine, February, 17, 1941.

image of China among American public opinion. As historian Robert E. Herzstein observed, he used his media outlets "as a kind of secular pulpit from which he preached the virtues of American engagement in Asia." Much of the material used in his media outlets was also reproduced by one of the most influential relief agencies at the time: United China Relief (UCR). The UCR was created by Luce and although it was not a political organization, its aim was to raise money in support of the Nationalists' cause by spreading positive propaganda about Jiang.[7]

Other media tycoons, although not officially members of the China Lobby, used their publications to foster a positive image of Jiang Jieshi and the Nationalists' cause among US public opinion. Roy Wilson Howard, president of the Scripps-Howard press, which included 19 daily newspapers and the United Press wire service, was a close friend of Madame Jiang Jieshi. The numerous Hearst newspapers also endorsed and promoted that Americanized picture.[8]

The most active member of the China Lobby was, however, Alfred Kohlberg, a New York importer. Kohlberg's infatuation with China and his concern about US-China policy earned him the title: "The China Lobby Man." He founded several organizations for the specific purpose of promoting the Nationalists' cause. Established in 1946, the American China Policy Association was the most important and active one. Until 1953, Kohlberg paid most of the organization's costs, including printing and distributing of letters, pamphlets, brochures, and books. Moreover, he traveled extensively to China and reported about his trips in letters to the President, Secretaries of State, members of Congress, and newspapers and magazines' editors. He also subsidized *the Plain Talks* magazine, an official mouthpiece of the China Lobby.[9]

[7] Patricia Niels, *China Images in the Life and Times of Henry Luce* (Savage: Rowan and Littlefield, 1990); 52–190; Jespersen, *American Images of China*, 43; Robert Herzstein, *Henry R. Luce, Time and the American Crusade in Asia* (Cambridge: Cambridge University Press, 2005), 1–48.

[8] Steven Casey, *Selling the Korean War: Propaganda, Politics and Public Opinion, 1950–1953* (Oxford: Oxford University Press, 2008), 14; Vance Trimble, *The Scripps-Howard Handbook* (Cincinnati: E.W. Scripps, 1981), 3–8, 171–215.

[9] Koen, *The China Lobby in American Politics*, 50–78; Charles Keely, *The China Lobby Man: The Story of Alfred Kohlberg* (New York: Arlington House, 1969); Herzstein, *Henry R. Luce, Time and the American Crusade in Asia*, 44; Bachrack, *The Committee of One Million, "China Lobby" Politics*, 12.

The China Lobby's job had also been made easier by Washington's political, military, and economic support for Jiang during World War II. President
Franklin D. Roosevelt envisioned that Japan, once defeated, would be
stripped of its empire and reduced to an island nation again. Anticipating a
more powerful Soviet role in Northeast Asia, he regarded a democratic, pro-
US China as an asset. As part of his strategy to raise Jiang to the status of
world leader, President Roosevelt insisted on making China a permanent
member of the United Nations (UN) Security Council.[10] President Roosevelt
contributed to the Nationalists' propaganda in the US by instructing the War
Department to issue a manual for the Motion Picture Industry recommend-
ing that war-time movies should portray China as a "great nation, cultured
and liberal, with whom, inevitably, the US would be very closely bound" in
the future. The Department also produced a documentary, for release in
theatres around the country, entitled *The Battle of China*. The film was
directed by Academy Award winner Frank Capra and was a series of compari-
sons between the US and China to show the American people that, thanks to
the generous US aid, China had finally become like America.[11]

Jiang also had critical support from the so-called China bloc in Congress.
The group included: Representative Claire Booth Luce (R-CT), wife of the
influential publisher; Representative Walter H. Judd (R-MN), formerly a
medical missionary in China in the 1920s; Senator William F. Knowland
(R-CA), former editor and publisher of the *Oakland Tribune*, later to be
known as "The Senator from Formosa" for vehemently opposing
Communist China's admission to the United Nations; Senator Styles
Bridges (R-NH); and Senator Alexander Smith (R-NJ). Those Congressmen
were carefully orchestrated by Jiang Jieshi's public relations specialist,
William J. Goodwin. As Goodwin explained in an interview with Edward
Harris for the *St Louis Post Dispatch* in 1950, his job was to spread Nationalists'
propaganda to convince the American people, and particularly the members of Congress, to send US financial and military aid to Jiang. He estimated that he had met with approximately one hundred Congressmen and
had managed to persuade at least one half of them to support Jiang.[12]

[10] John Gaddis, *Strategies of Containment* (Oxford: Oxford University Press, 1982),
10–11.
[11] Clayton Koppes and Gregory Black, *Hollywood Goes to War: How Politics, Profits and
Propaganda Shaped World War II Movies* (New York: Free Press, 1987), 68; Jespersen,
American Images of China, 77–78.
[12] Koen, *The China Lobby in American Politics*, 46–78: China Telegram, January through
June 1950, Records of the Office of Public Opinion Studies, State Department, 1943–1975,

The rosy propaganda spread by the Nationalists and their supporters in the US overwhelmed the few dissenters who had tried to portray the actual situation in China more realistically. When the civil war between the Nationalists and the Communists resumed at the end of World War II, some journalists and academics tried to warn Americans against Jiang. Echoing Nathaniel Peffer's 1943 article in The *New York Times* magazine, *New York Times* military expert Hansin W. Baldwin wrote a critical article for *Reader's Digest* entitled: "Too Much Wishful Thinking about China." Another expert on China, Harvard Professor John F. Fairbank, warned that the Nationalist regime was corrupt and unable to provide its people with economic security. Nobel Laureate and best-selling author Pearl S. Buck drew attention to the atrocities of the Civil War, particularly the Nationalists' suppression of civil liberties. Those admonitions had little effect on popular attitude. In the summer of 1947, a National Opinion Research Center (NORC) poll found that only 25% of respondents had an unfavorable opinion of Jiang. By equating China and everything Chinese so closely with ideals and events familiar to most Americans, Jiang and his supporters had succeeded in creating a distorted image of China.[13]

In that respect, it is fair to say that, as political scientist Amy Kaplan has suggested, that idealized image of China was so easy to sell because that was what the American people wanted to believe. Nonetheless, those illusions ill-prepared them for the events that followed the Communists' take-over of mainland China in 1949 and Jiang's withdrawal to Taiwan. That belief triggered a bitter and painful search for the culprits who had lost China, which had negative consequences on Sino-American relations for the next twenty years.[14]

WHO LOST CHINA?

Jiang's defeat was the inevitable consequence of his lack of leadership and his refusal to implement much-needed agricultural and economic reforms. Instead, most of the US dollars he had received in aid went into real estate

AI568P, box 26, National Archives II, College Park, Maryland. (Hereafter, CT followed by date, DOS, file reference, box number, and NAII).

[13] Hansin Baldwin, "Too Much Wishful Thinking About China," *Reader's Digest*, September 1949, 13; John Fairbank, *China Perceived* (New York: Alfred A. Knopf, 1974) 3–18; CT, July through December 1947, DOS, AI568P, box 26, NAII.

[14] Any Kaplan, "Left Alone with America," in *Cultures of United States Imperialism*, ed. Amy Kaplan et al. (Durham: Duke University Press, 1993), 16.

investment in New York City. The Communists, on the other hand, had brought social, political, and economic reforms to the areas under their control, thus gaining the Chinese people's trust and support. It is no surprise that the population ultimately favored the Communists. In just eight years, the Chinese Communist Party managed to assemble an army of almost one million troops, control over one fourth of Chinese territory, and govern over one hundred million people.[15]

As the Communists swept to victory, the Truman administration moved quickly to distance itself from the Nationalist regime. It published the *China White Paper*, a 1054-page review of Sino-American relations over the previous decade. The document's aim was to exonerate the administration from any responsibilities for the "loss of China" by demonstrating the Nationalists' record of incompetence and corruption. It comprised major treaties, reports of diplomatic missions, high-level communiqués, and a narrative to put them in context. It concluded that "the unfortunate but inescapable fact is that the ominous result of the civil war in China went beyond the control of the Government of the United States." In other words, Jiang had brought defeat on himself.[16]

The publication of the *White Paper* strengthened feelings of disappointment and frustration toward the Nationalist leader among US public opinion. In a very short time, Jiang's reputation went from enlightened Christian hero to corrupt dictator. This was reflected in a series of public opinion polls. An October 1949 NORC poll found that 50% of those interviewed now had "an unfavorable impression" of Jiang. A November 1949 Gallup poll revealed that more than one half of the respondents believed that "there was nothing the US could do" to help the Nationalist regime and did not favor sending any further economic or military aid. By the end of 1949, Jiang was so discredited that 75% of poll respondents expected an imminent loss of the island of Taiwan to the Communists.[17]

[15] Koen, *The China Lobby in American Politics,* 12; Michael Schaller, *The United States and China in the Twentieth Century* (New York: Oxford University Press, 1990), 185–203.

[16] The China White Paper was originally issued as United States Relations with China, with special reference to the period 1944–1949 (Washington, DC: State Department Publication 3573, Far Eastern Series 30, 1949), xvi; Hannah Gurman, "Learn to Write Well: The China Hands and the Communist-ification of Diplomatic Reporting," *Journal of Contemporary History* 45 (2010): 430–453.

[17] CT, June through December 1949, DOS, AI568P, box 26, NAII; "Special Report About US Popular Opinion on China", December 1949, DOS, AI568Q, box 33, NAII.

A State Department "Special Report about US Popular Opinion on China" revealed, however, that the *White Paper* had failed to silence public criticism of the administration. When asked "What is your opinion of the way our Government has handled the China situation?" 54% of the respondents disapproved of Washington's handling of the situation. Disapproval could be found among the press too. Many wondered how the US became involved with such a corrupt leader in the first place. *The St Louis Post Dispatch* pointed its finger at the China Lobby. Following Senator Styles Bridges' admission that he had accepted a campaign contribution from Alfred Kohlberg, the paper called for an investigation of the China Bloc in Congress and for a wider investigation into Kohlberg's relations with other members of Congress. *The Detroit Free Press* stressed the role played by William Goodwin: "The Chinese Nationalist Government has employed at $25.000 a year a certain William Goodwin, as Washington lobbyist to get more American dollars for China."[18]

Rejecting criticism of Jiang, the "Bloc in Congress" counter-charged that his defeat was the result of sabotage, even treason, within the State Department. *Time* magazine called the *White Paper* one of the "lowest of low points in modern US foreign policy" and "a betrayal of Jiang." Luce's protestations of Jiang's innocence were, not surprisingly, supported by the entire religious community. Catholic weeklies *American* and *Commonwealth* and Protestant weekly *Christian Century* endorsed Methodist Bishop Fred Corson's letter to The *New York Times*, in which he called Jiang "a great leader." Accusing Truman of "selling out the Nationalists" in favor of the administration's Europe-first policy, Styles Bridges called for an investigation of the Government's China policy. The Hearst and Scripps-Howard papers echoed this view: "The State Department's present position does not make sense. If international Communism is a threat to us, and clearly it is, this country should be opposing it everywhere, not making concessions to it in Asia, while trying to block it in Europe." Finally, Senators Smith and Knowland embarked on a long tour of East Asia. On their return they declared that there was still much life in the Nationalist regime and "The US had an obligation to support such a long time and loyal friend."[19]

[18] Ibid.
[19] CT, January through June 1950, DOS, AI568P, box 26, NAII: Herzstein, *Henry R. Luce, Time and the American Crusade in Asia*, 110.

In the meantime, Goodwin organized a series of dinners in Washington and in New York for wealthy and influential businessmen, which led to the formation of the China Emergency Committee, later to be known as the Committee to Defend America by Aiding Anti-Communist China. Its purpose was to oppose US recognition of "any Government imposed by force of arms upon the Chinese people" and support "any US aid, both economic and military, to anti-Communist forces in China." In other words, it advocated new appropriations for the Nationalist Government. Claire Booth Luce was one of the board members.[20]

That rancorous debate over the "loss of China" proved to be one of the key factors for the rise of a little-known Wisconsin Republican Senator, Joseph R. McCarthy. On February 9, 1950, in a speech at Wheeling, West Virginia, he charged that the State Department employed a high number of Communists. They were being protected, he asserted, by Secretary of State Dean Acheson, "This pompous diplomat in striped pants with a phony British accent." McCarthy had no original evidence to support his allegations. He had embraced the issue of communist subversion in Washington, not because he believed in the cause but for political motives. Nonetheless, for a country in search of culprits for the "loss of China," his reckless charges sounded quite plausible.[21]

The first target of that crazy witch-hunt was General George C. Marshall. During the Chinese civil war, President Truman had sent Marshall to China to negotiate a compromise between the Nationalists and the Communists and create a coalition government. McCarthy, along with Senator William E. Jenner (R-IN) accused Marshall of being a traitor and having worked in favor of the Communists. He then moved on to diplomat Philip C. Jessup, who had made an extensive official trip to Asia during the winter of 1949–1950 and was active in the formulation of American policy in the Orient. McCarthy labeled him a man with "unusual affinity for communist causes."[22]

The Wisconsin Senator eventually singled out Owen Lattimore, a China scholar at John Hopkins University and editor of the Institute of Pacific Relations' official journal *Pacific Affairs*, as one "of the principal architects of our Far Eastern policy" and "a top Russian espionage agent." Lattimore's involvement with the Institute of Pacific Relations had earned him Alfred

---

[20] CT, January through June 1950, DOS, AI568P, box 26, NAII.

[21] Richard Rovere, *Senator Joseph McCarthy* (New York: Harper and Row, 1973), 32–75.

[22] Ibid. Herzstein, *Henry R. Luce, Time and the American Crusade in Asia*, 125–139.

Kohlberg's eternal hate. Kohlberg believed that the Institute was infiltrated by Communists and had played a significant role in Jiang's fall. As Herzstein wrote: "In McCarthy, Kohlberg found an avenging angel," and he, therefore, provided him with plenty of ammunition to bring down Lattimore. There was never really any evidence that Lattimore ever exerted any influence in Washington. However, his case marked the apex of McCarthy's witch-hunt. Persecuted by the Wisconsin Senator or loyalty boards, China experts became almost invisible. Young officers avoided the Far East desk for fear that their careers would end before they properly began. As a result, the State Department was deprived of competent experts on China for almost twenty years.[23]

Despite the tense atmosphere, the Truman administration decided to carry on disengaging from the Nationalists. On January 5, 1950, the President, who had never liked Jiang, publicly announced that the US Government, in keeping with the Cairo agreements "consider Taiwan to be Chinese territory." Given that condition, he added, "The American Government has no reason to consider supplying the Nationalist forces on Taiwan with weapons." Later in the day, Secretary of State Dean Acheson reiterated Truman's massage and added, in words that would soon come to haunt him, that the US did not consider either Taiwan or Korea part of the US defense perimeter in the Pacific. A poll completed eight days after Truman's January 5th speech found that the general public endorsed the "hands-off" policy by a five to three majority.[24]

"Hands-off" from Taiwan did not mean embracing the People's Republic of China (PRC). From the beginning, US public opinion showed a strong hostility against establishing diplomatic relations with the Beijing (Peiping) regime. In January 1950, a Gallup poll found that recognition was opposed by a 41–19% among the informed public and by a 54–32%

[23] Ibid. Gurman, "Learn to Write Well: The China Hands and the Communist-ification of Diplomatic Reporting," 450–453.

[24] At the Cairo Conference, held from November 22 to 26, 1943, in Cairo, Egypt, President Franklin D. Roosevelt, British Prime Minister Winston Churchill, and Nationalist leader Jiang Jieshi agreed that at the end of the war, all the territories Japan had taken from the Chinese, such as Manchuria, Taiwan and the Penghus islands (Pescadores), should be restored to the Republic of China (ROC) and that in due course Korea should become free and independent. Harry S. Truman "United States Policy toward Formosa", *Department of State Bulletin*, 22, January, 16, 1950, 79. (Hereafter *DSB*, followed by issue number, date and page). Dean, Acheson, "United States Policy Toward Formosa", *DSB*, 22, January 16, 1950, 80; Monthly Survey 105, January 1950, DOS, AI568L, box 12, NAII; Kusnitz, *Public Opinion and Foreign Policy*, 31.

among the college educated. According to a NORC poll conducted during the same month, opposition was even higher, at 62–12% among the public. Moreover, 78% of respondents opposed Beijing's admission into the UN. There were similar findings on the issue of trade with the PRC. The Gallup poll revealed that of the 76% of the respondents informed on the issue, only 29% favored trade relations with the PRC. Public hostility toward the new regime was so strong that it prompted the American Board of Foreign Missions to call upon Christians in America "to withhold hostility judgment on China" and continue to aid the Chinese people "under whatever form of Government they strive to work out their national salvation."[25]

The Truman administration's public efforts to link the Chinese Communists with the on-going communist drive for world power also fueled the public's antagonism. The White House made no distinctions between Chinese Communism and Soviet Communism in portraying a monolithic red menace. It fostered the idea that Chinese Communists were thoroughly indoctrinated by and totally subservient to the Soviet Union. State Department Policy Planning Staff Director, George F. Kennan, declared in a mid-1949 interview for CBS radio, that the Communists in China were "being utilized as a means of inducing" the Chinese people to accept a disguised form of foreign rule. After Mao Zedong (Mao Tse-tung) traveled to Moscow to sign the Sino-Soviet Treaty of Friendship in December 1949, Acheson publicly called the pact "an evil omen of imperial domination."[26]

That sentiment became so widespread that one poll found a five-to-one majority agreeing with the statement that the Chinese rebels "take their orders from Moscow." Of course, that propaganda was also easy to sell because, as a State Department's special review of public opinion revealed, 80% of Americans interviewed believed that the Communist regime had been imposed on the "freedom-loving Chinese people." In fact, the administration was always careful in its public utterances to distinguish between the Chinese Communists and the Chinese people and made clear that the unhappy state within the Soviet orbit was not the choice of the Chinese people, who were also victims of the communist conspiracy.[27]

---

[25] CT, January through June 1950, DOS, AI568P, box 26, NAII.
[26] George F. Kennan, "The International Situation", DSB, 21, December 5, 1949, 324; CT, January through June 1950, DOS, AI568P, box 26, NAII.
[27] Ibid.

Despite the administration's rhetorical excesses, a more sophisticated view of Asia existed in Washington. Officials in both the White House and the State Department agreed that there were some differences between the Soviet Communists and the Chinese Communists that could be exploited to US advantage, but disagreed on how to do so. For example, Charles Yost, a State Department official, believed a hard line policy toward Beijing could force a split between China and Moscow, in a similar vein as Yugoslavia's break from the Kremlin. He argued: "Titoism does not arise because it was encouraged by the West but because pressure from the Russians became intolerable to the local Communist regime." On the other hand, another group of Foreign Service officers, like Edmund Clubb and Raymond Fosdick, believed that the best way to create a split was through flexibility. Fosdick suggested that the West, particularly the US, keeps in touch with China as much as possible because by showing American "ideas and ideals" to the Chinese people, they would see the benefits of choosing the American way of life and possibly revolt against the Communist regime.[28]

When reports of those internal discussions emerged in the press, they triggered a heated debate among the public. Led by Roger D. Lapham, the former Republican mayor of San Francisco and president of the American Hawaiian Steamship Company and Chief of the Economic Cooperation Administration in China from May 1948 to June 1949, the West coast business community became quite vocal in pressing Washington to establish a constructive relationship with the new Mao regime. His views were endorsed by the San Francisco Chamber of Commerce, *The St Louis Post Dispatch*, *The New York Compass*, and *The San Francisco Chronicle*, which also stressed the importance of the China market for the Japanese economy.[29]

Completely opposed to the idea of recognition was the China Lobby. From its perspective, that would deny Jiang Jieshi any possibility of ever returning to the mainland. According to Alexander Smith, "For generations we have been partners with the people of China in their quest for free and peaceful national life. Now, in their time of crisis, we must do what we can to help and encourage Chinese leaders who are devoted to constitu-

---

[28] Gordon Chang, *Friends and Enemies: The United States, China and the Soviet Union, 1948–1972* (Stanford: Stanford University Press, 1990), 42–80.

[29] Ibid.; Shu Guang Zhang, *Economic Cold War: America's Embargo Against China and the Sino-Soviet Alliance, 1949–1963* (Stanford: Stanford University Press, 2001), 17–49.

tional principles. I am definitely opposed to any recognition of the Chinese Communist Government." China Lobby supporters were also particularly critical of Great Britain's decision to recognize the PRC in 1949 for the sake of its economic interests. Claire Luce expressed concern that the US might also be forced to recognize Communist China in the interest of world trade. Disapproving of the "British eagerness to make a deal with the Chinese Reds," Scripps-Howard media outlets charged that the UK Government should have presented a united front with Washington.[30]

Truman and Acheson decided to take a middle ground between Yost and the advocates of flexibility. The administration wanted to avoid providing the Chinese Communists with any excuse to incite anti-Americanism as a means of rallying the people behind them. But to the dismay of the business community, in addition to policies of non-recognition and prevention of the PRC's representation in the UN, the President and the Secretary of State also decided to expand the multilateral controls on strategic trade with the Soviet Union and its European satellites to Communist China.[31]

THE KOREAN WAR: THE BREAKDOWN IS COMPLETE

The outbreak of the Korean War on June 25, 1950 put an end to any possibilities of establishing diplomatic and trade relations between the US and the PRC. The Truman administration's decision to respond to the North Korean attack, under UN Security Council Resolution 82, was fully supported by the public. A Gallup poll showed that 81% of the mass public supported the action. Letters to the White House were ten to one in favor of sending US help to Korea. An Associated Press newspapers survey found "no well-known papers opposing the President's policies." Even the Republican Party released a *White Paper* to call for everyone to unite behind the administration. There was a unanimous feeling in the US that Korea, thus far considered a peripheral interest, had become a vital symbol of American prestige in the world. In fact, as historian Steven Casey had demonstrated, support for what the President described as "a police action" was so strong that one of the administration's priorities was to dampen down the popular mood in case of demands for unwise escalation.[32]

[30] CT, January through June, 1950, DOS, AI568P, box 26, NAII.

[31] Chang, *Friends and Enemies*, 59–63; Zhang, *Economic Cold War: America's Embargo Against China and the Sino-Soviet Alliance, 1949–1963*, 24–30.

[32] Gallup, "Survey Finds 8 out of 10 Voters Approve of US Help to Korea", *The Washington Post*, July 2, 1950; Gaddis, *Strategies of Containment, A Critical Appraisal of American*

Trying to prevent an enlargement of the war area as well as stop any Chinese Nationalists' plan to exploit the conflict, Truman decided to interpose the US Seventh Fleet between the island of Taiwan and the Chinese mainland. The move complicated Taiwan's position. The administration no longer stated that it considered Taiwan as an integral part of the mainland and it no longer argued that determination of the island's future had to await a peace settlement with Japan. The public came to favor military supplies to Taiwan by a 48% to 35% plurality. Opinion polls, however, showed that this increased acceptance of aiding the Nationalists was not the result of a positive re-evaluation of Jiang Jieshi, but rather a "general increase of public willingness since the Korean War began to take positive action against communist aggression wherever it appeared," even if that meant re-engaging with the corrupt Nationalist leader.[33]

In October 1950, Truman ordered General Douglas MacArthur, commander-in-chief of the UN command in South Korea, to cross the 38th parallel and "roll back" Communism in North Korea. That proved to be one of the most disastrous decisions in American history, but as historian John Lewis Gaddis has explained, limiting the military operations below the 38th parallel would have projected an image of US weakness to the rest of the world. At the time, therefore, in the words of Dean Acheson, it appeared that "a greater risk would be incurred by showing hesitation and timidity."[34]

On November 26, 1950, the People's Liberation Army responded with a massive attack on UN forces that pushed them back below the 38th parallel. The Chinese attack divided US public opinion. A State Department opinion poll found that 50% of respondents wanted to bomb China, and the rest wanted to withdraw. The administration studied a wide range of possibilities, from total withdrawal to expanding the war to mainland China, and even using the atomic bomb. Abandoning South Korea, Acheson argued, "would make us the greatest appeasers of all times." Expanding the war, on the other hand, might bring in the

National Security Policy During the Cold War, 107–108; Casey, *Selling the Korean War, Propaganda, Politics, and US Public Opinion, 1950–1953,* 23–36.

[33] Harry S. Truman, *Memoirs: Years of Trial and Hope,* vol. 2 (New York: Doubleday and Co., 1956), 334; CT, June through December 1950, DOS, AI568P, box 26, NAII; Special Report on American Opinion, "Public Attitudes Concerning Formosa", September 26, 1950, DOS, AI568Q, box 33, NAII.

[34] Gaddis, *Strategies of Containment, A Critical Appraisal of American National Security Policy During the Cold War,* 106–115.

Russians. In the end, President Truman decided to stabilize the front near to the 38th parallel and then negotiate a ceasefire. He set aside any plans to liberate North Korea and exponentially increased American aid programs to Taiwan. By the middle of 1951, approximately $100 million in aid had been allocated to the Nationalist Government. The US also stepped up aid to Nationalists' covert operations and began to train and arm Tibetan rebels.[35]

According to the Gallup poll, support to send military aid to Taiwan became the majority position in the US after the Chinese crossed the Yalu River. Military aid was favored by a 54% to 32% margin. Opinion polls also overwhelmingly showed that "national support existed for continued recognition of the Nationalist Government and opposition to recognition of the Communist regime and its admission to the UN." The American public's view of the PRC was so negative that Guomindag (GMD) attacks on the mainland were supported by a four-to-one margin among the public. According to the NORC, seven different polls from 1951–1952 showed that most respondents were in agreement "on US planes bombing Communist supplies inside China." A State Department's national survey found that a vocal majority of commentators and a majority of the public favored such additional steps as more US aid to Jiang Jieshi to enable him to carry the war against the Chinese Communists to the mainland.[36]

Public hostility toward Beijing also reflected Washington's increasing efforts in building support for the war. By early 1951, the stalemate that followed the stabilizing of the front at the 38th parallel had seriously eroded public support. Opinion polls showed the extent of public disillusionment with the Korean adventure to be quite significant. According to a State Department's special review of public opinion, 66% of the Americans interviewed wanted to pull out of Korea. Washington hoped to stiffen the resolve of American people to carry on with the war by increasingly painting China's leadership as Soviet "puppets," a view that by then was accepted by 80% of the public, and as monsters who committed the most terrible atrocities. In line with that, at least a third of the reports

[35] Ibid.; In 1951, Truman reportedly approved an attack by 10,000 Nationalist troops, who had fled to northern Burma in 1949, into China. These troops received a large amount of covert aid channeled through the CIA. See Thomas Powers, *The Man Who Kept the Secrets: Richard Helms and the CIA* (New York: Pocket Books, 1981).
[36] State Department's Special Survey on Public Opinion Trends Toward Communist China, "Advocates of Strong US Support for Chinese Nationalist Government", DOS, AI568Q, box 33, NAII; CT, June through December 1950, DOS, AI568P, box 26, NAII.

issued by the UN between July 1950 and October 1951 contained descriptions and images of cruel communist acts against prisoners of war. Finally, in February 1951, the US led the way in getting the UN to brand the Chinese as "aggressors" in Korea. Three months later, it imposed a total embargo on trade and a travel ban to the mainland. The US press was also unanimous in taking an anti-Beijing line that stressed PRC servitude to Moscow and the "foreign nature" of its leaders.[37]

Although the administration was successful in keeping enough public support to continue the war effort, it was poorly positioned for the upcoming elections. The Republican Party now saw in the Korean War its best chance to regain control of the White House, which it had lost for almost 20 years. Republican right wingers, captained by Ohio Senator Robert A. Taft joined forces with the China Lobby to batter the Truman administration on its apparent "softness on Communism" and raise questions about the war strategy.[38]

General Douglas MacArthur, a hero figure to Truman's critics, publicly criticized the administration for not sharing his view that Asia had become "the decisive theatre of action of the Cold War." "This group of Europhiles," he complained in December 1950, "just will not recognize that if all Asia falls, Europe would not have a chance—either with or without American assistance." In MacArthur's view, the United States should blockade the Chinese mainland, make use of Chinese Nationalist manpower in Korea and elsewhere, bomb industrial targets in China, and even use the atomic bomb if necessary. It was, of course, the repeated public expression of those sentiments against explicit official orders that brought about his relief from command in April 1951.[39]

The dismissal of MacArthur turned out to be a public relations disaster. On his return to the US, only 28% of Americans approved of his discharge. Press statements such as "Thanks to General MacArthur, Japan, who was our enemy is now our friend, while thanks to the State Department, China, who was our friend is now our enemy" became more frequent. The

[37] By an 81 to 5% margin the public believed that China had entered Korea "on orders from Russia", see Gallup Poll on Red China and UN, December 28, 1950, DOS, AI568Q, box 33, NAII; CT, June through December, 1950, DOS, AI568P, box 26, NAII; Chang, *Friends and Enemies*, 80.

[38] Robert Divine, *Foreign Policy and US Presidential Elections, 1952–1960* (New York: New Viewpoints, 1974), 3–41; John Greene, *The Crusade: The Presidential Election of 1952* (New York: University Press of America, 1985), 9–20.

[39] Ibid.

idea that the Truman administration had lost China became more and more popular, and Senator McCarthy's reckless ideas more plausible. In a December 1951 review of US public attitudes on China policy, the State Department found:

> The advent of the Korean conflict, the entry of Red China into the fray and the dismissal of General MacArthur have served great spurs of public interest in the Far East. With the increased awareness of the region has come a heightened realization of the loss of China to Communism. And there has developed an increased tendency among the public to agree with vocal critics that US policy failed or erred badly in dealing with China.[40]

In the end, hundreds of thousands of Chinese and Koreans, and 34,000 Americans lost their lives in the conflict, according to UN estimates. However, beyond the appalling cost of human life, the war transformed East-West relations and Cold War policies. The Korean War was proof for the US that the Communists aimed at world domination. The White House reassessed the importance of the Nationalist regime on Taiwan and the significance of the island for American security. The Joint Chiefs of Staff (JCS) recommended that the US retain Taiwan "as the island was essential in the strategic defense of our offshore islands chain stretching from Japan to the Philippines." In other words, the Korean conflict chained US Far East policy to Jiang and Taiwan.[41]

The Chinese Communist leadership seemed a demonic threat for the American public. A June 1952 State Department special analysis reported that 85% of Americans who were interviewed described the Chinese Communists as "oblivious to death," attacked in "human waves," and "brainwashed" American prisoners. The same survey found that 87% of the respondents opposed establishing diplomatic relations with Beijing, 83% opposed the PRC's admission to the UN, and 79% supported the total trade embargo and travel ban to the Communist mainland (see Fig. 2.1).[42]

Furthermore, the war left the American public frustrated. On one hand, it was tired of the stalemate on the battlefield and wanted to bring "the boys home." On the other hand, however, it wanted a firm stand against

[40] "A Summary of US Attitudes on China Policy, 1949–1951", December 1951, DOS, AI568Q, box 33, NAII.

[41] Chang, *Friends and Enemies*, 80.

[42] "A Summary of US Attitudes Towards Communist China", June 1952, DOS, AI568Q, box 33, NAII.

US public opinion toward the PRC

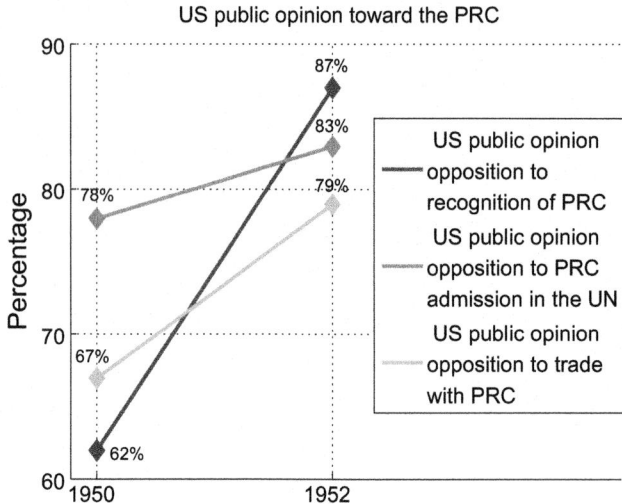

Fig. 2.1   US opposition to the establishment of diplomatic and trade relations with the PRC was further exacerbated by the outbreak of the Korean War. Source: "A Summary of US Attitudes Towards Communist China", June 1952, DOS, AI568Q, box 33, NAII

Communist expansionism. The lack of progress in the post cease-fire negotiations convinced many Americans that Truman was no longer the right person to handle the situation. His approval rating fell to 25%. In the autumn of 1952, the American people clearly wanted a new President who could stand up against the Communists and end the disastrous Korean experience.[43]

The 1952 Presidential Campaign and the China Issue

Only one man could fulfill that briefing: five-star General Dwight D. Eisenhower. His tasks as Supreme Allied Commander in Europe during World War II and then as NATO (North Atlantic Treaty Organization) first Supreme Commander in 1951 made him an international hero. His popularity among the American people was unparalleled, so much so, that 1948 Republican candidate Tom Dewey declared that Ike "was a public

[43] Divine, *Foreign Policy and US Presidential Elections, 1952–1960*, 7–8.

possession." Eisenhower was not just a military man–his humility, warm personality, and charming smile projected an image of a fatherly figure that could comfort the nation during a time of crisis.[44]

Whether he was interested in running for office or not has been a subject of debate among scholars. Historian Stephen Ambrose reported that in November 1952, Truman had offered to join Ike for the Democratic ticket and was even willing to run as his Vice-President. Eisenhower refused because of ideological differences, particularly regarding domestic issues. He wrote in his diary: "I could never imagine feeling any compelling duty in connection with a Democratic movement of any kind." Indeed, Eisenhower was an internationalist Republican. It was his concerns over Republican Senator Robert Taft's (OH) anti-NATO and pro-isolationism stance and his belief that the Republican Party needed to win the election to save the two-party system after twenty years of Democrats that prompted Ike to announce his candidacy in June 1952.[45]

Eisenhower launched his bid for the presidency in his hometown of Abilene, Kansas. Up until that time, not much was known about his views on China and Korea. From his private correspondence and diary, however, we learn that he considered Europe, not Asia, the real battleground of the Cold War. He saw Korea as another Soviet attempt at provoking the West: "The attack in Korea greatly alarmed the weaker nations exposed to Russian attack and produced a feeling in some areas of complete defeatism." He also believed the US had intervened for legitimate and justifiable reasons: "Had we allowed the South Korean Republic, which was sponsored by the free nations, to go under, we would have been by this time kicked out of South-East Asia completely."[46]

[44] Mara Oliva, "The Oratory of Dwight D. Eisenhower," in *Republican Orators from Eisenhower to Trump. Rhetoric, Politics and Society,* ed. Andrew Crines et al. (London: Palgrave Macmillan, 2017), 11–39.

[45] Greene, *The Crusade: The Presidential Election of 1952,* 50–53; Stephen Ambrose, *Eisenhower: Soldier and President* (New York: Simon & Schuster Paperbacks, 1990), 249–261; Richard Melanson, "The Foundation of Eisenhower's Foreign Policy," in *Re-Evaluating Eisenhower: American Foreign Policy in the 1950s,* ed. Melanson Richard et al. (Urbana: University of Illinois Press, 1987), 35–59; Eisenhower Dwight D., *The White House Years: Mandate for Change: 1953–1956* (Garden City, NY: Heinemann, 1963), 17–18.

[46] Letter from Eisenhower to Swede Hazlett, November 14, 1952; Letter from Eisenhower to Eugene Pullman, February 4, 1952; Letter from Eisenhower to George Sloan, March 20, 1952; Dwight D. Eisenhower Papers, Private Correspondence Series, 1948–1952, box 10, Dwight D. Eisenhower Library, Abilene, Kansas (hereafter DDE Papers, followed by file reference, box number, DDEL); Martin J. Medhurst, "Text and Context in the 1952

Eisenhower made his views publicly known on June 5, 1952, during his first press conference as a presidential candidate. He honestly declared that he did not have a solution to bring the war to an end but he believed that it was impossible for the US to retreat at this point: "We have got to stand firm and stand right there and try to get a decent armistice." More interesting, however, was what the General did not say in his remarks. Unlike the Republican right-wingers, he did not attack President Truman and did not link the outbreak of the Korean War to the "loss of China."[47] Nevertheless, Eisenhower needed support from Asia firsters and Western Republicans to win the nomination and then gain support from Congress if elected President. In Ambrose's words, for the GOP "of all the infamies committed by the Democrats in their twenty years of treason: the greatest were Yalta and the loss of China." The problem for Ike was that he had been one of Roosevelt's principal agents in carrying out his foreign policy in Europe during World War II, and Truman's JCS Chair in 1949. As NATO Supreme Commander, he was also a Europe firster. He was, however, willing to reach some form of compromise and adjust some of his opinions to please those GOP diehards whose support was necessary to win and then govern.[48]

His first step was to endorse the foreign policy plank of the Republican platform, which had been written by John Foster Dulles. As Richard Immerman wrote; "Dulles had trained all his life to become Secretary of State." He had been a symbol of bipartisan cooperation on foreign policy, alternating his duties at the UN and State Department—most recently in connection with the Japanese Peace Treaty—with his services to the Republican Party. However, by 1952, he had emerged as the chief foreign policy spokesman for the GOP. The son of a Presbyterian minister, Dulles' view of international relations and the US role in the world was deeply influenced by his own religious beliefs. His hatred of Communism derived mainly from the threat of moral bankruptcy that it represented. "A United States which could be an inactive spectator while the barbarians overran

Presidential Campaign: Eisenhower's "I Shall Go to Korea" Speech," *Presidential Studies Quarterly* 30 (2000):464–484.

[47] Eisenhower's press conference of June 5, 1952, the *New York Times,* June 6, 1952, p. 1; Medhurst, "Text and Context in the 1952 Presidential Campaign: Eisenhower's "I Shall Go to Korea" Speech," 464–484.

[48] Ambrose, *Eisenhower: Soldier and President,* 269.

and discredited the cradle of our Christian Civilization would not be the kind of US which could defend itself."[49]

Like Eisenhower, Dulles believed that the Soviet Union was the real focus of the Cold War and did not consider the loss of China as a tragic event. Moreover, in an interview for *CBS* in June 1949, he had not held the Truman administration responsible for what had happened in China. At the same time, he opposed recognition of the Beijing Government in the belief that international pressure could make the Communist regime collapse. However, he did not think it was necessary to break off all trade with the Chinese Communists.[50] As for Taiwan, in a memorandum to Assistant Secretary of State for the Far East Dean Rusk prior to the Korean War, he asserted the island should be neutralized under the aegis of the UN. When war broke out he revised his opinion to advocate that the US should retain Taiwan as part of the Pacific defense perimeter. Convinced that the attack had been orchestrated by the Soviet Union, he believed that Truman's response had been the correct one.[51]

By 1952, however, Dulles' public stance on the Truman administration had become considerably more critical. Perhaps because of his desire to become Secretary of State, his foreign policy platform adopted the Old Guard's critique of the Democrats. The opening line read: "This administration has, in seven years, squandered the unprecedented prestige, which was ours at the end of World War II." After listing all the friendly nations that had been lost to Communism, he focused on the situation in the Far East. Dulles accused the Truman administration of having abandoned China to the Communists by denying the Nationalists aid that had been authorized by Congress and was crucially needed to save China. Consequently, a US ally had been "substituted with a murderous enemy." He then charged that with foresight that the Korean War could have been avoided, but the administration's "Asia-last" policy had invited an attack

[49] Richard Immerman, *John Foster Dulles and the Diplomacy of Cold War* (Princeton: Princeton University Press, 1990), ix; Dulles' speech to the American Association for the United Nations, New York, December 29, 1950, *DSB*, 15, January 15, 1951, 88.

[50] Transcript of Dulles' interview for *CBS*, June 29, 1949, John Foster Dulles Papers, MC016, Duplicate Correspondence, 1949, box 40, Seely G. Mudd Manuscript Library, Princeton University, New Jersey (hereafter JFD papers, followed by record reference, box number, ML).

[51] Dulles to Dean Rusk, January 12, 1950, and "Notes on Initial Reaction to the Korean Development", November 30, 1950, JFD Papers, Duplicate Correspondence, 1950, box 47, ML.

I had committed the nation to fight back "under unfavorable conditions." He concluded by promising that the Republican Party would not sacrifice the East to gain time for the West. "We should end neglect of the Far East which Stalin had long identified as the real victory."[52]

Eisenhower's choice of running mate was also influenced by his desire to find a *modus vivendi* with the Old Guard. As a member of the House Committee on Un-American Activities, Richard M. Nixon had won the respect of the Republican right for his role in exposing Alger Hiss, yet he had consistently supported an internationalist foreign policy. He was also a relatively young man which counterbalanced Eisenhower's age. And as a Senator from California, he was a man from the West that counterbalanced Eisenhower's association with the East-coast Establishment.[53]

In the meantime, Illinois Governor Adlai E. Stevenson became the nominee for the Democratic Party. The party's foreign policy platform was unanimously adopted by the full convention. It praised the Truman administration's success in containing Soviet expansionism both in Europe and in Asia, and it declared that Korea had been a victory for collective security: "The Communist aggressor has been hurled back from South Korea."[54]

After defeating Senator Taft to win the nomination, Eisenhower took the last week of July and the first three weeks of August to plan the autumn campaign and choose his staff. Robert Humphreys, who had been the national affairs editor for *Newsweek* magazine from 1944 to 1948, was the public relations director of the Republican National Committee. On August 1, 1952, he presented a comprehensive campaign plan to Eisenhower and his team at the Brown Hotel in Denver, where the General had established his headquarters and took full advantage of the latest mass communication technology developments, especially television, and used the power of Madison Avenue to bring the Republican candidate to every American home. Barton, Batten, Durstine, and Osborne (BBDO) became a key GOP partner in 1952. All agreed that the Republican strategy had to be a full-blown attack on Truman and his disastrous foreign policy. It had to

---

[52] Republican Party Foreign Policy Platform, John T. Woolley and Gerhard Peters, *The American Presidency Project* [online] Santa Barbara, CA: University of California (hosted), Gerhard Peters (database). Available from World Wide Web: http://www.presidency.ucsb.edu/ws/?pid+254837. Retrieved: June 1, 2011. (Hereafter *The American Presidency Project* followed by retrieved date).

[53] Ambrose, *Eisenhower, President and Soldier*, 272–273.

[54] For an analysis of the Democratic candidate see: Divine, *Foreign Policy and US Presidential Elections*, 3–41; Greene, *The Crusade: The Presidential Elections of 1952*, 49–70.

play on the voters' emotions by stressing the danger of the international situation "today that causes Americans to fear for their security and lives." That was the only way to push those "stay-at-homes who vote only when discontent stirs them to vote against current conditions." That meant ignoring Stevenson to focus the attack on Truman. The Democratic candidate was always to be referred to as "Truman's candidate" or "Truman's successor." The Republican National Committee and Citizens for Eisenhower-Nixon would prepare pamphlets identifying Stevenson as a candidate pledged to carry on Acheson's disastrous foreign policy and proposing Eisenhower as the best solution for US problems. "If any man can bring the Korean War to a honorable end" one pamphlet asserted "that man is Eisenhower." Another read "Ike's worldwide prestige and experience make him the man most feared by Russia. He is our best hope to prevent World War III."[55]

Humphreys was very optimistic about the campaign strategy. He knew that the majority of the media would support Eisenhower. First and foremost, among his supporters in the press was Henry Luce. As one of his editors-in-chief noted, he "was deeply in love with Eisenhower's candidacy." To Luce, there could not have been a better candidate. The General was a Republican and an internationalist. His endorsement of the Republican foreign policy platform was a sign for Luce that Eisenhower would be a friend of the China Lobby. In working to elect him, he called upon his powerful friends, especially wealthy fund-raisers such as Thomas J. Watson of IBM and Winthorp Aldrich of the Chase Manhattan Bank. He also loaned the General his best editors and writers. C.D. Jackson, for example, took over a shaky speechwriting team and vastly improved the result. Eisenhower thanked Luce for sending him a "God-send." The brilliant *Life* editor Emmet Hughes also joined Eisenhower's speechwriting team.[56]

As a public figure, the General had already formed friendships with numerous publishers, and he counted Roy Howard among his close friends. He had also socialized and vacationed with William E. Robinson, the vice-president of the *New York Herald Tribune*. One of his bridge partners was *New York Times* publisher Arthur H. Sulzberger, nominally a Democrat but one who supported presidential candidates of both parties

[55] Divine, *Foreign Policy and US Presidential Elections*, 42–45; David Blake, *Liking Ike: Eisenhower, Advertising, and the Rise of Celebrity Politics* (Oxford: Oxford University Press, 2017): 71–80.

[56] Herzstein, *Henry R. Luce, Time and the American Crusade in Asia*, 156–165.

according to their policies. He endorsed Eisenhower right from the start of the campaign. Eugene Meyer's *Washington Post* also publicly declared its support for Eisenhower. Other friendly publishers included brothers Garner and John Cowles, whose family controlled *Look* magazine as well as newspapers in Minneapolis and Des Moines; Malcom Murs, president and editor-in-chief of *Newsweek*; Eugene C. Pullman, publisher of the *Indianapolis Star* and *The News and the Arizona Republican and Phoenix Gazette*; Palmer Hoyt, editor and publisher of the *Denver Post*; Virgil Pinkley, editor and publisher of the *Los Angeles Mirror*; and Senator Knowland's *Oakland Tribune*.[57]

In the words of Robert Divine, Eisenhower "was however determined to set limits on the exploitation of foreign policy for political expediency." The General let his campaign team capitalize on his immense personal popularity and agreed to be presented as the only man with enough experience to restore US prestige in the world. He accepted the Republican Party foreign policy platform but refused to endorse MacArthur's ideas regarding how to end the Korean War and to attack Truman for his handling of the Korean War. A major question about how long that could be maintained was one that could only be answered during the autumn campaign.[58]

The Autumn Campaign

Ike began his bid for the Presidency on September 4, 1952 with a speech in Philadelphia that clearly made the "loss" of China and its consequences the major issue of the autumn campaign. The opening line asserted: "We are at war in Korea because this administration abandoned China to the Communists." Referring to Acheson's January 1950 speech that had excluded both Taiwan and Korea from the Pacific defense perimeter, the General condemned the administration for publicly writing off the Far East. Eisenhower then introduced two themes that, as historian David Anderson has suggested, became standards of his campaign rhetoric: strength and peace. According to Eisenhower, the US was in Korea because Truman's foreign policy had made America look weak. The General announced that

---

[57] Daniel Douglass K. "They Liked Ike: Pro-Eisenhower Publishers and His Decision to Run for President," *Journalism & Mass Communication Quarterly* 77 (2000): 393–404.

[58] Divine, *Foreign Policy and US Presidential Elections*, 46; Medhurst, "Text and Context in 1952 Presidential Campaign: Eisenhower's "I shall go to Korea" Speech", 867–893.

through US and military strength, he would be able to restore American prestige in the Far East. However, he also reassured his audience that strength did not mean war. On the contrary, being fully aware of the public discontent with the war, he reassured his listeners that if elected, he would work hard to respond to the Communist threat but he would not involve the US in another war because "the people of America don't want war."[59]

Eisenhower's speech was enthusiastically received by most of the press. "Ike's first major speech of the campaign has made foreign policy the big issue of the campaign, as it should be. The voters will be wise to choose a presidential candidate of unrivalled know-how in the field," commented an *Arizona Republic* editorial. The *Houston Chronicle* declared, "Eisenhower put the blame for the Korean War where it belongs." In a public survey conducted a few days after his address, a Gallup poll revealed that 67% of the respondents thought Eisenhower "could handle the Korean situation better," while only 9% said Stevenson could, with 5% seeing no difference between two.[60]

The Eisenhower-Nixon Research Service weekly report confirmed that the Philadelphia speech had been a success in putting Stevenson on the defensive and recommended that: "It is of vital importance to keep the pressure on the Democratic candidate." It predicted that Stevenson and Truman would probably adopt differing campaign roles. In that scenario, the President would defend his own past record and at the same time attack and smear the Republican Party, thereby allowing the Democratic nominee to focus on the future while being progressive and constructive without being connected with the past Democratic record. The report was adamant that that had to be countered: "Instead, the past record must be tied blatantly on the tail of Stevenson's evening coat." The document ended with instructions for the press. Cartoonists were encouraged to keep Stevenson in a high hat and tail-coated evening clothes. Meanwhile, journalists and editorialists were urged to repeat that the success of a foreign policy depended on how it was put into practice, and assert that of the two candidates "only Ike has had first hand successful experience with national Governments in Europe on the spot."[61]

---

[59] The *New York Times*, September 5, 1952, p. 12; David Anderson, "China Policy and Presidential Politics, 1952," *Presidential Studies Quarterly* 10 (1980): 79–90.

[60] Monthly and Bi-weekly Summaries of Public Opinion, September 1952, DOS, AI568P, box 28, NAII.

[61] Eisenhower-Nixon Research Service Weekly Report, issue 25, September 17, 1952, Reid Family Papers, box 1, Library of Congress, Washington, DC (Hereafter LoC).

On September 8th in Indianapolis, Eisenhower again referred to the issue of the "loss" of China. He focused on Beijing's obedience to Moscow and said that the freedom-loving, peace-loving, and individualist Chinese had been enslaved by a dictator who was clearly Stalin's puppet and charged that the Truman administration had abandoned "700,000,000 human beings to the Communist slave world." It is not clear whether that monolithic presentation of the communist world accurately reflected Eisenhower's views. There is no reference to that in his private documents prior to his entry into the White House. Nevertheless, the Republican candidate knew that 80% of the American population believed Mao took his orders directly from Moscow.[62]

Stevenson responded to Eisenhower's accusations in San Francisco on September 9th. In defense of the administration's actions, he declared that Truman's foreign policy had been the right strategy to contain Soviet expansionism, particularly in the Far East where Moscow threatened Asia's hopes for freedom and decent living. He reiterated that US intervention in Korea offered proof that containment was successful and that the US had built a collective security system in the Pacific. Turning to China, the Illinois Governor argued that the Republican Party was proposing a "hindsight" war. "I don't think that tearful and interminable post-mortems about China will save any souls for democracy in the rest of Asia." Instead, Stevenson suggested that the US should focus on other countries under communist threat, such as India and Pakistan, and provide them with economic and technical aid to defend themselves against Soviet expansionism and allow them to develop.[63]

Long-standing critics of the administration's policy in the Pacific declared that Stevenson's speech "misinterprets the Communist threat in the Far East" and labeled it an "alibi" for Truman's failures. William Knowland claimed Stevenson was seriously mistaken if he thought a collective security system had been built as a result of the Korean War "when the US has carried 90 percent of the burden." The *Christian Science Monitor, Minneapolis Tribune* and *Detroit News*, however, welcomed Stevenson's San Francisco speech as "something to look forward and not backward." More acute commentators complained that despite the harsh rhetoric, neither presidential candidate had actually constructively

---

[62] The *New York Times,* September 10, 1952, 19.
[63] Adlai E. Stevenson, *Major Campaign Speeches of Adlai E. Stevenson 1952* (New York: Deutsch, 1953), 92.

addressed the Korean issue. Walter Lippmann wrote in his column for the *New York Herald Tribune* that "both parties and both candidates have been shadow boxing carefully to avoid candid and informative discussion of Korea because both parties are inextricably involved in every mistake made before and since the North Korean aggression."[64]

Taft, however, was still a problem for Ike. After losing the battle for the GOP nomination, the Senator from Ohio had promised he would help Eisenhower to win the election but instead, he decided to withdraw to his private island in Canada and refused to participate to any campaign events. Acknowledging the vital role that the party regulars could play in securing victory, Eisenhower asked Taft for a meeting which eventually took place on September 12, 1952 at Morningside Heights in New York City. The meeting was dubbed by the press as "the surrender of Morningside Heights" and was clearly a success for Taft and his supporters because immediately after the meeting, Eisenhower's attacks on the administration's foreign policy in the Far East became even harsher.[65]

On September 22nd in Cincinnati, Ohio, the General charged that the Democratic administration had "no single coherent policy in Asia," and the loss of China and the war in Korea were proof of that. He cited mid-nineteenth-century Secretary of State William Seward on the importance of China for the US. He again picked up Secretary of State Dean Acheson's speech of January 5, 1950 that had excluded Taiwan and Korea from America's vital defense perimeter in the Pacific and accused Truman of making an attack on South Korea unavoidable. In conclusion, he charged that Stevenson avoided answering questions on the administration's China record by talking of India. *New York Times* Washington correspondent, James Reston, called Eisenhower's Cincinnati speech "the sharpest attack on foreign policy in the last decade."[66]

Ike's charges were promptly endorsed by the Scripps-Howard and Hearst presses. The *Houston Chronicle* declared that "The Secretary of State gave the green light to Soviet aggression." Walter Lippmann and the *Washington Post* questioned the administration's wisdom in having made public the definition of the American perimeter. Lippmann wrote, "Eisenhower criticized Acheson for the wrong reason, the mistake may or

[64] CT, June through December 1952, DOS, AI568P, box 28, NAII.
[65] Divine, *Foreign Policy and US Presidential Elections*, 58–62; Greene, *The Crusade: The Presidential Elections of 1952*, 174–176.
[66] The *New York Times*, September 23, 1952, 1–17.

may not be in excluding Korea from the defensive perimeter but surely lies in the Secretary's treating American military policy as a formal public commitment of our foreign policy." A few, however, accused the General of deliberately misquoting or misinterpreting Acheson's remarks.[67]

Acheson defended himself, declaring that Eisenhower "tortures the facts on Korea," and pointed out that in January 1950, Ike was the Army Chief of Staff and, therefore, he had supported the decision regarding the Pacific defense. Similarly, in his September 27th Louisville speech, Stevenson asserted that Eisenhower knew that nothing less than military intervention could have prevented the Communist victory in China. He reminded his audience that the General agreed with the administration's decision to "let the dust settle in China." He then publicly questioned Eisenhower's motivation for endorsing the issue. "My distinguished opponent has certainly begun to parrot the charge of some of his recently acquired political tutors that the administration abandoned China to Communism. He did not talk this way once; but then he has changed in a good many respects of late. Maybe he is competing for the title of Mr. Republican as well as Mr. President."[68]

Gordon Englehart of the *Louisville Courier Journal* labelled Stevenson's speech "the sharpest personal attack yet on his GOP opponent." On his weekly program *See it Now on CBS*, Edward Murrow showed that the Pentagon's records were clearly stating that the General had agreed with the defense policy outlined by the Secretary of State at that time. To prevent further attacks on Eisenhower, the *Washington Post* called upon the General to "lay bare his participation in the pre-Korea period once and for all."[69]

Ignoring the *Washington Post*'s request, Eisenhower persisted with his charges that the Secretary of State had been mistaken in excluding Korea from the defense perimeter. Extra help came from the stalemate in Korea. The lack of progress in the peace talks and a steady, although low, number of casualties increased frustration among the American people as confirmed by several opinion surveys. According to a Roper poll, 53% of the Americans interviewed were so disappointed by the Truman administra-

---

[67] CT, June through December 1952, DOS, AI568P, box 28, NAII.
[68] The *New York Times*, September 27, 1952, 1; Stevenson, *Speeches*, 183.
[69] CT, June through December 1952, DOS, AI568P, box 28, NAII.

tion's management of the talks that they were even willing to support another military offensive just to get out "of this feeling of stagnation."[70]

Encouraged by such polls, Eisenhower continued his aggressive strategy. On October 5th, the Republican National Committee issued a statement challenging Stevenson's assertion that only American military intervention could have prevented a Communist takeover of mainland China. That labeled the Democrat's claim as a public admission that the financial and military aid given to Jiang Jieshi had been a waste. It further questioned Stevenson's contention that the administration had been successful in stopping Soviet expansionism in Asia. "Can this be serious? Can an administration, frankly confessing that it could not prevent the loss of China, the whole heart of Asia, have the audacity to boast no less than having blocked the Communists in Asia?"[71]

The GOP campaign team then decided Eisenhower had to exploit more the people's weariness of the war. In line with that, in a speech in Illinois, the General declared, "There is no sense in the UN, with the Americans bearing the brunt of things—this is the job of Koreans" and he called for intensifying the training of "twenty million South Koreans" or "those that are necessary to hold the front line." He then asserted that UN and US forces "must be brought back into reserve—if there must be a war there, let it be Asians against Asians, with our support on the freedom side." Senator Taft echoed his plea. In a speech in Rochester, New York, John Foster Dulles urged the US to arm and train South Koreans so that the "bulk of American troops can be withdrawn." Governor Dewey declared that "within a year of Eisenhower's election 9 out 10 of Korean battle front would be manned by Koreans."[72]

The *New York Post* bitterly assailed Eisenhower for playing politics with war, thereby "raising cruel and illusionary hope his election would overnight reunite every American family." Stevenson countered that "this view misses completely the significance of the Korean war." The Communist attack on South Korea was not an isolated event but a "Soviet-directed drive."[73] The General ignored any criticism and carried on with his tough rhetoric. He even gave up his plan to denounce McCarthy's witch-hunt by

[70] Adams, Sherman, Papers 1952–1959, box 26, DDE; Divine, Foreign Policy and US Presidential Election2, 1952–1960, 69–71.

[71] The *New York Times*, October 5, 1952, 80.

[72] Adams, Sherman, Papers 1952–1959, box 37, DDEL.

[73] CT, June through January 1952, DOS, AI568P, box 28, NAII.

paying a personal tribute to General George C. Marshall, who had been one of his mentors and a victim of McCarthy's accusations of disloyalty. Instead, in Milwaukee, Wisconsin, with McCarthy on his campaign train, Eisenhower made no reference to Marshall but charged that the loss of China and subsequent war in Korea were the direct consequence of communist infiltration in the Truman administration. "Their penetration of the Government," he stated, "meant treason itself."[74]

Truman, who thus far had been on the sidelines of this bitter debate, now stepped in to defend his action. "By meeting aggression in Korea," he declared "We have saved the free nations of Asia from catastrophe." And he added that the fact that the UN forces had been able to push back to North Korean army proved that "Communism was not invincible." A few days later, Truman challenged Eisenhower to offer a solution to the conflict in Korea, "If he knows a remedy and has a method for the situation, it is his duty to come and tell me what it is, and save lives right now."[75]

The General responded to Truman's challenge on October 24th, when he delivered his famous "I shall go to Korea" speech. That exerted a decisive effect on the campaign. The *New York Herald Tribune* wrote that "in one sentence Eisenhower has raised the spirits of men and cast a sudden ray of hope over a scene that has been obscured by uncertainty and doubt." By promising to make a personal trip to the battlefield, he fundamentally told the American people that if elected, he could successfully repeat what he had done during World War II: bring peace to the nation and restore American prestige in the world. That became clear on Election Day, when Eisenhower garnered an impressive 55.1% of vote compared with Stevenson's 44.4%.[76]

Eisenhower had enjoyed a clear advantage in the 1952 Presidential contest. His shrewd campaign strategy allowed him to chain Stevenson to an administration that had lost China and, consequently, was then stuck in a stalemate war in Korea. That coupled with the General's personal popu-

---

[74] Ambrose, *Eisenhower, Soldier and President,* 282–285; Divine, *Foreign Policy and Presidential Elections,* 58–62.

[75] The *New York Times,* October 17, 1952, 1.

[76] Medhurst, "Text and Context in 1952 Presidential Campaign: Eisenhower's "I Shall Go to Korea" Speech", 867–893; Oliva, "The Oratory of Dwight D. Eisenhower", 11–39; Steven Casey, "Confirming the Cold War Consensus: Eisenhower and the 1952 Election," in *US Presidential Elections and Foreign Policy: Candidates, Campaigns, and Global Politics from FDR to Clinton,* ed. Andrew Johnstone et al. (Lexington: The University Press of Kentucky, 2017): 82–105.

larity and the need for a change after twenty years of Democrats was a recipe for success. Stevenson was left with no choice but to defend Truman. The contest also revealed the extent to which Eisenhower was willing to bend to meet the public's favor. Despite his initial desire to "stay true to his opinions," as the November 4th polling day approached, he seemed increasingly willing to do whatever was necessary to win the election, including renouncing the opportunity of publicly denouncing McCarthy in defense of George Marshall.

More importantly, Eisenhower's campaign strategy showed the dilemma that characterized US-China policy for the next twenty years. On one hand, he did not want to appear soft on Communism. His campaign speeches always conveyed a message of firmness against the Chinese Communists. He was the candidate that could restore the lost prestige and credibility of the US in the Far East. On the other hand, despite the rhetoric, he reassured the American people that he would not involve the country in another war because he was fully aware that Americans were afraid that conflict with the PRC could escalate into World War III. Figuring out how to resolve that dilemma would be one of his priorities as soon as he entered the White House.[77]

REFERENCES

Acheson, Dean. *Present at Creation: My Years in the State Department.* New York: W.W. Norton & Company, 1987.

Ambrose, Stephen. *Eisenhower: Soldier and President.* New York: Simon & Schuster Paperbacks, 1990.

Anderson, David. "China Policy and Presidential Politics, 1952." *Presidential Studies Quarterly* 10 (1980): 79–90.

Bachrack, Stanley. *The Committee of One Million, "China Lobby" Politics.* New York: Columbia University Press, 1976.

Blake, David. *Liking Ike: Eisenhower, Advertising, and the Rise of Celebrity Politics.* Oxford: Oxford University Press, 2017.

Casey, Steven. *Selling the Korean War: Propaganda, Politics and Public Opinion, 1950–1953.* Oxford: Oxford University Press, 2008.

———. "Confirming the Cold War Consensus: Eisenhower and the 1952 Election." In *US Presidential Elections and Foreign Policy: Candidates, Campaigns, and Global Politics from FDR to Clinton,* edited by Andrew

[77] Anderson, "China Policy and Presidential Politics, 1952", 79–90; Ambrose, *Eisenhower, Soldier and President,* 284.

Johnstone and Andrew Priest, 82–105. Lexington: The University Press of Kentucky, 2017.

Chang, Gordon. *Friends and Enemies: The United States, China and the Soviet Union, 1948–1972*. Stanford: Stanford University Press, 1990.

Divine, Robert. *Foreign Policy and US Presidential Elections, 1952–1960*. New York: New Viewpoints, 1974.

Douglass, Daniel K. "They Liked Ike: Pro-Eisenhower Publishers and His Decision to Run for President." *Journalism & Mass Communication Quarterly* 77 (2000): 393–404.

Eisenhower, Dwight D. *The White House Years: Mandate for Change: 1953–1956*. Garden City, NY: Heinemann, 1963.

Fairbank, John. *China Perceived*. New York: Alfred A. Knopf, 1974.

Gaddis, John Lewis. *Strategies of Containment*. Oxford: Oxford University Press, 1982.

Greene, John. *The Crusade: The Presidential Election of 1952*. New York: University Press of America, 1985.

Gurman, Hannah. "Learn to Write Well: The China Hands and the Communistification of Diplomatic Reporting." *Journal of Contemporary History* 45 (2010): 430–453.

Herzstein, *Robert. Henry R. Luce, Time and the American Crusade in Asia.* Cambridge: Cambridge University Press, 2005.

Hunt, Michael. *Foreign Policy and Ideology*. New Haven: Yale University Press, 1987.

———. "East Asia in Henry Luce's 'American Century'." *Diplomatic History* 23 (1999): 321–353.

Immerman, Richard. *John Foster Dulles and the Diplomacy of Cold War*. Princeton: Princeton University Press, 1990.

Jespersen, Christopher. *American Images of China*. Stanford: Stanford University Press, 1996.

Kaplan, Amy. "Left Alone with America." In *Cultures of United States Imperialism*, edited by Amy Kaplan and Donald Pease, 3–21. Durham: Duke University Press, 1993.

Keely, Charles. *The China Lobby Man: The Story of Alfred Kohlberg*. New York: Arlington House, 1969.

Koen, Ross. *The China Lobby in American Politics*. New York: Octagon Books, 1974.

Koppes, Clayton and Gregory Black. *Hollywood Goes to War: How Politics, Profits and Propaganda Shaped World War II Movies*. New York: Free Press, 1987.

Medhurst, Martin J. "Text and Context in the 1952 Presidential Campaign: Eisenhower's "I Shall Go to Korea" Speech." *Presidential Studies Quarterly* 30 (2000): 464–484.

Melanson, Richard. "The Foundation of Eisenhower's Foreign Policy." In *Re-Evaluating Eisenhower: American Foreign Policy in the 1950s*, edited by Melanson Richard and Mayers David, 35–59. Urbana: University of Illinois Press, 1987.

Niels, Patricia. *Images in the Life and Times of Henry Luce*. Savage: Rowan and Littlefield, 1990.

Oliva, Mara. "*The Oratory of Dwight D. Eisenhower.*" In *Republican Orators from Eisenhower to Trump. Rhetoric, Politics and Society*, edited by Crines Andrew and Sophia Hatzisavvidou, 11–39. London: Palgrave Macmillan, 2017.

Powers, Thomas. *The Man Who Kept the Secrets: Richard Helms and the CIA*. New York: Pocket Books, 1981.

Rosenberg, Emily. *Spreading the American Dream*. New York: Hill & Wang, 1982.

Rovere, Richard. *Senator Joseph McCarthy*. New York: Harper and Row, 1973.

Schaller, Michael. *The United States and China*. New York: Oxford University Press, 2002.

Sheridan, James. *China in Disintegration: The Republican Era in Chinese History, 1912–1949*. New York: Free Press, 1977.

Spence, Jonathan. *The Search for Modern China*. New York: Norton, 1999.

Stevenson, Adlai E. *Major Campaign Speeches of Adlai E. Stevenson 1952*. New York: Deutsch, 1953.

Swanberg, William. *Luce and His Empire*. New York: Scribner, 1972.

Trimble, Vance. *The Scripps-Howard Handbook*. Cincinnati: E.W. Scripps, 1981.

Truman, Harry S. *Memoirs: Years of Trial and Hope*. New York: Doubleday and Co., 1956.

Zhang, Shu Guang. *Economic Cold War: America's Embargo Against China and the Sino-Soviet Alliance, 1949–1963*. Stanford: Stanford University Press, 2001.

CHAPTER 3

Keeping Promises

During the 1952 presidential campaign, Eisenhower had skillfully tailored his opinions to meet the voters' desires and at the same time appease the Republican Party right wing. Setting aside his views on foreign policy, he had endorsed the harsh GOP rhetoric in accusing the Truman administration of having abandoned millions of people to Communism in favor of a Europe-first policy and having involved the country in a stalemated war against the People's Republic of China (PRC). Fully aware of the American public's frustration regarding the Korean conflict, he had promised not only to bring peace but also to stand firm against the Chinese Communist threat and restore US prestige and credibility in the Far East.

When he entered the White House on January 20, 1953, however, he made it clear that he was no longer willing to be a pawn of the party or the bureaucratic machine. Rather, he would be in full control of the policy-making process and its public relations management. Unlike his predecessor, he would make full use of the National Security Council (NSC) which would be chaired by the President and would meet regularly every week. A firm believer in the necessity of support from public opinion for any foreign policy to be successful, he was also keen on establishing a public

Parts of this chapter were originally published in Mara Oliva, "Beaten at Their Own Game: Eisenhower, Dulles, US Public Opinion and the Sino-American Ambassadorial Talks of 1955–1957," *Journal of Cold War Studies* 20 (2018): forthcoming.

relations strategy capable of generating and maintaining popular support for the administration's policies. As he told his Cabinet in 1956, 'Our first task is to educate the American people and Congress. The National Security Council could be as wise as so many Solomon and yet end in complete failure if we cannot convince the public and the Congress of the wisdom of our decisions."[1]

This chapter explores the Eisenhower administration's first year in the White House. First, it considers President Eisenhower's and Secretary of State John Foster Dulles' sensitivity to and perception of public opinion. It then examines the opinion-tracking channels they developed, the credence they gave to them, and the information they conveyed. Finally, it discusses the impact that those mass attitudes had on the administration's formulation on foreign policy toward Communist China and the extent domestic public opinion determined the choices Eisenhower and Dulles made in 1953.

Great Expectations

The public had considerable expectations for the new President and the Secretary of State. According to a State Department nationwide cross-section survey done in the latter half of November 1952, 51% of respondents declared that foreign policy had been the key issue in determining their presidential election vote. The same survey revealed that 59% of those interviewed approved of the new administration's foreign policy ideas. Of the foreign policy problems facing Eisenhower, ending the Korean War was obviously the top priority, but 60% of Americans who were interviewed also expected the new President to be firmer with the Communist bloc.[2]

---

[1] Steven Casey, *Selling the Korean War: Propaganda, Politics and Public Opinion in the United States, 1950–1953* (Oxford: Oxford University Press, 2010), 340; Robert Bowie and Richard Immerman, *Waging Peace: How Eisenhower Shaped an Enduring Cold War Strategy* (New York: Oxford University Press, 1998), 84–92; Minutes of Cabinet Meetings, May 17, 1953. Dwight D. Eisenhower Papers, Cabinet Series, box 1, Dwight D. Eisenhower Presidential Library, Abilene, Kansas (hereafter DDE Papers, followed by file reference, box number, DDEL).

[2] "Popular Expectations on the new Administration's Foreign Policy", December 1952, Records of the Office of Public Opinion Studies, Department of State, 1943–1975, AI568J, box 1, National Archives II, College Park, Maryland (hereafter survey title followed by date, DOS, file number, box number, NAII).

According to the State Department, the press generally agreed that foreign policy had played a decisive part in determining the outcome of the 1952 election. Editorial pages turned from criticism of Truman's past and present blunders in Asia to speculation on the incoming administration's policies. The *US News and World Report* predicted an escalation of tensions with Communist China, even a possible bombardment of the mainland and a naval blockade. *Newsweek* concurred that "Eisenhower will fight more aggressively and more effectively." More moderate commentators such as columnist Walter Lippmann and the *Wall Street Journal*, however, urged colleagues to tone down their statements, fearing these might hurt the administration even before it took office.[3]

The China Lobby also had expectations. Henry Luce, particularly believed that after his tremendous contribution to Eisenhower's campaign and the fact that two of his best editors, Emmet Hughes and C.D. Jackson, had become members of the White House staff, he would develop a special relationship with the President. Wasting no time, just a few days after the election, he wrote Eisenhower urging him to include Taiwan (Formosa) in his forthcoming trip to Korea. "From all I can learn," Luce wrote, "the Nationalist Government has done a fine job in the last two or three years." He added that millions of "overseas" Chinese throughout Southeast Asia were swinging back to support Jiang Jieshi (Chiang Kai-shek). "A visit to Formosa, therefore, would be a morale-builder in many countries." Roy Howard's *Washington Daily News* joined Luce in urging Eisenhower to visit Taiwan and "prepare the way for using Chinese Nationalist forces." William Hearst Jr. suggested in his *New York Journal-American* that General Douglas MacArthur should accompany Eisenhower to Korea.[4]

The President was, however, determined not to let popular opinion and the press dictate his foreign policy decisions. It was clear from his private and public papers that Eisenhower had a realist approach toward the public and the media. In a private letter to the US Ambassador to France, Clarence Dillon, he wrote that policy makers should formulate foreign policy without taking public opinion into consideration because the public

[3] China Telegram, November 6 through 18, Records of the Office of Public Opinion Studies, Department of State, 1943–1975, AI568P, box 28, National Archives II, College Park, Maryland (hereafter CT, followed by date, DOS, file reference number, box number, NAII).

[4] Letter from Henry Luce to president-elect Eisenhower, November 10, 1952, DDE papers, Diary Series, box 25, DDEL; CT, November 6 through 18, DOS, AI568P, box 28, NAII.

lacked sufficient information to make a wise decision. He confided to an associate, Sigurd Larmon, "Americans understand it [foreign policy] less than anything else."[5]

Eisenhower also thought that public opinion was volatile, mood-driven, and consequently could be easily manipulated. He argued, "much of our so-called public opinion is merely a reflection of some commentators' reports which, as you well know, bear little relations to the truth. By the same token, I believe that public opinion based on such flimsy foundations can be changed rapidly." For those reasons, he thought it was the government's duty to select policies without reference to their popularity and then generate public support for those policies. He clearly outlined his philosophy in a memorandum to top administration officials:

> We have a task that is not unlike the advertising and sales activity of a great industrial organization. It is first necessary to have a good product to sell; next it is necessary to have an effective and persuasive way of informing the public of the excellence of that product.[6]

Although he did not want public opinion to affect foreign policy formulation, he considered its support of a foreign policy necessary for its success, especially for issues of major importance such as national security and war. For Eisenhower, a united, bipartisan foreign policy supported by the entire spectrum of public opinion would enhance American leadership and prestige abroad. On the other hand, any sizable public disagreement on the fundamentals of foreign policy would necessarily lead to difficulties and project an image of weakness to the world.[7]

Secretary of State Dulles also had a realist approach toward public opinion. Like the President, he believed that its influence on foreign policy should be limited to election time. As he put it, "national elections give the opportunity to translate the public's will into action." Dulles also reasoned that the public did not have enough information to make rational

---

[5] Letter from Eisenhower to Clarence Dillon, January 8, 1953, DDE Papers, Name Series, box 7, DDEL; Memorandum of Conversation with Sigurd Larmon, September 2, 1955, Sigurd Larmon Papers, Administration Series, box 20, DDEL.

[6] Eisenhower to Hughes, December 10, 1953, DDE Papers, Diary Series, box 4, DDEL; Eisenhower to Humphrey, Summerfield, Lodge, Adams, Hall, and Stephens, November 23, 1953, DDE Papers, Diary Series, box 3, DDEL.

[7] Douglass C. Foyle, *Counting the Public In: Presidents, Public Opinion and Foreign Policy* (New York: Columbia University Press, 1999), 33–40.

and sensible decisions on foreign policy. He concurred with Eisenhower that a successful foreign policy required popular support:

> There is no question that we need public opinion support for our foreign policies. We can't get too far ahead of public opinion, and we must do every-thing we can to bring it along with us. Any United States foreign policy to be effective, has to have a compelling majority of American public opinion behind it.[8]

For all those reasons, both the President and the Secretary of State were convinced that the administration had to make every possible effort to shape popular opinion in support of its goals. Devising an efficient public relations strategy that presented the government's case in an effective and convincing way to the American people was therefore one of their priori-ties upon taking office.

The linchpin of that strategy would be public information programs. Through speeches, press conferences, radio, and television talks, adminis-tration spokesmen would educate and inform Americans to create suffi-cient support for the government's decisions. Eisenhower thought the President was particularly suited for this task. As he explained to a friend, the four-year electoral cycle gave him more freedom and maneuverability to make the public support a certain foreign policy. Because he was not under the constant pressure of a political campaign, he had a "longer assured opportunity to teach an unpleasant fact" and convince the public of the validity of his arguments. Members of the House of Representatives, by contrast "must be elected every two years and they are sensitive indeed even to transitory resentments in their several districts."[9]

Key to that strategy was the maintenance of the President's public approval. Eisenhower believed that a popular President could change the views of public opinion. Accordingly, he deemed it essential not to become involved in public controversies or to be exposed to personal attacks that would damage his credibility and personal standing with the American people. That consideration shaped his relationship with the press and Congress.[10]

---

[8] Dulles' Speech "On Unity", February 27, 1952, John Foster Dulles Papers, box 306, Seely G. Mudd Manuscripts Library, Princeton University, New Jersey (hereafter JFD Papers, followed by record reference, box number, ML).

[9] Eisenhower to Dillon, January 8, 1953, DDE Papers, Name Series, box 7, DDEL.

[10] Eisenhower to Hughes, December 10, 1953, DDE Papers, Diary Series, box 4, DDEL.

The President appointed his campaign press adviser, James C. Hagerty, as Press Secretary. Eisenhower found Hagerty intelligent, hard-working, politically shrewd, and with a "canny capacity for judging people." Furthermore, having been a reporter himself, Hagerty knew how the media worked and had the respect of White House correspondents. The new Press Secretary agreed that it was vital for Eisenhower to preserve his popularity. The first mistake to avoid was to let the press dictate the administration's agenda. Hagerty wanted, instead, to find a way to use reporters as a channel to disseminate White House information. He suggested that the President expand his news conferences format to allow direct quotations of his statements. That decision, enthusiastically welcomed by the media, paved the way for the subsequent tape recordings to the radio networks, and then authorization of live television coverage of the press conference. As historian Craig Allen commented, "With these moves Eisenhower took a stride toward achieving a routine of placing his exact words before the public and having them stand alone against potential journalistic distortion or interpretation."[11]

Eisenhower and Dulles also accepted Hagerty's advice "to present their case to the public as often as possible" by holding a regular weekly press conference on Tuesday and Wednesday, respectively. The two events were closely coordinated. Prior to the President holding a press conference, the State Department Bureau of Public Affairs (SDBPA) always prepared questions that might come up as well as answers to them. In the same way, when Dulles had a press conference and knew that certain issues were going to arise, he would first check with the President and tell him what he expected to say.[12]

Every morning at 10 o'clock, Hagerty would also meet with reporters to brief them on the President's schedule for the day and answer their questions. A SDBPA official would do the same at 12:30. In addi-

[11] Dwight D. Eisenhower, *A Mandate for a Change, 1953–1956* (London: Heinemann, 1963), 232–234; Craig Allen, *Eisenhower and the Mass Media, Peace, Prosperity and Prime-Time TV* (Chapel Hill: North Carolina University Press, 1993), 43–54; Stephen E. Ambrose, *Eisenhower, The President, 1952–1969* (London: Allen & Unwind, 1984), 292–306.

[12] Hagerty, James C. President's Press Secretary, Eisenhower Administration Project: Oral History, 1962–1972, Columbia Center for Oral History, Butler Library, Columbia University, New York (hereafter DDE Oral History, followed by CUNY); Berding, Andrew H. Director of the State Department's Bureau of Public Affairs, John Foster Dulles Oral History Project, Seely G. Mudd Manuscripts Library, Princeton University, New Jersey (hereafter JFD Oral History, followed by ML).

tion to those regular meetings, the President, the Secretary of State, and other members of the administration would promote the government's foreign policy through public speaking engagements such as interviews, official addresses, and radio and television appearances. The State Department's Office of Public Service estimated that it handled an average of 1200 to 1500 speaking engagements a year. The goal of that strategy was not only to keep the public informed, but also to feed the press. The more material the administration put out, the less time the journalists had to snoop around digging out scoops. In combination with the press routine in the 1950s, that guaranteed that the administration's message was always reported.[13]

It was also routine in the 1950s for journalists to form "confidential" relationships with officials in the White House and the State Department with the hope of obtaining leads on news items. Eisenhower left that private side of public relations entirely to Dulles, who held dinners with selected foreign affairs correspondents. The dinners took place periodically and usually at Dulles' home in Georgetown or occasionally in the Washington home of one of the reporters. They were not social occasions. Either Dulles had a point he wanted to put out for use without attribution, or the journalists wanted issues clarified for their own purposes. Depending on his schedule, the Secretary of State was also available to meet reporters individually in his office or speak with them by telephone. Philip Crowe, a State Department official, helped Dulles develop a favorable reception by the press for his foreign policies. His job was to have lunch with American publishers and editors to explain on a person-to-person basis what Dulles' policies were, get their reactions, and report back.[14]

Historians Stephen Ambrose and Fred Greenstein have already convincingly demonstrated how President Eisenhower employed a rhetorical strategy to protect himself from public controversies and personal attacks in the press. Although the President had an excellent command of the English language, he preferred to use "jumbled syntax" and "long, inappropriate and impossibly confusing answers" to defuse controversial questions from pressing journalists. Eisenhower also looked to shield himself from Congress, especially GOP legislators who had little experience of

---

[13] Hagerty, DDE Oral History, CUNY; Berding, JFD Oral History, ML; for more details on press working routine in the 1950s see also Chap. 1.
[14] Berding, JFD Oral History, ML; Crowe, Philip, Department of State Public Relations Assistant, JFD Oral History, ML.

supporting the White House. As he explained to his Cabinet, "Congressional Republicans have been so used to a Democratic President that their instinct is to automatically oppose anything that comes from the executive branch." Instead, Eisenhower wanted to educate them to support his policy.[15]

To that end, he appointed Major General Wilton B. Persons as Head of the Congressional Liaison Office. Like the role he had played in the army, his job was "to keep the members of Congress, both Republicans and Democrats, happy." Persons was to keep legislators informed about the administration's activities, but in such a way that made them feel that the White House valued their opinions and input. If any controversies arose, he had to "smooth problems" so that the administration did not have a Congressional rebellion in its hands. For the same reasons, Eisenhower appointed three well-known supporters of Jiang Jieshi and friends of the China Lobby to relatively significant positions in the new administration. Walter Robertson, a protégé of Congressman Walter H. Judd (R-MN), became Assistant Secretary of State for the Far East; Admiral Arthur Radford, was made Chairman of the Joint Chiefs of Staff (JCS); and Karl Lott Rankin became Ambassador to Taipei.[16]

But who was the target of this public relations machine? What did Eisenhower and Dulles consider as public opinion? What channels did they use for monitoring it? And, how sensitive were they to the data they received? It is clear from the administration's papers that both the President and the Secretary of State valued the general mass public, the media, and Congress as three equally important sources of opinion.

To monitor the mass public the White House and the State Department made extensive use of opinion polls. Two New York advertising agencies, Batten, Barton, Durstine, and Osborn (BBDO) and Young and Rubicam, worked in the official scheme of the White House. BBDO introduced the "tracking" procedure to the President's public opinion research staff. That technique, although unscientific, had been used to test and market products for the agency's clients. Every Sunday night since 1953, agency representatives from BBDO's 12 branches phoned 50 to 100 people

[15] Ambrose, *Eisenhower, The President*, 292–306; Fred Greenstein, *The Hidden-Hand Presidency: Eisenhower as a Leader* (New York: Basic Books, 1992), 25–38; Minutes of Cabinet Meeting, January 12, 1953, DDE Papers, Cabinet Series, box 1, DDEL.

[16] Emmet J. Hughes, *The Ordeal of Power: A Political Memoir of the Eisenhower Years* (New York: Atheneum, 1963), 66.

across the nation to establish the public's interests and concerns on both foreign and domestic issues. They then tabulated the results and sent them to the White House the following day. George Gallup, the famous pollster, was also hired as a consultant for the new administration. Eisenhower often invited him to the White House to discuss in more detail the results of his opinion surveys. When he believed he did not have enough information, the President called his friend Roy Howard to obtain his research data from polls undertaken by his many publications throughout the country.[17]

The SDBPA prepared daily, weekly, and monthly analyses of American public opinion on international topics based on editorials from 100 representative daily newspapers throughout the country, columns by leading writers, and news stories and feature articles from 60 magazines and periodicals. Those reports also included Congressional opinion, nationwide polls of the American Institute of Public Opinion (Gallup), and the National Opinion Research Center at the University of Chicago. The Bureau sometimes also used polls from individual states, notably Iowa, Minnesota, and Texas that were thought to mirror the national trend. Those reports included a sample of letters sent to the State Department by private citizens and statements of political or other leaders interested in foreign affairs. Finally, the SDBPA also prepared the China Telegram: a weekly analysis of Congressional, press, and public opinion on foreign policy issues in Asia.[18]

Despite President Eisenhower's claim that he never looked at any newspapers, Assistant Press Secretary Murray Snyder, among others, considered him an avid reader of them. He usually scanned the *New York Herald Tribune* (by far his favorite), *the New York Times*, and the Washington newspapers every morning over breakfast. He was keen on learning the opinion of editorialists and top columnists; people who had the power to shape the political debate, notably Walter Lippmann, whose razor-sharp reflections on topical issues were syndicated in around 160 newspapers with an estimate circulation of about eight million.[19]

---

[17] "Notes on Monitoring American Public Opinion", December 1953, Hagerty Papers, box 3, DDEL. Allen, *Eisenhower and the Mass Media, Peace, Prosperity and Prime-Time TV*, 37–38.

[18] "Department of State Criteria for Public Opinion Surveys", DOS, AI568L, box 12, NAII; Berding, JFD Oral History, ML.

[19] Snyder, Murray, White House Assistant Press Secretary, DDE Oral History, CUNY. Allen, *Eisenhower and the Mass Media, Peace, Prosperity and Prime-Time TV*, 50–51.

Dulles was also an omnivorous reader of newspapers. He had the Washington papers, the *New York Times,* the *New York Herald Tribune,* and the *Wall Street Journal* delivered to his home so that he could read them quickly over breakfast. He considered the *New York Times* the most important because not only did it have the largest circulation in a country with no real national newspaper, but also it was the one newspaper that went to every embassy in Washington. He worried about its State Department's correspondent, James Reston, whom he considered very influential in Washington and a liberal critic of the administration.[20]

Both the President and the Secretary of State used the information on public opinion as warning signs to determine whether popular opposition was building against a policy. Their concern was to verify if the administration's message was well received and understood, rather than to reshape policy. If the polls, opinion analyses, and newspapers revealed public concern or opposition were building up against a policy or action, then Eisenhower and Dulles would chart out some sort of campaign to counter it. As Hagerty explained:

> Most of the time, Eisenhower would say "Well, that may be so but I am going to do what I think is right." Now, if the polls agreed with what he was doing, well and good. If they didn't, it didn't make the slightest difference in what he thought was best for the nation or the world on whatever he was proposing. But he would call a meeting with Dulles to discuss what could be done to improve public's understanding of his decision.[21]

Similarly, the former SDBPA director, Andrew Berding, and the Special Assistant to Secretary of State, William Butts Macomber, reported that Dulles was very keen on reading the SDBPA analyses of American public opinion to check for potential opposition.[22]

UNLEASHING JIANG JIESHI

President Eisenhower's Inaugural Address was the first step toward regaining control of the foreign policy process. Delivered on January 20, 1953, the speech very much mirrored his campaign rhetoric. He reminded Americans that they were living in a country founded on cherished prin-

[20] Berding, JFD Oral History, ML; McCardle, Carl, Department of State Public Relations Assistant, JFD Oral History, ML.

[21] Hagerty, DDE Oral History CUNY.

[22] Berding, JFD Oral History, ML; Macomber, William B. Special Assistant to Secretary of State, JFD Oral History, ML.

ciples of faith, truth, and freedom, values now threatened by terrible enemies who "tutor men in treason and feed upon the hunger of others." He vowed that his administration would meet that threat "not with dread and confusion but with confidence and conviction." Abhorring war as a chosen way to balk the purposes of the enemies, he declared himself ready to engage in any other effort to achieve secure peace for all. On the other hand, Eisenhower insisted, "We shall never placate the aggressor by the false and wicked bargain of trading honor for security."[23]

The President then warned that the US could not meet the Communist threat alone. Collective security was vital for the survival of the American way of life. To that end, he rejected the idea of a "Fortress America" championed by Senator Taft and his supporters in the Republican Party, in reaffirming his support for the United Nations as "the living sign of all people's hope for peace" and the necessity of a free Europe, not least for the importance of its markets. Finally, Eisenhower's Inaugural speech cemented the relation with the right wing of his party and the China Lobby in reiterating criticism of the Truman administration's Europe-first policy.[24]

According to a State Department's "Special Review of the Press," Eisenhower's address received enthusiastic praise from almost all segments of opinion. Among those lauding the speech as a reflection of the kind of "inspirational leadership" the President could provide, the *Christian Science Monitor* declared, "There was an over-all impression of more dynamic effort to combat Communism." "If the new President was trying to get across one thought, it was this," the *New York Times* declared, "there will be a sudden end to the vacillation which has marked America's foreign policy for years past." The *Cleveland Plain Dealer* added, "Freedom and the cause of the free world received a shot in the arm."[25]

Just a week later, on January 27th, Secretary of State Dulles gave his first televised address to the nation. Unveiling a map of a vast area that stretched from "Kamchatka, near Alaska, the northern islands of Japan and right on to Germany, in the center of Europe," he reminded the American people that thanks to events in China since 1949, Soviet Russia

[23] Eisenhower's Inaugural Address, January 20, 1953, *Public Papers of the Presidents: Dwight D. Eisenhower, 1953–1961*, ed. Galambos Louis and D. Van Ee (Baltimore, John Hopkins University Press, 1996), 6 (hereafter EPP followed by page number).
[24] Ibid.
[25] "Press Reaction to President Eisenhower's Inaugural Address", February 1953, DOS, AI568K, box 6, NAII.

now controlled one third of all the people of the world. The United States faced a "gigantic conspiracy designed to overthrow our Government by violence." Those 800 million people were being forged into a vast weapon of fighting power backed by industrial production and modern weapons that included the atomic bomb. He then reaffirmed the importance of collective security.[26]

After painting such a bleak picture, the second part of his speech was a real shot of optimism. He reassured the American people that they had elected the right man to face that terrible threat. He repeated several times that the administration would never choose war as an instrument of policy, that he and the President were absolutely opposed to any such policy, and that, of course, all his associates in the State Department and Foreign Service were against it. But at the same time, he reiterated the principle of firmness. The American Government would not be intimidated, subverted, or conquered: "Our nation must stand as solid as a rock in a storm-tossed world."[27]

Editors throughout the land and many columnists and radio commentators were enthusiastic in their reaction to Secretary Dulles' first report to the nation on general foreign policy. A State Department's survey of some 134 newspapers from all the sections of the country revealed that 121 lauded the report, while the remaining 13 were "lukewarm," although not sharply critical of any point. Almost all welcomed the address as evidence of "transition" from a passive to an active conduct of foreign policy. "The Secretary's masterful exposition of the tasks that face this nation foreshadowed bold and dramatic actions, a seizure of initiative that we had in 1945," said *Newsweek* in a representative commentary.[28]

Some controversy arose over the Secretary's simplified presentation of general foreign policy problems. On one hand, many listeners applauded it as a "refreshing change" from usual "diplomatic double talk" which marked the arrival of a "new firmer hand in control of the State Department." "Whatever his policies are going to be," said Josh Harsch of the *Christian Science Monitor* in a representative commentary, "they are going to be presented more effectively to the public than were those of his

[26] "Dulles' Radio and Television Address to the Nation", January 27, 1953, *Department of State Bulletin*, 18, February 9, 1953, 212–217 (hereafter *DBS* followed by issue number, date and page).

[27] Ibid.

[28] "Press Reactions to Secretary Dulles' first report to the Nation", January 27, 1953, DOS, AI568J, box 1, NAII.

predecessor." Congressman Walter Judd (R-MN) expressed the hope that the Secretary "and other officials will make such frank and informal broadcasts to the people of America and of the world frequently." On the other hand, there were some observers, like James Reston of the *New York Times*, and columnist Walter Lippmann, who took exception to the Secretary's "controversial and colloquial style" on grounds that "it either gives the appearance of talking down to the public" or was "a dangerous" method, in that so complex a subject as foreign policy could not be simplified without inevitable misunderstandings on the part of foreign and domestic audiences.[29]

On February 2, 1953, President Eisenhower delivered his first Annual Message to Congress on the State of the Union and made the explosive announcement that he would remove the Seventh Fleet from patrolling the Taiwan Straits. Historians have often dismissed the decision as a "puff of smoke," which neither led to any concrete development in the Far East nor brought the Korean War to an end. True, the conditions of Beijing's proposal to resume talks in response to Eisenhower's message were unacceptable and the stalemate did carry on for several months more. Yet, from a public relations point of view, it was a success. In declaring, "The free world cannot indefinitely remain in a posture of paralyzed tension, leaving forever to the aggressor the choice of time and place and means to cause greatest hurt to us at least cost to himself," the speech delivered exactly what he had promised during the presidential campaign. It was time to regain the initiative. The US would no longer prevent the Chinese Nationalists from attacking the mainland. The President reassured his audience, however, that there was no aggressive intent on the American side.[30]

The majority of observers in the press, radio, and Congress vigorously endorsed President Eisenhower's decision. The move was hailed as "logical" and "a positive first step" toward regaining the "initiative" in the Far East. Columnist David Lawrence of the *US News and World Report* stressed, "The initiative now is passing from Moscow to Washington, orders of Seventh Fleet mark positive, dynamic element too often lacking in our foreign policy." *The Philadelphia Inquirer* declared, "It is not an aggressive move against

[29] Ibid.
[30] Eisenhower's State of the Union Address, John T. Woolley and Gerhard Peters, *The American Presidency Project* [online] Santa Barbara, CA: University of California (hosted) Gerhard Peters (database). Available from World Wide Web: http://www.presidency.ucsab.edu/ws/. Retrieved: July 4, 2011 (hereafter *The American Presidency Project* followed by retrieved date).

the Chinese Communists. It is, however, employment of American strength
as an affirmative means of supplying pressure on Reds, instead of negative
method of preserving the status quo." A *New York Times* editorial said the
President "is right and wise." *The Wall Street Journal* added, "Logic and
sense dictate this decision; they are the marks of a reasoning man confident
that in any war, foreign policy must fail, if it leaves the enemy the choice of
time, place and action." *Business Week* and the *San Francisco Chronicle*
declared that it was the first blow in a war of nerves against Red China.[31]

The China Lobby was rapturous. In his Lincoln Day speech in St. Paul,
Minnesota, Senator Styles Bridges (R-NH) called for atomic bombing in
Korea and attacks on Red bases in Manchuria. He also suggested a naval
blockade of the Chinese mainland and "fuller use of Anti-Communist
Asian armies." Senator William F. Knowland (R-CA) put forward a plan
that included having Jiang Jieshi send troops to Korea, requesting all
nations that were part of the United Nations (UN) to withdraw recognition of Communist China, and demanding that Russia stop furnishing
support to North Koreans. Henry Luce declared that the Nationalists
were living completely for the purpose of liberating China from the
Communist regime. "The time has come," he believed, "to join hands
with the Nationalists in their struggle to free the mainland." According to
Bob Considine of the *New York Journal-American*, "Chiang will want to
throw high hand one against the mainland as quickly as possible, so
devoured is he by the desire to strike back...hold your breath."[32]

Those pro-Jiang hawks were supported in their bellicose statement by
public opinion. The President's decision to remove the Seventh Fleet
received immediate approval from the public. According to a State
Department special spot-check of national sentiment, 65% of those interviewed approved of "the plan to permit Nationalist forces on Formosa to
make raids on the mainland Communist China" and six out of 10 respondents favored giving military supplies to Jiang for attacking the Chinese
Communists. A Gallup poll revealed that 61% of respondents would approve
of the US supplying more warships to the Chinese Nationalists for them to
blockade the coast of Communist China and 62% supported supplying
more airplanes to the Nationalists to use for bombing the mainland.[33]

---

[31] CT, February 4 through 16, 1953, DOS, AI568P, box 28, NAII.
[32] Ibid.
[33] "Special Spot-Check Report of the Nation", February 8, 1953, DOS, AI568J, box 1,
NAII.

Some commentators, however, expressed some words of caution. A *Washington Post* editorial observed that advocates of a blockade were "deceiving" the American public in their assurances that such action would not disturb peace. *The Post* added that "a blockade is warlike, indeed it is doubtful whether under international law the US could declare a blockade of Communist China without declaring war." *The New Orleans Times-Picayune* noted that "the China Lobby is doing a good job in advocating the very policy Chiang has openly admitted gives him the only chance to regain power on the mainland that is US action against Red China." *The Louisville Courier Journal* similarly wondered if the President was ready "to risk an all-out war with China." And, Frank Edwards of *MBS* worried whether the US would "defend Formosa in case of a Communist attack."[34]

Despite the administration's bold rhetoric, its private views were considerably more moderate. Eisenhower and Dulles no longer believed that Jiang Jieshi cut an important figure in Asia, in comparison with Mao Zedong (Mao Tse-tung) and India Prime Minister Jawaharlal Nehru. Neither trusted the Generalissimo, whom they feared would drag the US into a major war against Communist China. The US Ambassador to Taipei, Karl Rankin, was therefore instructed to inform Jiang that the removal of the Seventh Fleet did not signify any change in US policy regarding the extension of military and economic assistance to the government of the Republic of China. Additionally, he was to inform the Nationalists not to go ahead with any significant attack on Communist-held territories without first consulting the US. In his discussions with Jiang, Rankin also had to make clear that the US would continue to defend Taiwan and the Penghu (Pescadores) Islands, but that Washington would not undertake any commitment to counter Communist military actions that were the consequence of Chinese Nationalist offensive operations undertaken without the prior concurrence of US authorities.[35]

Moreover, the administration wanted Rankin to inform Jiang that the US would participate in the defense of the other Nationalist-held islands only in the event Taiwan and the Penghu Islands were also attacked. Finally, Rankin had to convey to the Generalissimo a list of "requests." The Nationalists should give immediate thought to, and plans should be

---

[34] CT, February 17 through 23, 1953, DOS, AI568P, box 28, NAII.

[35] Memorandum of Conversation with the President, May 31, 1953, Karl Lott Rankin Papers, Administration Series, box 7, DDEL; Department of State Telegram to US Ambassador to Taipei Rankin, February 3, 1953, *FRUS*, XIX, 1952–1954, 135–145.

made to blockade the China mainland, with respect to Chinese Communist shipping only, from Swatow on the Communist coast to the Dechen (Techen) Islands, both inclusive. Plans should also be made to increase the frequency of raids, not only from the offshore islands, but also from Taiwan and the Penghus, and that both small and large raids be planned and executed on a wide front to obtain prisoners and worry and confuse the Communist coastal defenses.[36]

A furious Jiang understood well that his much advertised "unleashing" was in reality a mere public relations move that would only benefit the US. He knew that the administration was using him to confuse Beijing, but it did not want to risk a global war for his dream of returning to the mainland. In response to US requests, he asserted that a blockade of the stretch of China coast between the Dechen Islands and Swatow for interception of Communist vessels would not justify the effort because of the small amount of shipping which would be affected. The only way possible was to block the entire coast.[37]

Jiang's reply troubled Washington. The JCS were particularly worried by the imminent delivery of US F84 aircrafts to the Nationalists. Radford reminded the NSC: "As you know very well Chiang wants to broaden the conflict…He may well be tempted to undertake some adventures with his F84 either with or without deliberate intention of involving the US in a broader war with Communist China." A meeting between Dulles and Nationalist Chinese Foreign Minister George Yeh further fueled anxiety about Jiang's irresponsible behavior. Yeh complained about the exaggerated statements being made by Senator Knowland and Congressman Judd. He told Dulles he had not tried to stop them because of their known friendliness toward Nationalist China, but the Nationalists had no intention of sending their troops to Korea. He insisted that Jiang's strategy was to hold on to Taiwan and make it an increasing source of potential pressure against the Communist mainland. Fearful that the situation might get out of hand, Eisenhower ordered delivery of further aircrafts to be halted until Jiang committed to US conditions, which he did in April 1953.[38]

[36] Ibid.
[37] Ibid.
[38] Notes on NSC Meeting, March 2, 1953, DDE Papers, NSC Series, box 13, DDEL; Memorandum to President Eisenhower from Dulles on Dulles' meeting with Chinese Foreign Minister Yeh, March 2, 1953, JFD Papers, Subject Series, box 8, DDEL.

None of that ever surfaced in public. While speculations about viable future actions continued, the administration made no official declarations of its real intentions. It did not clarify, for example, how the US would respond to a Communist attack on the offshore islands. Eisenhower and Dulles even deliberately confused the public regarding the blockade question. In his very first press conference the President was asked by Richard Wilson of Cowles Publications if he was considering a blockade of China, the President replied that as far as he was concerned the matter had been only discussed in the press and not by his administration. The following day, however, in his press conference, Dulles answered the same question stating that a naval blockade of China was under consideration, among other possibilities.[39]

That was all part of Eisenhower's strategy to gain control of the foreign policy-making process. He had given Americans what they wanted: a bold action to show that the US was no longer to be intimidated, but not so bold as to risk World War III. Meanwhile, he had retained enough maneuverability. Because details of the administration's policy were never publicly clarified, not only the public, but also the enemy, were left guessing about what Jiang's unleashing really meant. Confirming success from a public relations perspective, a SDBPA poll in mid-February found that 71% of the respondents approved of the way the State Department was handling foreign affairs. The efficiency and dispatch with which the President acted in taking up his great burden appeared to be a source of satisfaction and reassurance. Eisenhower's approval rating was up to 78%, and only one American out of 10 interviewed did not agree with the President's foreign policy ideas.[40]

STALIN'S DEATH

The administration was soon on the defensive. On March 5, 1953, Soviet leader Joseph Stalin died. A few days later, the new chair of the Soviet Council of Ministers, Georgy Malenkov, publicly hinted at Russia's desire for a new phase of détente in Soviet-US relations. In April, the Chinese

---

[39] Eisenhower's press conference, February 18, 1953, The American Presidency Project, [retrieved June 8, 2009]; Dulles' press conference, February 18, 1953, DOS, AI568X, box 5, NAII.

[40] "Approval of State Department's Job", February 15, 1953, DOS, AI568N, box 20, NAII.

Communist negotiators in Panmunjom accepted the American offer to exchange sick and wounded prisoners of war (POWs). A breakthrough in the truce talks now seemed possible.[41]

With a ceasefire appearing more likely than any previous time over the past two years, talks of a review of US Far East policy intensified. Speculation in the press increased regarding the future status of Korea, the problem of establishing diplomatic relations with the PRC, and what to do about Jiang Jieshi. Among several possibilities considered by the Administration was a trusteeship for Taiwan. In 1950, Dulles had collaborated with Assistant Secretary of State for Far Eastern Affairs, Dean Rusk on a similar plan to rid the island of Jiang and protect it against Communism by making it a UN trusteeship territory, but the scheme had failed to persuade Secretary of State Dean Acheson. The plan was being reviewed again, and the administration wanted to gauge public opinion reactions about such an eventuality.[42]

In early April, at an off-the-record dinner for a group of journalists, Dulles told Walter Waggoner of *The New York Times* "that a trusteeship for Formosa had been considered in the UN and might be considered again." The next day the latter passed the news to his newspaper's White House correspondent, Anthony Leveiro, who wrote a story that senior officials in the State Department were contemplating a trusteeship for Taiwan and a settlement with the Communists regarding Korea, which would result in the division of the peninsula.[43]

The article sparked off a bitter debate and outraged Jiang's supporters. Dulles' alleged trusteeship statement was the biggest item on the news agenda for several days, obscuring even the progress of talks regarding the POWs. William Knowland declared that a UN trusteeship "could not be anything but a roundabout device to surrender the island to the Reds." Styles Bridges was reported as saying "to agree to peace with Nationalist China confined to Formosa would certainly be regarded by all Asians as a tremendous Red victory." Other typically more moderate commentators also voiced opposition to such a possibility. *The New York Herald Tribune*, for example, wondered if peace in Asia could really be achieved without peace between

---

[41] Casey, Steven, *Selling the Korean War, Propaganda, Politics, and Public Opinion, 1950–1953*, 344; Stueck, William Jr. *The Road to Confrontation; American Policy Toward China and Korea, 1947–1950* (Chapel Hill: University of North Carolina Press, 1981), 308–309.

[42] Memorandum of Telephone Conversation, undated, JFD Papers, Telephone Conversations Series, box 1, DDEL.

[43] Memorandum of Telephone Conversation, April 9, 1953, JFD Papers, Telephone Conversations Series, box 1, DDEL.

Taiwan and the mainland. While conceding that the Secretary's trial balloon had been poorly conceived and executed, the *Detroit News* was one of the few newspapers to note that at least it had served to bring to public attention "the fact that if we want a try for peaceful settlement in Asia we will have to back down from demands that could be achieved only as a result of total victory." Placed uncomfortably on the defensive, the White House issued a firm denial about a trusteeship for Taiwan.[44]

While the public was still digesting the information, the administration came under fire over another issue. British Foreign Secretary Anthony Eden's statements favoring admission of Communist China into the UN after the signing of the Korean truce angered prominent Congressional supporters of Jiang and provoked a stormy media debate. Leading the attack, Knowland accused Britain of urging a "Far Eastern Munich," remarks that were vigorously endorsed by Scripps-Howard's *Washington Daily News*, Hearst's *New York Journal-American*, and the *Washington Times-Herald*. The *Times-Herald* and *Journal-American* also applauded Senator Joseph McCarthy (R-WI), who threatened the United Kingdom with economic reprisals and declared that if it was the British purpose to blackmail the US into accepting "Communist peace" by threatening to withdraw support in Korea, "then I say to them withdraw and be damned!" Although deploring such language, the media and legislators opposed admitting Communist China to the UN.[45]

The public opposition to seating the Chinese Communists in the UN paralleled leadership opinion. According to a State Department public opinion survey, 85% of Americans who were interviewed were against PRC admission to the world body. However, only 19% of the respondents approved of US withdrawal from the UN if Communist China was given a Security Council seat (see Table 3.1).[46]

Fearing a breach in the relationship with Britain, Eisenhower tried to shore up the foundations of the alliance at his press conference but only further irritated those opposed to Beijing's admission to the UN. Senator William Jenner (R-IN) called on the President to issue "a final statement" pledging that the US would not recognize the PRC or sanction its admission to the UN. The *Houston Chronicle* was alarmed that the President "seemed to leave the gate open for ultimate agreement with the British

---

[44] CT, April 16 through 22, 1953, DOS, AI568P, box 28, NAII.
[45] CT, April 22 through May 17, 1953, DOS, AI568P, box 28, NAII.
[46] Monthly Survey of Public Opinion, May 1953, DOS, AI568K, box 13, NAII.

Table 3.1 Detailed breakdown of US public opinion opposition to PRC admission to the UN

US public opposition to UN membership by PRC

"Would you approve or disapprove of letting Communist China become a member of the United Nations?"

	National	College educated	High school	Grammar school
Approve	6%	8%	6%	10%
Depends	6%	9%	7%	4%
Disapprove	85%	85%	75%	76%
No Opinion	3%	7%	6%	10%

"Suppose that most of the other countries should vote to admit Communist China into the UN. What do you think we should do about it?"

Intransigent opposition	Total: 19%	Intermediate qualified	Total: 17%	Accept majority decisions	Total: 40%
Pull out of UN	10%	Veto against	7%	Have to accept	18%
Take reprisals	2%	Try to negotiate	1%	Accept	10%
Veto It	2%	Mix	3%	Now favor admission	12%
Don't let them in	3%	Depends	6%		
Refuse to accept decision	2%				

Source: CT, May 14 through 20 1953, DOS, AI568P, box 28, NAII

position" at his press conference and "awaited" explanation from him. Knowland became so disturbed at Eisenhower's failure to take a firm stand, that he introduced a resolution to put Congress on record in favor of US withdrawal from the UN if Communist China should ever be admitted. A few days later, the Senate Appropriations Committee attached a rider to the resolution, cutting off the US contribution to the UN if Communist China were seated on the Security Council.[47]

The press condemned the rider as being too aggressive. In a representative commentary, the *Philadelphia Bulletin* declared, "If the Senate was out to lower the prestige of the US abroad, it could have hardly done a better job than make a threat to the UN." This was a useless gesture because the US could veto the admission of the PRC into the

[47] CT, May 14 through 20, 1953, DOS, AI568P, box 28, NAII.

UN. Eisenhower was furious, but decided to avoid a public confrontation. While publicly trying to evade questions on the Committee rider and give general, non-committed answers on the issue, he and his senior advisers privately made a concerted effort to convince Congressional leaders to change track. On June 2nd, after a long meeting at the White House, agreement was reached to scrap the rider in exchange for the President's promise to seek assurances from the Allies that they were not to use the Korean truce as justification for urging Communist China's membership in the UN. Eisenhower also stipulated that for as long as Red China was constituted of the present basis and under the present leaders, "so obviously serving the ends of Soviet Russia," he would never be a party to its recognition and its acceptance into the UN.[48]

The decision of the Senate Republican leaders to scrap the "offensive rider" in favor of a "non-controversial substitute" was reported as a victory for the President. Among the majority of those who had initially criticized it, Elmer Davis of *ABC* welcomed GOP Senators' capitulation to the President, but expressed concern that the "extremely bad public relations effect cannot be wiped off." Indeed, it was a victory for Eisenhower, but not a complete one. Through private consultations, he had avoided a public showdown and succeeded in having the rider removed, but his first taste of what it would be like to go against the China bloc in Congress demonstrated that his hand was not as free as he believed.[49]

Similarly, not everyone in Congress congratulated the administration on finally reaching a truce in Korea on July 26, 1953. Some Republicans, led by Senators Jenner and McCarthy, accused the White House of having given up on victory and Senator Lyndon Johnson (D-TX) noted that an armistice gave the Chinese Communists a free hand to attack somewhere else.[50]

A POLICY FOR CHINA

The end of the Korean War drastically changed US perceptions of China. Historian Gordon Chang remarked that "Americans had to acknowledge grudgingly that China, which fought them and their Allies to a stalemate,

---

[48] CT, May 27 through June 3, 1953, AI568P, box 28, NAII; Memorandum for the Secretary of State from President about meeting with Congressional leaders on Recognition of Red China, June 2, 1953, JFD papers, White House Memoranda Series, box 1, DDEL.

[49] CT, May 27 through June 3, 1953, DOS, AI568P, box 28, NAII.

[50] Ambrose, *Eisenhower, The President*, 328–331; Casey, *Selling the Korean War*, 365.

was a formidable, independent power in the world." Beijing's prestige, particularly in the Far East, had increased. America's superpower image had by contrast, received a big blow. A mid-1953 secret administration review of US policy toward the Communist bloc reflected the new view.[51]

Meeting in the White House Solarium, 18 top national security officials were divided into three groups to analyze various approaches in dealing with the Soviet Union and to establish US general foreign policy orientation. Group A looked at the possibility of continuing Truman's strategy of containment; group B examined a strategy of deterrence that drew lines around the periphery of the communist world and using nuclear weapons, or least the threat of doing so, against anyone crossing them; and group C examined liberating those countries already under the Soviet influence using political, psychological, economic, and covert operations. Eisenhower used the findings of all three groups to formulate his foreign policy.[52]

With respect to the Soviet Union, Project Solarium concluded that the US should not pursue a policy of liberation because such a strategy would be too risky and could easily escalate into another world war. Instead, it recommended acceptance that Moscow constituted a long-term challenge and opposition to its expansionist ambitions but not in a provocative way. In short, the advice to the Eisenhower administration was to continue Truman's containment strategy.[53]

Group A's 150-page report also included an evaluation of Communist China. In its judgment, the US position in the Far East had considerably weakened since the end of World War II for two main reasons. First, the Korean War outcome had elevated Communist China's image within the Soviet sphere and in South-East Asia, thereby diminishing US prestige. Second, Beijing was a threat to American interests in Asia and was successfully creating difficulties among the Western allies. The report from group A also observed that Communist China's growth in stature represented a dangerous threat for Moscow also and "was making the Kremlin uncomfortable." It therefore recommended that the US should adopt a hardline policy toward Beijing in the hope that the application of diplomatic and economic pressure could drive a wedge between the PRC and the Soviet Union. Nonetheless, the report cautioned that "A Communist China, even independent of

---

[51] Gordon Chang, *Friends and Enemies: The United States, China and the Soviet Union, 1948–1972* (Stanford: Stanford University Press, 1982), 89.

[52] "Notes on NSC Meeting", July 16, 1953, DDE Papers, Subject Series, box 9, DDEL.

[53] Ibid.

Moscow, predominant in the power equation of the Far East and attracting Asian support, is very much against our own interests." That radical reevaluation of China's role in international relations meant, as the report stated, that "the bipolarity which distinguished the immediate post-hostilities period" was losing much of its rationale. The United States must face "a more complex, fluid international situation, in which, many national entities are going to play an important part." It was clear that China would be one of them.[54]

The recommendations from Project Solarium provided the foundations for discussion of policy paper NSC166/1. One of the administration's first priorities was to exploit Mao's rise in status after Stalin's death to drive a wedge between Beijing and Moscow. Indeed, even prior to discussions of NCS166, Eisenhower had tried to put pressure on the relationship between the two Communist giants by authorizing a few covert propaganda operations through the Voice of America in the PRC. For example, in a broadcast celebrating the third anniversary of the Russian-Chinese alliance, a Chinese citizen reported that the festivities were very nice. "They ought to be. They were very expensive. We paid for it with Port Arthur, the Changchun Railway, Sinkiang and let's see…the war in Korea." Voice of America often broadcast messages about China's poor economic conditions and "underwhelming Soviet aid. Even so, Chinese soldiers were useful for Moscow's imperialist adventures."[55]

Secretary Dulles concurred with Eisenhower that the relationship between Moscow and Beijing was more complicated than it appeared in public and the differences between the two Communist giants could be exploited to US advantage. In his view, the best way to force a break in the alliance was by putting pressure on Communist China, as the US had done with Yugoslavia. He reasoned that "Tito did not break with Stalin because we [America] were nice to Tito. On the contrary, we were very rough to Tito. It seems to me that if China can win our favors while it is also working closely with Moscow, then there is little reason for it to change." In short, Dulles believed that keeping up pressure on Communist China would force the Chinese Communist Party (CCP) to ask the Soviets for more than they would give, which would eventually produce a break between the two Allies.[56]

[54] Ibid.

[55] Mayers, David, "Eisenhower and Communism: Later Findings", in Richard, Melanson, and David, Mayers, *Re-Evaluating Eisenhower: American Foreign Policy in the 1950s* (Urbana: University of Illinois Press, 1987), 89–90.

[56] "Notes on NSC Meeting", August 24, 1953, DDE Papers, Subject Series, box 9, DDEL.

Not everyone in the administration agreed with that view. The Ambassador to the Union of Soviet Socialist Republics (USSR), Charles Bohlen, argued that a flexible policy toward Beijing was a better solution to weaken its ties with Moscow. In his assessment, a policy of inducement was more likely to prompt a division. A third view, held by Nationalist supporters, denied the existence of tensions between the CCP and the Soviets. In the upper levels of the administration, only Assistant Secretary of State for Far Eastern Affairs, Walter Robertson, held such an opinion.[57]

During the NSC discussions, however, Central Intelligence Agency (CIA) Director, Allen Dulles, the Secretary of State's brother, contended that talks about driving a wedge between the two countries were hypothetical because no fundamental change in Sino-Soviet relations had occurred since Stalin's death. He stressed that China's position in the Soviet bloc was not that of a satellite but of a voluntary and genuine ally that willingly followed the Soviet lead in foreign affairs. Acknowledging that any successor to Stalin would not have the same prestige in Asia, and that Mao's stature as leader and theoretician had increased with the former's death, he pointed out that Soviet deliveries of military and industrial equipment and petroleum products were still 53% of the total PRC imports, with another 10% coming from Soviet satellites and only 28% from the West. Accordingly, the CIA director concluded that no early weakening in Sino-Soviet alliance was to be anticipated.[58]

The second item under discussion was trade policy. During the Korean War the US and its allies had imposed a total trade embargo against Communist China. Now that the fighting had stopped, America's allies were increasingly unwilling to support its stance and wanted to expand the volume of their trade rapidly. Furthermore, businessmen and exporters in the United States were fearful that rivals had an advantage over them.[59]

The administration's official answer to those pressures was that an end of fighting in Korea did not signify that Communist China was no longer intent on pressing its objectives through force. The threat of aggression would continue, particularly in Southeast Asia, while the Communists

---

[57] Ibid.

[58] "CIA Special Estimate on Probable Consequences of the Death of Stalin and the Elevation of Malenkov to Leadership in the USSR", CD Jackson Papers, March 10, 1953, box 1, DDEL; Memorandum of Discussion at 169 meeting of NSC, November 5, 1953, *FRUS*, XIX, 1952–1954, 347–369.

[59] Memorandum of Discussion at 169 meeting of NSC, November 5, 1953, *FRUS*, XIX, 1952–1954, 347–369.

sought to exploit the armistice as tactical device to weaken and divide the free world. It was, therefore, important to US national security as well as to the objectives of obtaining an acceptable settlement in Korea to maintain and develop political and economic pressures against Communist China during the immediate post-armistice period.[60]

In private, however, Eisenhower was skeptical about such a strict policy. During several NSC meetings, he voiced his belief that a more sensible course of action for the United States in that situation would be to apply the criterion of "net gain." To him, there was no profit in blindly adhering to a rigid set of rules and methods of dealing with trade with Communist China. Instead, the US should have the freedom to act in such a manner "as would contribute most to our own advantage in any transactions with Communist China." He even said he was willing to send jet aircrafts to the Chinese Communists "if it could be shown to our net advantage," although, of course, he could not conceive of any return to the US which would suitably balance jet planes.[61]

The President reminded the NSC that trade could be utilized as a diplomatic weapon to weaken the Sino-Soviet alliance. He also focused its attention on Japan's need for economic viability in any discussion of Communist China. If Japan could sell harmless manufactured goods to the PRC, such as "crockery, knives, and forks, and wholly non-strategic materials," that could serve the dual purpose of relieving Beijing's dependence on Russia and Japan's dependence on the US treasury.[62]

Eisenhower acknowledged that the greatest difficulty would be in the public relations aspect of any policy which involved trading with Communist China. "Demagogues would raise a hue and cry about building up economies of nations that used their resources to kill American soldiers." Public opinion polls were also clear on the matter (see Table 3.2). According to the latest survey from the State Department, 83% of Americans interviewed disapproved of any US or allies trade with Communist China, and another 56% believed that the US should insist that the allies stop all trade with Communist China, even if it involved non-strategic material only. Eisenhower was confident, however, of winning popular support for such a change in policy if required. He explained during a NSC meeting that a well-organized information campaign that

[60] NSC152/2 "Economic Defence", July 31, 1953, *FRUS*, XIX, 239–240.
[61] Ibid.; NSC122/1 Economic Defence Policy Toward Hong Kong and Macao, *FRUS*, XIX, 1952–1954, 267–277.
[62] Ibid.

Table 3.2   Detailed breakdown of US public opinion opposition on trading with Communist China

Trade with Communist China

"As you may know, our Allies have stopped selling war materials to Communist China, but some are still trading other goods with them. Do you approve or disapprove of our Allies carrying on this other trade with Communist China?"

	National	College educated	High school	Grammar school
Approve other trade	14%	19%	12%	13%
Disapprove	83%	81%	86%	82%
No Opinion	3%	–	2%	5%

"Do You think our Government should insist that our Allies stop all trade with Communist China, or should we let them decide these matters themselves?"

	National	College educated	High school	Grammar school
We should insist	56%	55%	57%	57%
Let them decide	24%	23%	27%	21%
No Opinion	3%	3%	2%	4%

Source: "Popular Attitudes on Allied Trade with Communist China", June 10, 1953, DOS, AI568J, box 1, NAII

enlisted the assistance of the business community would make the public understand the economic and national security benefits of trading with the PRC.[63]

Secretary of Commerce Sinclair Weeks and Secretary of the Treasury George M. Humphreys agreed with the President. Believing that East-West trade would ultimately need to be opened, they considered it impractical for the United States to stick to such a strict policy in the long term. Weeks was also very concerned about the humanitarian aspect of the embargo on antibiotics. Now that the fighting had ended, the US was going to be very hard pressed to withstand propaganda that it was deliberately withholding needed drugs from China. In contrast, Secretary of Defense Charles E. Wilson stated the opposing view that "we could not fight the Communists and love them at the same time." His view was shared by Dulles, whose support for a trade embargo was coherent with his strategy of pressure on China to drive a wedge between the CCP and the Soviets.[64]

---

[63] "Popular Attitudes on Allied Trade with Communist China", June 10, 1953, DOS, AI568J, box 1, NAII; Memorandum of Discussion at 160 meeting of NSC, August 5, 1953, *FRUS*, XIX, 1952–1954, 290–306.

[64] Ibid.

After several months of discussion, the NSC approved the last version of NSC 166/1 on November 6, 1953. The document endorsed Group A's conclusions: "The problem for US foreign policy in the Far East is to cope with the altered structure of power which arises from the existence of a strong and hostile Communist China, and from the alliance of Communist China with the USSR." It acknowledged that the Chinese Communists had succeeded in establishing strong, centralized political control over the mainland. The PRC's goal was to recapture historically held Chinese territories which at that time were under US or Western protection and to substitute Western influence in Asia for its own. NSC 166/1 further contended that regardless of resolution of Far Eastern issues to the satisfaction of Beijing, the Chinese Communists, as Communists, would continue to maintain a basic hostility for the West in general and for the US in particular.[65]

According to that policy document, the only solution for the US was to secure a reorientation of the Chinese Communist regime and ultimately to replace it by a regime that would not be hostile to the US. However, that was not possible at that time because China's military capacities made an invasion of its territory costly and required commitment of major US and Western resources. In the absence of further Chinese Communist aggression or a basic change in the situation, the main objective of US policy in Asia should be to weaken, or at least retard, the growth of PRC power in Asia. The document then specifically directed the United States to maintain the security of Taiwan and the offshore islands, to prevent the territorial expansion of the Chinese Communists, to continue recognition and support the Chinese Nationalists, to strengthen non-Communist Asia, and to continue to exert covert as well as "unconventional and overt pressures" against Communist China.[66]

NSC166/1 finally called for utilizing "all feasible means, covert and overt, to impair Sino-Soviet relations." Acknowledging the CIA estimate that US capabilities for exercising pressure were limited because Beijing was not actually interested in splitting from Russia, it still contended that economic restrictions on the part of the US and its allies would delay PRC efforts to achieve industrialization and obligate the USSR to continue to carry the burden of assisting Communist China. Furthermore, the docu-

---

[65] NSC 166/1 "US Policy Towards Communist China", November 6, 1953, *FRUS*, XIX, 1952–1954, 308–334.

[66] Ibid.

ment envisaged that US diplomatic and political measures would impede general international acceptance of the Chinese Communist regime, thus reducing Beijing's effectiveness in rendering propaganda to support the USSR and forestalling an increase of Chinese Communist prestige. In summary, NSC 166/1 sanctioned the policy of pressure advocated by Dulles.[67]

Records of NSC discussions show that public opinion did not have much influence on the formulation of US-China policy. It was never mentioned during meetings, except when Eisenhower brought up the hypothetical question of relaxing the trade ban, but even in that case the President felt confident that he would be able to generate support for change in policy. US national security considerations were clearly uppermost in establishing a hardline policy toward Beijing.

Public opinion did, however, play a role in determining the way the administration presented its China policy. Although the White House and State Department surveys showed it overwhelmingly supported a policy of total hostility toward the PRC, Eisenhower and Dulles did not want to take any chance. From September to December 1953, the two of them and other members of the administration gave no less than 250 press conferences, interviews, and official statements and addresses, all aimed at portraying Communist China in a negative light. Those public messages focused on five themes: the monolithic nature of the communist world; the Chinese people's suffering because of the Communist conquest of the mainland; US moral superiority; Beijing's aggressive record in the Far East; and US concern for American citizens still held in Chinese Communist jails since 1949.[68]

The reasoning behind the decision to present a monolithic view of the Communist world was clear. As Eisenhower explained during a NSC meeting on November 5th, despite the administration's more sophisticated opinion on Sino-Soviet relations, "It would be too difficult for the American public to understand the subtle and complicated differences between the Soviet Communist Party and the Chinese Communist Party." It was much easier to sell them a "black and white" image of the problem: all the Communists were the same and all the Communists were bad. Sentences like "The threat of the Bolshevik Plot" or "Beijing takes its

[67] Ibid.
[68] *DBS*, September through December 1953; DDE Papers, Speeches Series, box 3–4, DDEL; JFD papers, box 49–50, ML.

orders from the Bolshevik Communists" consequently became staples of the administration's public messages.[69]

Additionally, Eisenhower thought that presenting a monolithic view of Communism would help to limit the influence of those who supported an Asia-first policy. The President was afraid that if the Asia-first policy supporters convinced the public that the main source of danger for US national security came from Beijing, popular opinion would force the administration to divert military and economic resources to fight the Soviet Union in Europe in favor of the Far East. Reminding the American people that Moscow was still the greatest threat to the US was, therefore, necessary to guarantee continuation of aid programs for Europe, which the President still considered the real focus of the Cold War.[70]

Closely linked to that theme was the Chinese people's suffering from the Communist conquest of the mainland. That was a very familiar issue to the American people and one that Eisenhower had already exploited during the 1952 presidential campaign. Although their personal views on that score are unclear from their private papers, the President and Dulles wanted to capitalize on the American people's sentimental predisposition toward the Chinese by portraying them as victims of a "global Communist conspiracy." They also decided to continue fostering illusions about an eventual Chinese mass conversion to Christianity. Accordingly, sentences like "Christianity will save us and the Chinese people" became another standard of the administration's rhetoric.[71]

Finally, the administration publicly justified its policy of non-recognition, opposition to PRC admission into the UN, trade embargo, and total travel ban by reminding the American people of the Chinese Communist aggressive record in the Far East and the fact that 33 American citizens were still being held in Chinese Communist prisons.[72]

As for Taiwan, there was a vast discrepancy between the administration's private views and its public stance. President Eisenhower was especially fearful that Jiang would use any excuse to launch an attack to recapture mainland China and drag the US into it. It was therefore agreed that Washington should try to limit its engagement with Taipei. Publicly

[69] 170th Meeting of the NSC, November 6, 1953, *FRUS*, XIX, 1952–1954, pp. 308–334.
[70] Ibid.
[71] *DBS*, September through December 1953; DDE Papers, Speeches Series, box 3–4, DDEL; JFD papers, box 49–50, ML.
[72] Ibid.

however, the White House still showed support for the Generalissimo and still portrayed him as China's only hope for democracy. Additionally, Eisenhower sent Vice President Richard M. Nixon on a 70-day tour of Southeast Asia "to cultivate friendships and show the world our support for old Chiang."[73]

After a brief stop in New Zealand and Australia, Nixon flew to Indonesia, Malaya, Singapore, Indochina, and then Taiwan. When he landed in Taipei, the American press was ecstatic. "The Vice President's visit to Formosa shows the world exactly where America stands," declared a *Washington Daily News* editorial. A *New York Herald Tribune* editorial said: "This would make clear once and for all who our friends are." Every public detail of Nixon's stay was cabled back to the US, notably regarding the official banquet given in his honor by Jiang Jieshi; Mrs. Nixon's shopping trips to the local markets; and the Vice President's cordial relationship with the Generalissimo. What they did not report was Nixon's private meeting with Jiang, which lasted seven hours, with Madame Jiang serving as interpreter. Jiang spoke grandly of his hopes to invade the Chinese mainland and reunite the country under his leadership, but the Vice President responded that "American military power would not be committed to support any invasion he might launch."[74]

Extra help for the administration's propaganda campaign came from the newly established Committee for One Million against the Admission of Communist China into the United Nations (hereafter Committee for One Million or COOM). On October 22, 1953, Congressman Walter Judd met with President Eisenhower at the White House to present a petition against the admission of the PRC into the UN. As Judd explained, the idea had originated in the Far East Subcommittee of the House Foreign Affairs Committee, whose members had become increasingly concerned about the British insistence on admitting the Beijing regime to the world body.[75]

The COOM petition warned of the effect of PRC's admission into the UN. Not only would it "destroy the purposes and violate the spirit of the law" of the UN by admitting a country unable to carry out the obligations

---

[73] Ambrose, Stephen E. *Nixon: The Education of Politician, 1913–1962* (New York: Simon and Schuster, 1987), 319–327.

[74] Ibid.; CT, November through December 1953, DOS, AI568P, box 28, NAII.

[75] Memorandum for the President, October 23, 1953, DDE Papers, Dulles-Herter Series, box 1, DDEL. Letter from Eisenhower to Judd, October 24, 1953, DDE Papers, Diary Series, box 3, DDEL.

of the UN Charter, but it would also expel a charter member: the Chinese People's Republic, the duly constituted Government of China. Furthermore, the Beijing regime "has shown its unwillingness to carry out the obligations of the Charter by systematically disregarding every human right and violating every freedom and had proved itself an aggressor state by aiding in aggression upon South Korea and making war on the UN." Admission would destroy the prestige and the position of the UN and the Free World in Asia in turn encouraging Asian nations to "make fatal compromises with the communist bloc."[76]

The petition had already been signed by 210 prominent public figures, including former President Herbert Hoover, 49 members of Congress (Judd, Knowland, and Bridges prominent among them), 11 retired generals (including George C. Marshall and Lucius D. Clay), and 18 publishers and journalists (including William R. Hearst Jr). The list also contained religious leaders; scientists and educators; business, industry and finance executives; retired diplomats; and famous individuals from the arts, entertainment, and sports. After reading the document, the President reassured Judd that his administration had no intention of establishing any form of relationship with the PRC until it "demonstrated its intention to live according to civilized international rules."[77]

Eisenhower's meeting with Judd gave a huge popular boost to the Committee's cause. Its petition received widespread press coverage throughout the nation. The *New York Times* officially endorsed it, Roy Howard guaranteed "the continued support of his publications," and *Newsweek* dedicated a three-page feature to explain the importance of signing the document. By the end of December 1953, the COOM steering committee could report that around 180,000 petition forms had been distributed, approximately 100,000 signatures had been received, and $22,000 had been contributed. By March 1954, the number of signatures had reached 500,000.[78]

In recent years, however, new evidence has emerged that the formation of the Committee of One Million was, in reality, an early example of a

[76] Ibid.

[77] Ibid.

[78] "Drive Against Red China: Hoover Asks Signatures to Plea to Bar Nation from UN", the *New York Times*, January 25, 1954, 3; Letter from Howard to Judd, Roy Howard's Private Papers, box 263, Library of Congress, Manuscript Division, Washington, DC (hereafter Howard Papers, LoC); "The Petition Against Admission of Red China in the UN", *Newsweek*, November 17, 1953, 7–10.

covert CIA domestic political operation. The original idea came from Nicholas de Rochefort, once a French citizen and member of the Office of Strategic Services, the World War II predecessor to the CIA. In 1953, Rochefort became an American citizen and was employed by the CIA during the Committee's inception. He contacted Dr. Judd and succeeded in persuading him to present his plan on mobilizing domestic and international public opinion against Red China admission into the UN, at a meeting of the sub-committee for the Far East of the House Foreign Affairs Committee. Consequently, a group was formed, headed by Judd that launched the public appeal presented to the President on October 22nd.[79]

It is plausible that the CIA might have been behind the plan. Historians Shawn Parry-Giles and Kenneth Osgood have documented President Eisenhower's extensive use of covert operations to generate domestic and international support for his foreign policy. Regardless of its origins, the Committee helped promote the administration's strategy of hostility toward the PRC. In its quest to gather the one million signatures, it produced a vast amount of propaganda literature and organized many events to keep its cause at the forefront of the public debate. From its inception, it also officially replaced the work of the China Lobby.[80]

Eisenhower and Dulles had managed to gain control of the foreign policy making process by formulating a China policy based on what they thought was right for US national security, but, they had also kept their campaign promises. They had brought peace by ending the Korean War, and had taken some decisive steps in restoring US prestige and credibility in the Far East. An end-of-the year survey by the State Department on public attitudes toward the administration's China policy revealed that its public relations strategy had also been successful. Popular opinion fully supported the hardline policy against the PRC. Of those interviewed, 89% were against establishing diplomatic relations with the PRC, 84% opposed admission of Beijing into the UN, and 24% approved US withdrawal from that body if the Chinese Communists were given a seat in the Security Council, an increase of 5%. Additionally, 87% of those surveyed were in favor of continuing the total trade embargo and travel ban policy and dis-

[79] Stanley Bachrack, *The Committee of One Million, "China Lobby" Politics* (New York: Columbia University Press, 1976).

[80] Shawn J. Parry-Giles, "The Eisenhower Administration's Conceptualisation of the USIA: The Development of Overt and Covert Propaganda Strategies," *Presidential Studies Quarterly* 24 (1994): 263–276; Kenneth Osgood, *Total Cold War: Eisenhower's Secret Propaganda Battle at Home and Abroad* (Lawrence: University Press of Kansas, 2006).

approved of the Allies trading with Beijing; of those, 60% believed that the US should insist that the Allies cease trading.[81]

The State Department also reported that the administration's public stance had won the enthusiastic applause of press observers throughout the country. That included newspapers of every area: Democratic, Republican, independent, internationalist, and nationalist titles all agreed that the Administration's public statements represented "an American foreign policy declaration of first magnitude." Commentators found important messages in them for all peoples. They not only made the US position "clear to Allies and enemies alike" but also assured the American people that the US Government recognized its role as "leader" of the free world and had a "firm policy" in meeting the communist menace. The warnings to Communist China against new aggression in Korea and Indochina made the greatest impact of all and were strongly endorsed. For example, a *Baltimore Sun* editorial declared that the warnings gave emphatic new voice to a new and definite policy that will guide the government. Another *New York News* editorial opined that "Dulles' momentous speech marked a return to Americanism which will be welcomed and supported." The *New York Times*, the *Wall Street Journal*, the *New York Herald Tribune*, the *Boston Herald*, the *San Francisco Chronicle*, Scripps-Howard Press, and the *Kansas City Star* all endorsed those views.[82]

Henry Luce was the sole publisher who was disappointed with the administration's new policy, but did not figure in the State Department's report. Although the *Time* and *Life* owner supported Eisenhower's hardline policy against the PRC, he was troubled by his policy regarding Taiwan. His former editor, C.D. Jackson, had been appointed as Special Assistant to the President on psychological warfare. Regularly in attendance at NSC meetings, he kept his old boss thoroughly informed about discussions and decisions. Luce was, therefore, fully aware that the administration's public stance on the Nationalist Government did not reflect Eisenhower and Dulles' private views. He knew that the widely advertised unleashing of Jiang Jieshi was only a public relations gimmick that did not make any substantial difference to Jiang's quest to re-conquer the mainland. Despite personal disappointment, he decided to continue supporting the President via his publications because he was afraid that too much

---

[81] "Public Attitudes Toward the Administration's China Policy", December 1953, DOS, AI568K, box 1, NAII.

[82] Ibid.

criticism might put an end to his relationship with the White House. A loyal Republican, he also thought that was the right thing to do politically.[83]

The President's popularity among the American people remained untouched. In December 1953, his approval rating was up to 80%, Dulles' was up to 70%. Of course, overall, the administration's task had not been that difficult. Much of its China policy reflected what the public wanted and most of public opinion was already in favor of a hostile line toward the PRC, even before Eisenhower and Dulles formulated the policy. Still, they had done it without bowing to public pressure and had been able to create the right conditions to maintain that popular support. The reaction by the Chinese Communists to the tough policy and its consequences on American public opinion would be the real challenge for the Eisenhower-Dulles strategy.[84]

REFERENCES

Allen, Craig. *Eisenhower and the Mass Media, Peace, Prosperity and Prime-Time TV*. Chapel Hill: North Carolina University Press, 1993.
Ambrose, Stephen E. *Eisenhower, The President, 1952–1969*. London: Allen & Unwind, 1984.
Bachrack, Stanley. *The Committee of One Million, "China Lobby" Politics*. New York: Columbia University Press, 1976.
Bowie, Robert and Richard Immerman. *Waging Peace: How Eisenhower Shaped an Enduring Cold War Strategy*. New York: Oxford University Press, 1998.
Casey, Steven. *Selling the Korean War: Propaganda, Politics and Public Opinion in the United States, 1950–1953*. Oxford: Oxford University Press, 2010.
Chang, Gordon. *Friends and Enemies: The United States, China and the Soviet Union, 1948–1972*. Stanford: Stanford University Press, 1982.
Eisenhower, Dwight D. *A Mandate for a Change, 1953–1956*. London: Heinemann, 1963.

[83] Luce had a regular correspondence with Jackson from January 1953 to December 1954, when Jackson left the White House. They discussed the unleashing of Jiang Jieshi and Luce's disappointment with Eisenhower's views between February and November 1953. Evidence of this correspondence can be found among Henry R. Luce Papers, Private Correspondence, box 33, Library of Congress, Manuscript Division, Washington, DC (hereafter Luce Papers, LoC).

[84] "Public Attitudes Toward the Administration's China Policy", December 1953, DOS, AI568K, box 1, NAII.

Foyle, Douglass C. *Counting the Public In: Presidents, Public Opinion and Foreign Policy*. New York: Columbia University Press, 1999.

Greenstein, Fred. *The Hidden-Hand Presidency: Eisenhower as a Leader*. New York: Basic Books, 1992.

Hughes, Emmet J. *The Ordeal of Power: A Political Memoir of the Eisenhower Years*. New York: Atheneum, 1963.

Oliva, Mara. "Beaten at Their Own Game: Eisenhower, Dulles, US Public Opinion and the Sino-Ambassadorial Talks of 1955–1957." *Journal of Cold War Studies* 20, no. 1 (2018).

Osgood, Kenneth. *Total Cold War: Eisenhower's Secret Propaganda Battle at Home and Abroad*. Lawrence: University Press of Kansas, 2006.

Parry-Giles, Shawn J. "The Eisenhower Administration's Conceptualisation of the USIA: The Development of Overt and Covert Propaganda Strategies." *Presidential Studies Quarterly* 24 (1994): 263–276.

Stueck, William, Jr. *The Road to Confrontation; American Policy Toward China and Korea, 1947–1950*. Chapel Hill: University of North Carolina Press, 1981.

CHAPTER 4

Challenge One: Dien Bien Phu and the Geneva Conference of 1954

"I cannot afford to have the Democrats ask: who lost Vietnam?" President Dwight D. Eisenhower told his National Security Council (NSC) in January 1954 while discussing a possible US intervention in the French colonial war against the Communist-led Vietminh in Indochina. The military crisis at Dienbienphu and the subsequent peace conference in Geneva were the first challenge to the Eisenhower administration's hardline policy toward the People's Republic of China (PRC). They typified the dilemma outlined in the 1952 Presidential campaign. Public opinion was still reeling from the painful Korean War experience and was certainly not in the mood for another limited war, particularly if that might precipitate PRC involvement. But President Eisenhower correctly feared a repeat of "the loss of China" debate. Only this time, he would be accused of losing yet another country to Communism if he let the Vietminh take control of the Indochina peninsula.[1]

The vast revisionist literature on the Eisenhower administration's involvement in Indochina has advanced numerous interpretations of the influence those contradictory popular feelings had on the President's thinking. Without disputing Eisenhower's sound decision not to intervene in Dien Bien Phu, some scholars, such as Robert Divine, have suggested that President Eisenhower and Secretary of State John Foster Dulles skillfully used public opinion and particularly Congress to restrain those "impulsive administration advisers" who favored sending US troops

[1] Stephen Ambrose, *Eisenhower: The President* (New York: Simon & Schuster, 1983), 173.

© The Author(s) 2018
M. Oliva, *Eisenhower and American Public Opinion on China*,
https://doi.org/10.1007/978-3-319-76195-4_4

85

to Indochina. Others, like historian Stephen Ambrose, have observed that Eisenhower's strategy in Indochina was fashioned by his fear of the domestic repercussions of losing Vietnam. More recently, political scientist Douglas Foyle has argued that Congressional and public lack of support for US intervention forced the administration to review its policy of hostility toward the PRC and back down in Indochina.[2]

This chapter disputes those scholars' contentions. It argues instead that while the administration kept a careful eye on public opinion, neither Eisenhower nor Dulles were willing to sacrifice national security interests and review their hardline policy toward Beijing (Peiping) to appease the public. The popular outlook, and particularly that of Congress, narrowed the choice of policy options available and affected the way that the President and the Secretary of State implemented their national security strategy and how they presented it to the public, but it did not influence the administration's basic thinking about the enemy nor did it determine the policy choice.

1953: BACKGROUND TO THE DIEN BIEN PHU CRISIS

When Eisenhower took office in January 1953, the US was already substantially involved in the Indochina war. The conflict between France and the Communist-dominated nationalist movement, Vietminh, had started in 1946. The French were trying to recapture what they considered to be a colony lost to Japan during World War II. But the Vietminh, led by Ho Chi Minh, were fighting for independence. Fearing the Chinese Communists would use the war to spread their power throughout Southeast Asia, the Truman administration had been supplying military and economic aid to the French since May 1950. Within three years, US assistance reached $3 billion and included military and medical supplies. As historians Mark Atwood Lawrence and Frederick Logevall observed: "From 1950 onwards the Franco-Vietminh war was simultaneously a colonial conflict and a Cold War confrontation—a Sino-US war by proxy with the potential to escalate into a direct military confrontation."[3]

---

[2] Robert A. Divine, *Eisenhower and the Cold War* (New York: Oxford University Press, 1981), 39–51; Stephen Ambrose, *Eisenhower: Soldier and President* (New York: Simon and Schuster Paperbacks, 1990); Douglas C. Foyle, *Counting the Public In: Presidents, Public Opinion, and Foreign Policy* (New York: Columbia University Press, 1999).

[3] John Dumbrell, *Vietnam: American Involvement at Home and Abroad*, BAAS Pamphlets in American Studies 22 (British Association of American Studies, 1992), 9–11; Mark Atwood

The Eisenhower administration recognized the importance of Indochina, in terms of what would become known as the "domino theory." Just a few weeks after taking office, Dulles voiced concern to the Joint Chiefs of Staff (JCS) about the consequences that the loss of Vietnam would have on Japan. "If Southeast Asia were lost," he declared, "this would lead to the loss of Japan. The situation of the Japanese is hard enough with China being commie. You would not lose Japan immediately, but from there on out the Japs would be thinking of how to get on the other side." The Secretary's judgment of Indochina's importance received support a few months later from a special Congressional study mission to the Far East, headed by Representative Walter H. Judd (R-MN). Upon his return to Washington, Judd reported:

> The area of Indochina is immensely wealthy in rice, rubber, coal and iron ore. Its position makes it a strategic key to the rest of Southeast Asia. If Indochina should fall, Thailand and Burma would be in extreme danger. Malaya, Singapore, and even Indonesia would become more vulnerable to the Communist power drive... Communism would then be in an exceptional position to complete its perversion of the political and social revolution that is spreading through Asia. The Communists must be prevented from achieving their objectives in Indochina.[4]

Eisenhower acknowledged that Indochina "had probably the top priority in foreign policy, being in some ways more important than Korea because consequences of loss there could not be localized but would spread throughout Asia and Europe." However, the President did not believe that using military force, French or American, was the correct option to save Indochina from Communism. He was quite sure that the Chinese would quickly step in to help the Vietminh. Indeed, back in 1951,

Lawrence and Fredrick Logevall, *The First Vietnam War: Colonial Conflict and Cold War Crisis* (Cambridge, MA: Harvard University Press, 2007), 9–10; Melanie Billings-Yun, *Decision Against War: Eisenhower and Dien Bien Phu, 1954* (New York: Columbia University Press, 1988), 13–15; Melvin Gurtov, *The First Vietnam Crisis: Chinese Communist Strategy and United States Involvement, 1953–1954* (New York: Columbia University Press, 1967), 20–25.

[4] JCS Meeting, January 28, 1953, *Foreign Relations of the United States*, XIII, 1952–1954, 361 (hereafter FRUS followed by volume, year, and page number); *House Special Study Mission Report* 1953. US House of Representatives, Committee of Foreign Affairs, *Report on the Special Mission to Pakistan, India, Thailand, and Indochina*, H. Rpt. No 412, 83rd Congress, 1st session, May 6, 1953, 53.

he had written in his diary: "Even if Indochina were completely cleared of Communists, right across the border is China with its inexhaustible man-power." An intervention by the PRC in the conflict could not be ignored by the United States as that could have quickly turned a regional conflict into a global one.[5]

To prevent such a bleak occurrence, throughout 1953, Washington publicly notified Beijing that the US was ready to respond to any Communist aggressive action in the area and was willing to go beyond the Vietnamese border onto the China mainland. On April 16th, the President hinted before the American Society of Newspapers Editors that he had the full support of the international community. "The free world," he cautioned, "knows that aggressions in Korea and in Southeast Asia are threats to the whole free community to be met through united action." A few months later, at the annual Governors' conference, Eisenhower stressed again that a Beijing-sponsored movement in Vietnam represented a serious national security threat for the US; not least because a loss of Indochina would trigger a "chain reaction." The Malaya peninsula would follow quickly and the rest of Asia would be "outflanked." Consequently, Communist aggression in the area "must be blocked and must be blocked now."[6]

Believing in the effectiveness of making "one's intentions clear in advance," Dulles sent a very stark warning to the PRC on September 2nd. Speaking at the American Legion Convention, he declared:

> Communist China has been and is now training, equipping and supplying the Communist forces in Indochina. There is a risk that, as in Korea, Red China might send its own army into Indochina. The Communist Chinese regime should realize that such a second aggression could not occur without grave consequences which might not be confined to Indochina.[7]

[5] Memorandum of Conversation, March 24, 1953, *FRUS*, XIII, 1952–1954, 419; Dwight D. Eisenhower, *The Eisenhower Diaries*, ed. Robert Ferrell (New York: W.W. Norton & Company, 1981), 190; Memorandum of Conversation, April 2, 1953, Dwight D. Eisenhower Papers, Memoranda Series, box 2, Dwight D. Eisenhower Presidential Library, Abilene, Kansas (hereafter DDE Papers, followed by file reference, box number, DDEL).

[6] "Transcript of President Dwight D. Eisenhower's April 16 Address", the *New York Times*, April 17, 1953, 4; "Transcript of President Dwight D. Eisenhower's August 4 Address", the *New York Times*, August 5, 1953, 10.

[7] "Transcript of Secretary of State John Foster Dulles' September 2 Address," the *New York Times*, September 3, 1953, 4.

Verbal warnings were accompanied by increased US economic and military assistance for the French to offset China aid for the Vietminh. In March 1953, on JCS recommendation, the administration approved a plan to broaden the American role in Indochina by providing greater financial and material support. It was hoped that it would prevent Washington from becoming directly involved in the war. Eisenhower also reminded French Prime Minister, Rene Mayer, of the importance of public opinion in the US. He warned him that if he wanted American help, he needed to state clearly that Paris would grant full independence to Vietnam because "unfortunately many Americans continue to think of the war in Indochina as a French colonial operation rather than as a part of the struggle of the free world against the forces of Communism."[8]

Lack of support from the Americans for what they considered French colonialism was reflected in several opinion polls. In the summer of 1953, Eisenhower asked pollster Alfred Politz to conduct a survey on the Indochina issue. In his briefing to Politz, the President specifically requested him to ascertain popular feeling toward expanding the US role in the war, even if the conflict remained confined to the French and the Vietminh, and, how the American people would react to a US-armed response against a PRC-armed attack in Vietnam. Politz's subsequent memorandum to Eisenhower presented a very clear picture of the feelings of Americans toward the French fight against the Vietminh. His polls found that 83% of the respondents opposed "expanding US role in the war if the conflict remained confined between the two belligerents." However, results on a possible PRC intervention were more ambivalent. Asked if the United States should help fight if the Chinese Communists were going to invade Indochina, 47% of the respondents answered "yes", 32% answered "no", and 21% answered "I don't know." Those who had answered that "the US should help fight" or "I don't know" were then asked several follow-up questions regarding specific policy options to fight the PRC. Of those, 30% of respondents declared themselves in favor of sending "American soldiers to fight in Indochina," but 23% were "opposed," and 15% "did not know." Meanwhile, 39% were against the

[8] Memorandum for the Secretary of Defense, March 13, 1953, US Congress, House Committee on Armed Forces, *United States-Vietnam Relations, 1945–1967: A Study Prepared by the Department of Defense* (Washington, DC: Government Printing Office, 1971), book 9, 11–14; Minutes of Meeting Between President Eisenhower and Prime Minister of France Mayer, March 26, 1953, *FRUS*, XIII, 1952–1954, 429–432.

United States supplying money and men, and 42% opposed "unilateral US involvement without United Nations cooperation," but 46% of those surveyed favored" sending increased armament supplies to Indochina."[9]

Later surveys confirmed Politz's findings. A September 18, 1953 Gallup poll asked, "The United States is now sending war material to help the French fight the Communists in Indochina. Would you approve or disapprove of sending US soldiers to take part in the fighting there?" Eight percent of the respondents said yes, but an impressive 85% said no. Furthermore, an October 1953 State Department poll found that 53% of Americans approved of using air force "if it looked like the Chinese Communists might take over all Indochina."[10]

Those polls clearly showed the dilemma facing the Eisenhower administration. While an overwhelming majority of the public opposed expanding the US role in the war between the French and the Vietminh, popular feeling toward a PRC attack were less evident. Poll results failed to identify a distinct majority or minority in favor of or in opposition to a specific policy option. Support for increasing armament supplies, using air force, and sending US soldiers ranged from 30 to 53%, while opposition to the US supplying money and men, and unilateral US involvement without United Nations (UN) cooperation ranged from 39 to 42%.

The military crisis began to quickly precipitate in the autumn of 1953, when the French Commander Raoul Salan was replaced by General Henri Navarre. Navarre asked the White House for $400 million to implement a new plan to increase French forces and train native troops. He would then use that new and revitalized army to attack the Communists in the Red River Delta area. Neither the President nor the JCS thought this could bring a definite solution to the difficult situation in Indochina. But the administration had no choice: a refusal to back the plan would cause the French to withdraw, and Washington definitely did not want that. The consequence would be to either abandon Indochina or, as the Director of the State Department Policy Planning Staff, Robert Bowie,

---

[9] Jackson to Eisenhower, July 11, 1953, DDE Papers, Administration Series, C.D. Jackson 1953, box 21, DDEL.

[10] Gallup, George, The Gallup Poll, 1949–1958 (New York: Random House, 1972), 1146; "Special Report on American Opinion", November 1953, Record of the Office of Public Opinion Studies, Department of State, 1943–1975, AI568J, box 1, National Archives II, College Park, Maryland (hereafter survey title followed by date, DOS, file reference, box number, NAII).

observed: "Begin to consider most seriously whether we [US] should take over this area."[11]

Grudgingly, on September 9th, Eisenhower agreed to send the French an additional $385 million with Congress agreeing a few days later. However, the French Commander unfortunately decided not to implement his plan. Instead, in November 1953 he made the disastrous decision to send a sizable number of his best troops to the remote Dien Bien Phu fortress in northwest Vietnam, where he hoped to lure the Vietminh into a set piece battle. Eisenhower recalled being "horror stricken" that the French would try to defend such an isolated location: "I can't think of anything crazier. No experienced soldier would ever establish a force, in a place, in a fortress, and then ask the enemy to come and get it."[12]

UNDER ATTACK

Navarre's plan did not work out as originally planned. By early 1954, a Central Intelligence Agency (CIA) report had confirmed that he had managed to isolate his forces in the northeast corner of Vietnam. The NSC had no choice but to begin discussions about what to do in Indochina and what role the US should play. The chairman of the JCS, Admiral Arthur Radford, wanted the US to step in and "do everything possible to forestall a French defeat at Dien Bien Phu." However, other officials, led by Secretary of the Treasury, George Humphrey, were very disturbed by the idea of putting American troops in Indochina. Very poignantly, he asked: "how long would it be before we get into war? And can we afford to get in such a war?"[13]

At that point President Eisenhower expressed his strong opposition to using ground troops to confront the problem. The minutes of the meeting state:

---

[11] Report on the National Security Council by the Department of State, August 5, 1954, *FRUS*, XIII, 1952–1954, 714–717; Substance of Discussions of State-Joint Chiefs of Staff Meeting, September 4, 1953, *FRUS*, XIII, 1952–1954, 756.

[12] Substance of Discussions of State-Joint Chiefs of Staff Meeting, September 4, 1953, *FRUS*, XIII, 1952–1954, 756; Dwight D. Eisenhower, Eisenhower Administration Project: Oral History, 1962–1972, Columbia Center for Oral History, Butler Library, Columbia University, New York (hereafter DDE Oral History, followed by CUNY).

[13] "CIA Special Report on Situation in Indochina", January 1954, DDE Papers, NSC Series, box 385, DDEL; Memorandum of Discussion, 179 NSC Meeting, January 8, 1954, *FRUS*, XIII 1952–1954, 949–954.

For himself, said the President with great force, he simply could not imagine the United States putting ground forces anywhere in Southeast Asia, except possibly in Malaya, which we would have to defend as a bulwark to our off-shore island chain…I cannot tell you, said the President with vehemence, how bitterly opposed I am to such a course of action. This war in Indochina would absorb our troops by divisions.[14]

However, he was not completely opposed to the idea of sending "a little group of fine and adventurous pilots with unmarked US planes," if that could avoid a defeat at Dien Bien Phu, and more importantly, US direct involvement in the war. In opting for that solution, Eisenhower was thinking about American public opinion. As he reminded the NSC, it was going to be quite a challenge for the administration because the polls clearly showed that the public was very confused about Vietnam and did not know "what it wants." As Assistant to the President Sherman Adams recalled in his memoirs, Eisenhower was fully aware that the still fresh memories of the Korean War, under armistice for less than a year, remained on the popular mind. Additionally, in the 1952 presidential election, he had a run on a platform that had promised "no more Koreas." Indeed, he had exploited the very issue by accusing the Truman administration of having sent the country into war by losing China to Communism. He was then afraid he would be accused of having lost Vietnam.[15]

No agreement was reached by the end of the meeting. Eisenhower, therefore, decided that the CIA and the Defense Department would join forces and work out what other options were available to the US to help the French. In response, the two agencies produced a document which became known as NSC paper 5405. The document recommended that the US should "without relieving France of its basic responsibilities for the defense of the Associated States, expedite the provision of, and if necessary increase, aid to the French Union forces, under terms of existing commitments…and encourage further steps by both France and the Associate States to produce a working relationship based on equal sovereignty within the general framework of the French Union."[16]

[14] Ibid.

[15] Ibid.; Sherman Adams, *First Hand Report: The Story of the Eisenhower Administration* (New York: Harper, 1961), 118.

[16] Memorandum of Discussion, 179 NSC meeting, January 8, 1954, *FRUS,* XIII, 1952–1954, 949–954; Richard Immerman, "Between the Unattainable and the

In the meantime, the President asked Deputy Secretary of Defense Roger Keys, Special Assistant to the President C.D. Jackson, Under-Secretary of State Walter Bedell Smith, and CIA Director Allen Dulles to establish a special committee "to come up with a plan in specific terms, covering who does what and with which and to whom." Fundamentally, Eisenhower was complaining about lacking "an area plan" and wanted "any possible alternative lines of action" to be explored.[17]

At the first committee meeting on January 29, 1954, it was agreed that the US would send 400 mechanics and 20 additional B-26s to Indochina. Soon after, a furor erupted in Washington when Joseph and Stewart Alsop revealed in their *Washington Post* column that the NSC "has already taken the decision" to send 400 mechanics and maintenance experts from the US Air force. They pointed to that decision and to reports that the NSC was considering sending out air and naval support as a "measure of the gravity of the crisis." The next day, columnist Drew Pearson claimed that "Admiral Radford has persuaded Eisenhower to order 400 air force technicians and mechanics into Indochina" in answer to French requests.[18]

It is not clear how that information reached the Alsop brothers and Pearson, but the leak sparked speculation about what the US would do to help the French and the Vietnamese in their campaign against the Vietminh. Concerned that it would be just the beginning of a slow and steady US involvement in Indochina, Senator John Stennis (D-MS), a member of the Senate Armed Service Committee, became one of the most vocal critics of the plan. Others voicing their apprehension about a US move were Democratic Senators Robert Byrd (VA) and Walter George (GA). Warning that the next step would be requests by the French for US pilots and ground forces, the duo voiced opposition to such action.[19]

A *US News and World Report* charged that "step by step, the US is being dragged more deeply" into the Indochina war. Hearst's *New York Journal-American* also warned that "we might find ourselves embroiled in

Unacceptable," in *Re-Evaluating Eisenhower: American Foreign Policy in the 1950s*, ed. Richard Melanson et al. (Urbana: University of Illinois Press, 1987), 124–125.

[17] Memorandum by C.D. Jackson, Special Assistant to the President, January 18, 1954, *FRUS*, XII, 1952–1954, 981–982; Immerman, "Between the Unattainable and the Unacceptable," 125–127.

[18] China Telegram, January 23 through 31, 1954, Records of the Office of Public Opinion Studies, Department of State, 1943–1975, AI568P, box 28, National Archives II, College Park, Maryland (hereafter CT, followed by date, DOS, file reference, box number, NAII).

[19] Ibid.

another Asiatic war in territory not of our choosing." It confessed "to uneasy feeling that the administration and Defense Department have not been leveling with American people in their assurances that there is no possibility our men will be under attack." Columnist Constantine Brown argued against sending US air, naval, and ground forces into conflict. He suggested instead that Jiang Jieshi's (Chiag Kai-shek) forces be permitted to stage attacks against South China to relieve the pressure on Indochina.[20]

The administration acknowledged public uneasiness surrounding the issue but nevertheless on February 3th, at his weekly press conference, President Eisenhower announced that in the interest of US national security and world peace, additional mechanics and equipment would be sent to Indochina. Attempting to reassure the public, he stressed that "no American boy will take part in the fighting." He also called a meeting with the Congressional leadership. However, the following day on February 4th, a *CBS* broadcast grabbed the headlines again by revealing that a "special committee on Southeast Asia" was behind the decision to send extra help to the French and was considering further US involvement in Vietnam. The news was a massive blow for the administration's public image. It suggested that the White House had not been entirely up front with the American people and was ignoring Congress.[21]

Worried about the effect that would have on popular belief, the State Department Bureau of Public Affairs (SDBPA) carried out a "Nation Spot-Check" on the situation in Indochina. The results again presented a very contradictory impression. Asked if they were concerned that the administration was involving the country in a war without consulting Congress, 64% of respondents answered "yes", 27% answered "no" and 9% expressed no opinion. However, when asked what the US should do if the Chinese Communists attacked Indochina, most of those surveyed (74%) would have "the US help defend" the country, 19% would have the US stay out, and the remaining 7% stated that they did not know. Those who favored US action were fairly evenly divided as to whether Washington should stop the invasion just in the attacked country, or whether it should

[20] Ibid.

[21] Eisenhower's Press Conference of February 3, 1954, John T. Woolley and Gerhard Peters, *The American Presidency Project* [online] Santa Barbara, CA: University of California (hosted) Gerhard Peters (database). Available from World Wide Web: http://www.presidency.ucsab.edu/ws/. Retrieved: July 4, 2011 (Hereafter *The American Presidency Project* followed by retrieved date); CT, February 1 through 7, 1954, DOS, AI568P, box 28, NAII.

attack Red China itself. Significantly, only 11% would have it intervene alone and 50% said it should act with the UN.[22]

President Eisenhower was very displeased with those poll results and thought it was up to the administration to rectify the situation through an adequate information campaign. At his February 7th press conference, he vehemently declared: "No one could be more bitterly opposed to ever getting the United States involved in a hot war in the region as I am; consequently every move I authorize is calculated, so far as humans can do it, to make certain that does not happen." He reiterated the same message the following day while meeting with the legislative leaders. "Don't think I like to send them there," he said, "but after all we can't get anywhere in Asia by just sitting here in Washington and doing nothing. My God we must not lose Asia—we have got to look the thing right in the face." In discussing the issue with the Congressional leaders, he was particularly concerned that they would cut appropriations. In exchange for their support, he guaranteed that he would bring all American soldiers back by mid-June; although privately, he confessed to Dulles that if necessary, he was willing to recruit civilians to replace the technicians.[23]

Congress was not satisfied. The main concern was still the role of the "Special Committee on Asia" and that it might lead the country into a war no one wanted. The President made it clear at his February 17th press conference that he would never involve the US in a war without consulting with Congress. He also agreed to have top administration officials answer questions from both Executive sessions of the Senate Foreign Relations and House Foreign Affairs Committees. Undersecretary Smith and Admiral Radford reassured both committees that the US would not need to escalate its involvement in Vietnam because the French were not planning on pulling out. But should "we see ourselves suddenly confronted with the loss of Indochina, and possibly the resultant loss of much of Southeast Asia to the Communists, there will be a situation created

---

[22] "Special Nation-Spot-Check on the Situation in Indochina", February 5, 1954, DOS, AI568J, box 1, NAII.

[23] Eisenhower's Press Conference of February 7, 1954, *The American Presidency Project*, [retrieved: July 4, 2011]; James Hagerty Diary, February 8, 1954, James C. Hagerty Papers, DDEL; Eisenhower telephone conversation with Charles Wilson, February 8, 1954, DDE Papers, Whitman File, Diary Series, box 35, DDEL; Eisenhower to Dulles, February 10, 1954, DDE Papers, Whitman File, Dulles-Herter Series, box 23, DDEL.

which would make it necessary for the President to come to Congress and ask for its advice and consent to take more drastic means."[24]

Eisenhower's press conference and Smith and Radford's testimonies, however, failed in reassuring the public. Anxiety about the US role in Vietnam kept rising among the public with the Democrats being particularly vocal. Although the administration's foreign policy had enjoyed consistent bipartisan support throughout 1953, some were now seeing an opportunity to regain control of Congress in the mid-term elections of 1954. Similarly to how the Republicans had exploited the "loss of China" in 1952, the Democratic party was increasingly accusing the White House of not having a good enough strategy to solve the Indochina problem. Very poignantly, Senator Hubert H. Humphrey (D-MN) told Dulles, "As ye [sow], ya reap, and believe me you have so sown and so you reap." Senator Richard Russell (D-GA) charged that the State Department already had a plan on how to escalate American involvement in Indochina. Finally, Senator John F. Kennedy (D-Mass.) declared on *NBC* "Meet the Press" that the administration had made a mistake in sending technicians and additional equipment as those were unnecessary and would haste US involvement in the near future.[25]

The administration's public position worsened on February 18, 1954, when it was announced that the Indochina issue would be discussed at the forthcoming Geneva conference on Far Eastern problems, scheduled to begin on April 26th and that the PRC had been invited to participate. The announcement sparked the ire of the Committee for One Million Against the Admission of Communist China in the United Nations (Committee for One Million) and of the Republican right in the Senate. Both immediately charged that it was another "Far Eastern Munich" that would force the US to recognize the PRC and would open Beijing's way into the UN.[26]

---

[24] Eisenhower's Press Conference of February 17, 1954, *The American Presidency Project*, [retrieved: July 4, 2011]; February 16, 1954 session, *Executive Sessions of the Senate Foreign Relations Committee 1954* (Washington, DC: Government Printing Office, 1977), 6, 107–146; 18 February, 1954 hearing, *Selective Hearings of the House Committee of Foreign Affairs 1951–1956* (Washington, DC: Government Printing Office, 1980), 8, 99–123. Immerman, "Between the Unattainable and the Unacceptable", 127.

[25] Reichard, Gary W. "Division and Dissent: Democrats and Foreign Policy, 1952–1956", *Political Science Quarterly* 93 (1978), 51–60; CT, February 11 through 17, 1954, AI568P, box 28, NAII.

[26] "Public Opinion Reaction to Geneva Conference Announcement", DOS, AI568J, box 1, NAII.

The decision had basically been forced on Washington during the previous month at the Berlin conference. The US, the Soviet Union, Great Britain, and France had met for four weeks to discuss the problems of Germany and Austria. Right from the beginning of the summit, Soviet Foreign Minister Vyacheslav Molotov had proposed including Communist China in a five-power conference to settle Far East questions. Dulles immediately rejected the proposal and released a press statement to quash any rumors that the US might be softening their stance toward the PRC:

> Who is this Chou En-lai whose addition to our circle would make possible all that so long seemed impossible? He is the leader of a regime which gained de facto power on the China mainland through a bloody war, which had liquidated millions of Chinese...which so diverts the economic resources of its impoverished people to military efforts that they starve by millions, which became an open aggressor in Korea and was so adjudged by the United Nations; which promotes open aggression in Indochina by training and equipping the aggressors and supplying them with vast amounts of war munitions. Such is the man, Mr. Molotov urges would enable the world to solve all its problems and to gain lasting peace and mounting prosperity.[27]

But Molotov did not give up and eventually the US agreed.[28]

Agreeing to a meeting with PRC representatives went against the policy of total pressure sanctioned by NSC166 just a few months earlier. Dulles observed that it was "destined to have repercussions on the domestic scene." But the Allies, particularly France and Britain, had made clear that American cooperation on that front would be very welcome. In exchange, the White House hoped that Paris would finally join plans to create the European Defense Community and relax Franco-German hostility.[29]

In deciding to go along with the conference, the administration's desire to appease the Allies clearly prevailed on the Republican right's protestations. Knowing, however, that the announcement would create problems on the domestic front, Dulles insisted that the final communiqué stated clearly: "It is understood that neither the invitation to or the

---

[27] Press release 47 dated February 3, 1954, *Department of State Bulletin*, 30, February 15, 1954, 222–223 (Hereafter *DBS* followed by, issue number, date and page number).

[28] Gordon Chang, *Friends and Enemies: The United States, China and the Soviet Union, 1948–1972* (Stanford: Stanford University Press, 1990), 99–102.

[29] Gurtov, *The First Vietnam Crisis: Chinese Communist Strategy and United States Involvement, 1953–1954*, 82–94.

holding of, the above-mentioned conference shall be deemed to imply diplomatic recognition in any case where it has not already been accorded."[30]

The administration also began an intense public campaign to allay domestic fears. Before Dulles even left Berlin, the State Department published an article by Walter P. McConaughy, Director of the Office of Chinese Affairs, in the *Department of State Bulletin* entitled "China in the Shadow of Communism" which defended the Chinese Nationalist Government on Taiwan (Formosa) and denigrated the PRC. On the same day that the announcement on the Geneva Conference was made, Assistant Secretary for Far Eastern Affairs Walter Robertson gave a speech before the English-speaking Union in New York on why the US could not and would not recognize the "Communist dictatorship that oppresses the people of China mainland."[31]

Upon his return to Washington, Dulles explained in a radio and television report to the nation regarding why the decision had been made. In it, he somewhat overstated matters in declaring that the Berlin conference had been a "real success for the US." He went on to say that concern about a possible recognition of the Beijing regime was "a fear without basis." He also recounted how he stood up to Molotov: "I told Mr. Molotov flatly that I would not agree to meet with the Chinese Communists unless it was expressly agreed and put in writing that no United States recognition would be involved." Molotov had resisted that provision to the last and had sought by every artifice and device and through the Allies to force the US to meet with Communist China as one of the Great Five Powers. However, Dulles stated, "I refused and our British and French Allies stood with us." Accordingly, he concluded, "Under that resolution, the Chinese Communist regime will not come to Geneva to be honored by us, but rather to account before the bar of world opinion."[32]

[30] "Report to the Nation on the Berlin Conference", address by Secretary Dulles delivered to the nation over radio and television on February 24, 1954, *DBS*, 30, February 27, 1954, 343–347.

[31] McConaughy, Walter P. "China in the Shadow of Communism", February 13, 1954, *DBS*, 30, February 15, 1954, 323–326; "Responsibilities of the US in the Far East", address by Walter Robertson made before the English Speaking Union, New York City, February 18, 1954, *DBS*, 30, February 27, 1954, 348–349.

[32] "Report to the Nation on the Berlin Conference", address by Secretary Dulles delivered to the nation over radio and television on February 24, 1954, *DBS*, 30, February 27, 1954, 343–347.

Surprisingly, the Committee for One Million found the administration's reasoning plausible and decided to endorse it. In the ensuing weeks, it published a vast amount of literature for public distribution that, while emphasizing the government's official opposition to recognition of Beijing and its admission to the UN, supported the administration's decision "to listen to the Chinese Communists, before deciding anything without their participation." In early March 1954, a State Department public opinion survey noted that, "Thanks to the State Department's information campaign and the Committee's propaganda effort, the majority of the general public, 84 percent of the respondents, support the US decision to agree to the Geneva conference." At the same time, 8 out of 10 Americans surveyed still approved of the administration's firm position against establishing diplomatic relations with the PRC and admitting it into the UN.[33]

The Republican right wing and quite a few Democrats were, however, still disturbed about the prestige and degree of recognition accorded to Beijing and feared, as Senator George declared, that "The US would be forced in a position which might compel us to recognize Red China." Concern was heightened by Arthur Dean's declarations on the necessity of reviewing US-China policy and establishing trade relations between Washington and Beijing to drive the two Communist giants, China and Russia, apart. Dean had negotiated the armistice talks in Korea and he was also a personal friend of John Foster Dulles. His position in the administration caused his declarations to be perceived as semi-official, with the result that the State Department came under vicious attacks from the Nationalist supporters in Congress and in the press. Senator Herman Welker (R-ID) took the floor of the Senate to accuse Dean of promoting the same excuse about dividing the Communist giants long used by "pro-Red China apologists in the State Department." Welker demanded to know whether Dean spoke "with the blessing of the Secretary of State or the President of the United States." Senator Alexander Smith (R-NJ) warned against recognizing Communist China or permitting its admission into the UN "while it remains a satellite taking orders from Moscow." In a report on his recent tour of the Far East, he also stated that "while it

---

[33] Bachrack, Stanley, *The Committee of One Million, "China Lobby" Politics* (New York: Columbia University Press, 1976), 83–102; Publications Relating to the Committee of One Million Against the Admission of Red China to the United Nations, 1954–1966, Tamiment Library, New York University, NY (hereafter Tamiment Library, NYU); "Public Opinion's Reaction to State Department's Information Campaign on Geneva Conference", March 15, 1954, DOS, AI568J, box 1, NAII.

would be unrealistic to expect a successful all-out attack on Chinese mainland by the Nationalists," the forces on Taiwan could be "of very great
importance" if the Chinese Reds "precipitated a new crisis in the Far
East." The State Department therefore "should not abandon such a valuable ally."[34]

The very thought of recognizing the Chinese Communists remained
an anathema to Hearst's *New York Journal-American*, which continued to
hold that "Chinese Communists cannot be accepted under any conditions." Scripps-Howard's *Washington News* declared that "Achievement
of peace in Korea would not alone be enough to clear way of UN seat for
Red China."[35]

Dulles publicly denied that China policy was under review, and he pri-
vately assured Senate Majority Leader William Knowland (R-CA) that
Dean did not favor the recognition of China or its acceptance into the
UN, and that the administration's policy was one of total hostility toward
Beijing in any case. However, columnist Walter Lippmann and the
Christian Science Monitor found Dulles' declarations very disappointing.
Lippmann wrote in his *New York Herald Tribune* column, "We [the US]
should have an open mind towards Red China and take a new look towards
it." Similarly, a *Christian Science Monitor* editorial opined that "We believe
it fatuous (or worse) for the nation to tie its hand in advance by taking
irrevocable position on its China policy." The paper became the first major
publication to publicly withdraw support for the administration's hardline
policy toward the PRC and advocate establishment of diplomatic relations
between Washington and Beijing.[36]

United Action

After the Berlin conference, Washington anticipated and warned the
French about intensified Communist activity. As expected, in a series of
attacks beginning on March 13th, the Vietminh seized two major hill
outposts established by the French to protect the fortress and the airfield
below. The CIA estimated that at best there was an even chance that the

[34] CT, February 28 through March 3, 1954, DOS, AI568P, box 28, NAII.
[35] Ibid.
[36] Ibid.; Dulles to Knowland, March 1954, John Foster Dulles Papers, box 187, Seely
G. Mudd Manuscripts Library, Princeton University, New Jersey (hereafter JFD Papers, followed by record reference, box number, ML).

vulnerable French could hold out. It also reported that Chinese Communist assistance had "decidedly peaked up." Chinese Communist aid was approaching a peak of 4000 tons of war material a month, not including nearly 2000 tons of food being delivered monthly "despite widespread starvation in China." Eisenhower saw those developments as a PRC plan to obtain negotiating advantage in Geneva. A few days following the Dien Bien Phu attack, he wrote to his friend Swede Hazlett: "I suspect that this particular attack was launched by the Chinese Communists to gain advantage to be used at the Geneva conference."[37]

The White House believed its position was becoming more and more difficult and that it was running out of options. Should the US intervene or not? Should it intervene alone or ask support from the Allies? Would the use of air and naval forces be enough or were ground troops also necessary? On March 24th, Eisenhower informed Dulles that introduction of American ground troops was out of the question but he would not "wholly exclude the possibility of a single air strike, if it were almost certain this would produce decisive results." A week later, he referred to the idea again but stressed that such an operation would need to be covert and "we would have to deny it forever." Dulles was also in favor of some sort of US intervention But did not think an air strike was the right option. He believed, instead, that a Chinese attack could be offset through "harassing tactics from Formosa and along the Chinese seacoast," measures which "would be more readily within our natural facilities than actually fighting in Indochina."[38]

After further discussion, Eisenhower and Dulles agreed that although it would be best for the US not to intervene directly, it had also become necessary to show the Chinese Communists that the Western world was united and determined to protect its interests in Indochina. In practice, that meant putting together a coalition comprised of the US, France, Great Britain, New Zealand, Australia, the Philippines, Thailand, and the Associated States of Indochina. Those states would pledge to defend not only Vietnam but also the broader Southeast Asia against a Communist attack. The President and the Secretary of State hoped that the "United

[37] Gurtov, *The First Vietnam Crisis: Chinese Communist Strategy and United States Involvement, 1953–1954*, 81; Dulles's phone conversation with Allen Dulles, March 16, 1954, JFD Papers, Telephone Conversation Series, box 3, DDEL; Robert Griffith, *Ike's Letters to a Friend* (Lawrence: University Press of Kansas, 1984), 122.

[38] Memorandum of Conversation with Eisenhower, March 24, 1954, Records of the State Department, box 222. Lot 64D199, NAII.

Action" would be enough to deter any further Chinese move and, therefore, avoid further escalation of US involvement. However, as historians George Herring and Richard Immerman observed, if US intervention became necessary, United Action ensured "that Washington would do so under favorable circumstances."[39]

In line with the realist approach of both Eisenhower and Dulles toward public opinion, both men chose United Action as the policy that best addressed American national security interests. Believing that the support of the public was necessary, particularly in cases of war and commitment of American troops, the President and the Secretary of State also formulated a public education program to generate support for the chosen policy. Dulles noted that the numerous State Department opinion analyses showed that "if the public won't go along with a strong policy, it won't go along with appeasement. Neither policy is popular." Eisenhower agreed and added that Congressional reaction to the February press leaks indicated "some persuasion was needed in that area too." During the final week of March, therefore, they concentrated on presenting the United Action proposal to Congress and the public.[40]

In a March 29th televised address, Dulles publicly unveiled the concept of United Action in deliberately vague terms. He began by warning that the Chinese Communists now supported the Vietminh "by all means short of open invasion." The PRC was providing training, equipment, deliveries of artillery, and transport of munitions from the Czech Skoda to China for use in the war. Furthermore, 2000 Chinese soldiers were giving military and technical assistance "in staff sections of high command, at division level and in the specialized units, such as signal, engineering, artillery and transportation." Indochina was therefore in danger:

> If the Communist forces were to win uncontested control over Indochina, or any substantial part thereof, they would surely resume the same pattern of aggression against other free people in that area. The propagandists of Red China and Soviet Russia make it perfectly apparent that the purpose is to dominate all of Southeast Asia. Now Southeast Asia is an important part

[39] Ibid.; Dulles' telephone conversation with H. Alexander Smith, April 19, 1954, JFD Papers, Telephone Conversations Series, box 1, DDEL; George C. Herring and Richard H. Immerman, "Eisenhower, Dulles and the Dienbienphu Crisis: "The Day We Didn't Go to War" Revisited," *The Journal of American History* 71 (1984): 343–363.

[40] Telephone Conversation Between Eisenhower and Dulles, March 27, 1954, JFD Papers, Telephone Conversations Series, box 3, DDEL.

of the world. It is the so-called rice bowl. It is an area that is rich in many raw materials. And in addition to the tremendous economic values, the area has great strategic value. Communist control of Southeast Asia would carry a grave threat to the Philippines, Australia, and New Zealand...the entire Western Pacific area, including the so-called offshore islands would be strategically endangered.[41]

He concluded by declaring that a Communist attack "should not be passively accepted but should be met by United Action." Robert Bowie observed that Dulles had "deliberately" crafted the speech to sound "menacing without committing anybody to anything." Indeed, the Secretary thought he had successfully managed to send a strong warning to the Chinese Communists and at the same time, he had laid solid foundations to build public support for any necessary future US action.[42]

However, a SDBPA opinion analysis in early April 1954 reported that Dulles' address had not been the success he had hoped for, but had instead elicited mixed feelings. A majority of the press expressed disapproval of what it interpreted as a US "commitment" to the defense of Indochina no matter what cost. Some newspapers also pointed out that the Secretary of State had left unsaid what sort of United Action he had in mind. Similarly, many in Congress expressed anxiety about the US becoming involved in the war step by step. Leading off the debate, Senator Kennedy asserted that the American people had not been told "the blunt truth" about Indochina. Criticizing the administration for raising hopes of victory that could not be guaranteed, he voiced support for United Action, but warned that no amount of "money, material, and men" can bring victory in Indochina without the support of Indochinese or other Asians. Kennedy's speech was applauded by Senators Knowland, Henry M. Jackson (D-WA), and Stuart Symington (D-MO). Having initially endorsed Dulles' position, Knowland now called upon the administration to demand a "clear-cut" statement from other free nations on what they stood ready to do in Indochina if the Chinese Communists intervened directly. Jackson, meanwhile, made a strong plea for the administration to come before Congress and spell out policy for Southeast Asia.[43]

[41] "The Threat of Red Asia" Address by Dulles, March 29, 1954, JFD Papers, box 82, ML.
[42] Ibid.; Robert Bowie, Director of State Department Policy Planning staff, John Foster Dulles Oral History Project, Seely G. Mudd Library, Princeton University, New Jersey (hereafter JFD Oral History followed by ML).
[43] "Special Public Opinion Analysis on Popular Reaction to Secretary Dulles' speech of March 29 1954", April 1954, DOS, AI568J, box 1, NAII.

More significantly, the SDBPA opinion analysis noted that "Talks of escalating US involvement through a United Action had increased fear of wider US involvement in the war among the general public" and brought about a significant opinion change in what were until now ambivalent popular feelings. While most of the Americans interviewed still approved of sending military supplies to help the French, for the first time since February 1954, a SDBPA opinion poll noted that "A plurality of the general public would prefer a negotiated truce with the PRC over the continuation of fighting and increased aid." Likewise, a March 1954 Gallup poll revealed that even "if it looked like the Chinese Communists might take over," only 9% of respondents would favor sending US armed forces to Indochina, a 65% decrease in less than two months; 33% would favor sending more supplies but no soldiers or fliers, and 45% would favor "trying to arrange for an armistice." The remaining 17% made no choice among the alternatives proposed (see Fig. 4.1).[44]

Meanwhile, the situation in Dien Bien Phu had worsened considerably. Vietminh attacks had intensified and the French were steadily retreating. Even Admiral Radford, who had championed the possibility of a US intervention admitted that "The outcome at Dien Bien Phu would be determined within a matter of hours" and therefore "it does not call for any US participation."[45]

The question now was what would happen when the French finally succumbed to the Communists' attacks. Would it lead to a total withdrawal from Indochina? Should the US step in? And how would the Western powers' position at Geneva change? Despite the lack of public support, Eisenhower and Dulles decided to remain with United Action as the best response to protect American national security interests. The President instructed the Secretary of State to schedule a special meeting with the legislative leadership for Saturday, April 3rd to request Congressional endorsement of a broad, blank check resolution, that would give the President discretionary authority to use US air and sea power to prevent the "extension and expansion" of Communist aggression in Southeast Asia and to defend "the safety and security" of the United States. The authority would end on June 30, 1954 and would in "no way derogate from the authority of Congress to declare war."[46]

[44] Ibid.
[45] Memorandum of Conversation, April 2, 1954, DDE Papers, Daily Appointments Series, box 67, DDEL.
[46] Ibid.

Public opinion support for US intervention in Indochina

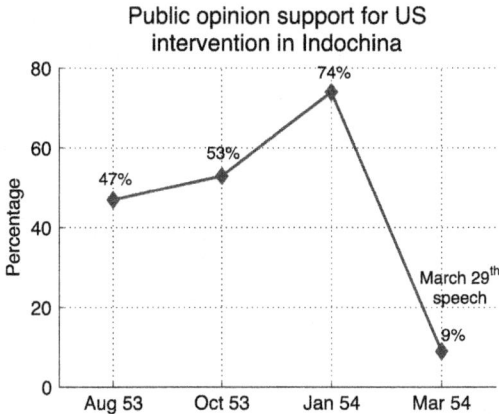

Fig. 4.1 US public support for American intervention in Indochina in case of a PRC attack increased until Dulles' March 29, 1954 speech. However, talks of escalating US involvement in the war aroused popular concern with a resulting 65% drop in support. Source: "Special Public Opinion Analysis on Popular Reaction to Secretary Dulles' speech of March 29, 1954", DOS, AI568J, box 1, NAII

According to Eisenhower and Dulles' reasoning, the resolution could act as a deterrent to the Communists and at the same time give a boost to French and Vietnamese morale. It could also strengthen the allies' position at Geneva and reassure them of America's commitment to preserving Indochina from Communism, thus increasing the chances of creating a United Action coalition. It was, therefore, of vital importance to bring Congress on board. Fearing that Congressional leaders might get the impression that a decision to push for intervention had already been reached without consulting them, the President insisted that "the tactical procedure should be first to develop the thinking of the Congressional leaders without actually submitting in the first instance a resolution drafted by ourselves."[47]

The meeting took place on April 3rd. Representing the administration were Dulles and Radford who asked for Congressional authority to use US sea and air forces but reassured the leaders that no US ground troops would be deployed. Despite an initial positive response from Senator

[47] Ibid.

Knowland, the Congressional leaders were not persuaded and insisted on a commitment from the Allies, particularly Britain, before granting any authorization. Poignantly, Senators Russell and Johnson stated "there must be no more Koreas with the United States furnishing ninety percent of the manpower." They were also keen on a French pledge to "internationalize the war" and finally grant independence to Indochina.[48]

The Congressional leaders had turned the tables on Eisenhower and Dulles. Although they had not declined their support, the conditions imposed by the latter forced the administration to reverse the order of its strategy, which in turn made Dulles' task more difficult. Although the leaders' request did not fundamentally change the substance of United Action, it affected the way it was to be carried out by making it dependent upon British support and French concessions, "each of which" as Dulles noted "would be very difficult to obtain prior to activity by Congress."[49]

The Congressional specifications also narrowed the available choice of policy options. The leaders' refusal to approve the plan prior to consultations with the British and the French forced the administration to finally abandon the possibility of US unilateral intervention. "There is no possibility whatsoever of US intervention in Indochina," Eisenhower told the NSC, "and we best face the fact. Even if we tried such a course, we would have to take it to Congress and fight it like dogs, with very little hope for success." Instead, a new plan for the creation of a "regional grouping to defend Southeast Asia" began to take shape. Both the President and the NSC believed that was a necessary action, even if Indochina was lost.[50]

In the meantime, the administration continued its efforts to build public support for United Action. In speeches and press conferences, it repeatedly portrayed Communist China as an extremely dangerous threat to Indochina and all Southeast Asia. On April 5, 1954, Dulles presented unmistakable evidence before the House Committee of Foreign Affairs that the Chinese had been involved in supporting the Vietminh in Dien Bien Phu with all possible means, including supplies, artillery, munitions, and equipment for prosecution of the attack. A few days later, at his weekly press conference,

---

[48] Memorandum for the File of the Secretary of State, April 5, 1954, FRUS, XIII, 1952–1954, 1224–1225; Memorandum of Conference with Congressional Leaders, April 5, 1954, JFD Papers, Chronological Series, box 4, DDEL.

[49] Telephone Conversation with Eisenhower, April 3, 1954, JFD Papers, Telephone Conversation Series, box 2, DDEL.

[50] Memorandum of Discussion, 192 NSC Meeting, April 6, 1954, FRUS, XIII, 1952–1954, 1250–1265.

President Eisenhower discussed the vital importance of saving Indochina to protect the rest of the region from Communist influence. In what later became known as "the Domino Theory," he explained that if Dien Bien Phu was lost, the rest of Southeast Asia would "go over quickly."[51]

In addition to those efforts, the State Department began an intensive information program to generate support among the American public for US intervention. Journalist Richard Rovere, who attended one of those sessions, commented that Dulles was "conducting undoubtedly what must be one of the boldest campaigns of political persuasion ever undertaken by an American statesman. Congressmen, political leaders of shadings of opinion, newspapermen, and radio and television personalities have been rounded up in droves and escorted to lectures, briefings on what the State Department regards as the American stakes in Indochina."[52]

Meanwhile, Dulles traveled to Europe to meet first with British Foreign Minister Anthony Eden and then with the French Foreign Minister George Bidault to persuade them to join the United Action Plan. Unfortunately, neither meeting was successful. The British believed Indochina could not be saved and were especially afraid that any intervention would trigger a war with China. The best hope was to negotiate a settlement in Geneva that would grant independence to Indochina. They did, however, agree to begin multilateral discussions that could lead to the creation of a collation to protect the area from further Communist influence. Similarly, the French considered Geneva the best opportunity to finally remove themselves from Vietnam and, therefore, could not agree to any actions that might interfere with the conference.[53]

United Action received its final blow a few days later, on April 16, when Vice-President Richard M. Nixon declared that the US was ready to "take the risk" of sending American soldiers if the French failed in Indochina. It is still not clear whether Nixon's remarks were a trial balloon to test how the US public would react to such a possibility or whether his statement

---

[51] Dulles' Testimony Before the House Committee of Foreign Affairs, April 5, 1954, *DSB*, 30, April 19, 1954, 579–583; Eisenhower's Press Conference of April 7, 1954, *The American Presidency Project* [retrieved: July 4, 2011].

[52] Richard H. Rovere, *Affairs of State: The Eisenhower Years* (New York: Farrar, Straus & Cudahy, 1956), 3.

[53] Memorandum of Conversation Between Secretary Dulles and British Foreign Minister Anthony Eden, April 12, 1954, FRUS, XIII, 1952–1954, 1311–1315; Memorandum of Conversation with George Bidault, April 14, 1954, JFD Papers, Dulles-Herter Series, box 2, DDEL.

had not been authorized. Regardless, the prospect of "putting our boys in" met with both sharp and widespread public opposition. A SDBPA opinion analysis of reactions to Nixon's speech revealed that both parties in Congress reacted negatively, based on concerns that the administration had once again cut them out of foreign policy decision making. The American and world press labeled the speech "a serious provocation that could lead to World War III." The SDBPA report also found that among the public, 84% of those surveyed condemned the Vice-President's statement and opposed sending US ground troops to Indochina. Additionally, 68% also favored negotiating an armistice rather than continuing to fight, a 23% increase since March 1954. Even worse, Nixon's explosive statement led the British to pull out from the multilateral talks scheduled for April 20th aimed at creating a coalition to protect Southeast Asia.[54]

As the situation in Dien Bien Phu worsened, requests by the French for US intervention were repeatedly declined. The administration was not convinced that an air strike would save the fortress. More importantly, without British support, Congress would not have authorized such an action. In Eisenhower's words: "without Allies, the leader is just an adventurer like Genghis Kahn." At that point, it was probably easier to let Dien Bien Phu fall. The President conveyed the decision to the NSC on April 29.[55]

During his press conference on that same day, he told the American people that from now onward, the US would try to find a "modus vivendi" in Southeast Asia. Because he could not accept a Communist conquest of the area and developing a relationship with the Chinese was impossible, the only other solution was "to work out a practical way of getting along."[56]

The administration's strategy had, as historian Mark White observed, "foundered on the rocks of British recalcitrance" and French unwillingness to make concessions. While public opinion, and particularly Congress, did influence the way Eisenhower and Dulles implemented their plan, United Action ultimately failed because of the Allies' refusal to go along with it. Congress did narrow the available policy options by

---

[54] "Special Report on Public's Reaction to Vice-President Nixon's April 16 speech", April 1954, DOS, AI568J, box 1, NAII.

[55] John Foster Dulles to State Department, April 25, 1954, JFD Papers, Dulles-Herter Series, box 1, DDEL; Memorandum of NSC Meeting, April 29, 1954, FRUS, XIII, 1952–1954, 1431–1433.

[56] Eisenhower's Press Conference of April 29, 1954, The American Presidency Project, [retrieved: July 4, 2011].

ruling out US unilateral intervention, but it did not determine the policy choice. The President and Secretary of State had already identified United Action as the option that best addressed US national security interests. The conditions imposed by the Congressional leaders at the April 3rd meeting only reversed the order of the strategy, but did not fundamentally change the substance of the plan because they coincided with the administration's own view.[57]

Similarly, Eisenhower and Dulles' continuous efforts to generate public support for United Action, even after the disastrous public response to the Secretary of State's March 29th speech prove first that, the administration put national security ahead of popular feelings, and second that it was confident enough to be able to eventually sway the public. President Eisenhower wrote in an unpublished draft of his memoirs:

> Indeed had the circumstances lent themselves to a reasonable choice of victory or a chance to overt a defeat of freedom, then I feel that the task of explaining to the American people the necessity for sacrifice would have been a simple one indeed. But this was the wrong war for such actions. The jungles of Indochina would have swallowed up division after division of US troops.[58]

Eisenhower clearly believed he could have led the public to support US ground force intervention had he favored such an action but because Britain and France refused to be part of the plan, the President had decided not to intervene. Although initially showing support for US intervention if the PRC attacked Indochina, the public ultimately came to favor a negotiated agreement. The American decision sealed the destiny of Dien Bien Phu. The French surrendered after 52 days of heroic resistance. The attention of the belligerents and of the interested outside parties immediately shifted to Geneva, where the Indochina phase of the conference was to begin the following day.

---

[57] Mark J. White, *Against the President, Dissent and Decision Making in the White House: A Historical Perspective* (Chicago: Ivan r. Dee, 2007), 154.

[58] John Burke and Fred I. Greenstein, *How Presidents Test Reality* (New York: Russell Sage Foundation, 1989), 160–167.

THE GENEVA CONFERENCE

Eisenhower's April 29th declarations were deceiving because he had no intention of finding a *modus vivendi* with the PRC. At Geneva, the US behaved in a consistently obstructive manner and resisted giving the negotiations the slightest opportunity. The French told the Communist Chinese representatives, "The US intends to sabotage the entire conference and then place the blame on China."[59]

The day before the conference on April 26th, the State Department published an article by Alfred le Sense Jenkins, Officer in Charge of Chinese Political Affairs, entitled "Present United States Policy toward China." It recited the administration's indictments against the Chinese Communist government on the mainland. First, the regime did not represent the "will of the people it controls;" second, it was dedicated "to the proposition of world Communist revolution under the leadership of the Soviet Union" and "followed no recognized standards of international conduct;" and finally, it was "a ruthless police state with all that that implies." For those reasons, among others, "it is hardly surprising that the firm policy of the US is one of strong opposition to the Chinese Communist regime. We cannot recognize this regime, and we shall continue vigorously to oppose attempts to accept it in the United Nations Organization as representing the Chinese people."[60]

Political policy thus covered, Jenkins spelled out economic policy—in short total trade embargo against Communist China—before broaching Geneva. In his scenario, the Berlin Conference's plans for a multi-power conference would not produce "as the Communists are claiming, a five-power conference. Communist China, far from attending the conference as a great power, will not in our view even attend as a government." He then asserted that "the time, place and composition of the Conference are entirely as we wanted. We do not fear this conference...we will not be prepared at Geneva to allow the aggressors to achieve at the conference table what they have failed to achieve in battle. This applies not only to territorial considerations but to any deal which would...trade a United Nations seat and an end to the trade controls for an agreement by

[59] Quoted in Jian, Chen, "China and the Indochina Settlement of the Geneva Conference of 1954", in Lawrence, Mark Atwood, and Fredrick, Logevall, *The First Vietnam War: Colonial Conflict and Cold War Crisis* (Cambridge, MA: Harvard University Press, 2007), 240–262.

[60] Jenkins, Alfred le Sense, "Present United States Policy Toward China", *DBS*, 30, April 26, 1954, 456–458.

Communist China to stop supplying the Vietminh...we do not contemplate any action at Geneva or anywhere else which would damage the
cause of the Government of the Republic of China."[61]

Once in Geneva, Dulles put on a display of total hostility toward the
Chinese Communist delegation. First, he refused to sit at a table with
Zhou En-lai (Chou En-lai) or near any Communist delegation, forcing
the organizers to rearrange seating into an auditorium style, thus also
affecting the well-established alphabetic seating system for diplomatic
conferences. The unenviable task of negotiating the new conditions fell to
the US Ambassador to Prague, U. Alexis Johnson. Dulles had asked him
to take part in the conference because of his knowledge of Far Eastern
Affairs, gained from holding various positions in the Department of State's
Far Eastern Bureau and having participated in the talks on the Korean
armistice. The Russians were obviously not pleased with the new arrange-
ments because they hindered their plan of having Communist China join
the conference as an equal.[62]

That became even more difficult when Dulles blocked the PRC from
chairing part of the conference and thus recognize it as an equal. Then,
during the recess of the first session on Korea, an incident occurred which,
according to Johnson, "plagued our relations with Peking for many years."
Dulles refused to shake hands with Zhou En-lai when they both walked
into the Palais des Nations lounge. Apparently, when the Secretary saw
that the photographers and the press were ready to record the historic
moment, he decided to ignore Zhou's outstretched arm. Finally, on May
3rd, Dulles departed Geneva leaving Undersecretary of State Smith, an
inferior in ranking, in command of the US delegation.[63]

Those gestures, which the Chinese interpreted as "vilifying" and "arro-
gant", combined with Dulles' and Smith's refusal to meet privately with
Zhou or make any concessions, and their continuous efforts toward imple-
menting United Action ended in a US defeat at the diplomatic table. In
the absence of American cooperation, the PRC, the Soviet Union, France,
Britain, Cambodia, Laos, and North Vietnam managed to reach a compromise that was acceptable to all parties. On July 21st, they signed agree-

[61] Ibid.
[62] Johnson, Alexis U. *The Right Hand of Power* (Englewood, New Jersey: Prentice Hall Inc. 1984), 204–226; Alsop, Joseph, "Dulles Blocks Reds at Geneva", the *Washington Post*, April 27, 1954, 1.
[63] Ibid.

ments that ended the 8-year war in Southeast Asia. The document also acknowledged the sovereignty of Cambodia, Laos, and Vietnam. It divided Vietnam at the 17th parallel and established that free elections should be held by 1956. The United States and South Vietnam refused to be signatories.[64]

Historians Gordon Chang and Stephen Ambrose have argued that the administration adopted such a hostile strategy during the conference because it feared that the China Lobby and domestic conservatives would accuse it of having joined yet another "Munich" debacle. Dulles wanted to show the public both at home and abroad that the administration had not embraced appeasement. Acknowledging the PRC as an equal partner or shaking Zhou's hand, therefore, had to be avoided. Furthermore, according to the Secretary's sister, Eleanor Lansing Dulles, Washington also feared that a photograph capturing a friendly gesture between the American and Chinese delegations might be used by the Soviets to generate confusion within the Soviet bloc about US China policy.[65]

While the administration was certainly keen on protecting its anti-communist credentials, it seems, however, that domestic public opinion was not a major concern, quite the contrary. On the eve of Dulles' departure for Geneva, the SDBPA had prepared a special report on US public's feelings regarding the conference. While the document reported that "the usual section of conservative press and Congressmen" is warning against "the hundreds of traps laid at Geneva that might force the US to recognize the PRC," it also stated that "The majority of the national and international press and US public see the imminent meeting in a highly favorable light" because "they hope the talks will help diffuse international tensions and avoid war." Furthermore, a National Opinion Research Center poll clearly showed that the public did not share the Republican right's concern about a possible PRC recognition. Seventy-eight percent of Americans who were interviewed had full confidence in Dulles' skills as a diplomat and believed that he would not give in to Soviet and Chinese pressure. Twelve percent of the respondents thought the Allies might force the Secretary to reach a compromise on a UN seat for Beijing and the remaining 10% had no opinion. The report

---

[64] Ibid.

[65] Chang, *Friends and Enemies*, 99–101; Ambrose, Stephen, *Eisenhower: Soldier and President* (New York: Simon and Schuster Paperbacks, 1990), 183–185.

concluded that Dulles "can take with him to Geneva the full support of the majority of the nation."[66]

The administration did not perceive any strong public opposition to force it to adopt a policy of hostility. It seems more likely, as Johnson explained in his memoirs, that consistently throughout the conference, Washington rejected any contact with the Chinese delegation because it was determined not to lose Southeast Asia to the Communists. Both Eisenhower and Dulles believed that "dizzy with victory because of the fall of Dien Bien Phu," the Communists expected to secure France's prompt departure from all Vietnam and international recognition of their legitimacy on the country's government. The US wanted to avoid precisely that. A policy of hostility would deny the Communists' aim of becoming a key player in world politics. That combined with the creation of a military agreement that could guarantee Southeast Asia security would hopefully deter the Chinese from any further of expansion.[67]

Furthermore, a policy of hostility was what NSC166 had sanctioned just nine months earlier. One of the tactics recommended by the paper was to use "diplomatic and political measures…to impede general international acceptance of the Chinese Communist regime…" thus weakening, or at least retarding, the growth of its power in Asia. The document had also recommended adopting measures "which tend to require Chinese negotiations with the USSR, as means for attaining a split between Moscow and Peiping." A combination of firm diplomacy and military threat could produce the requisite pressure to exacerbate dissension among the Communists.[68]

The strategy, however, failed to work. Disagreements with the Allies throughout the conference only led to further tensions and made Washington appear isolated and out of touch with world politics. The real winner in the Geneva was the PRC. Its borders were secured and the world had to acknowledge its position as an emerging power. A *People's Daily* editorial on July 22nd stated, "The international status of the People's Republic of China as one of the big world powers has gained universal recognition."[69]

---

[66] "Special Nation Spot-Check on the Eve of Secretary Dulles' Trip to Geneva", April 1954, DOS AI568J, box 1, NAII.

[67] Johnson, *The Right Hand of Power*, 204–226.

[68] NSC166/1 "US Policy Towards Communist China", *FRUS*, XIX, 1952–1954, 308–334.

[69] Quoted in Chang, *Friends and Enemies*, 102 and Mayers, David A. *Cracking the Monolith: U.S. Policy Against the Sino-Soviet Alliance, 1946–1955* (Baton Rouge: Louisiana State University Press, 1986), 133–134.

The disappointment of the outcome of the conference made the administration vulnerable to bipartisan criticism. Dulles was specifically taken to task for having failed to adequately consult with a number of Congressional leaders, for having consulted Congress only after announcing United Action, and for having gambled and lost on the chance that the Allies would support United Action, thus eventually turning the Geneva conference, in the words of Senator Knowland, "into one of the greatest Communist victories of the decade."[70]

The administration replied to those charges by presenting a new security framework for Southeast Asia. Saving Indochina from a Communist conquest was no longer a priority. Instead, the collective defense organization plan that Eisenhower and Dulles had been working quietly on became the main objective of US policy.[71] Throughout June and July 1954, the White House and the State Department focused on generating public support for a Southeast Asia Treaty Organization (SEATO). Press conferences and speeches centered on two messages: first, the falling domino principle could be easily offset once nations joined together in collective defense; second, hostility toward the PRC was still the right policy as the only deterrent against Communist expansion.[72]

The new strategy did not succeed in assuaging public disappointment regarding the outcome of the conference, but it did quickly shift popular attention from Geneva to SEATO. Headlines about Red gains in prestige, land, and human resources were soon replaced by supportive statements in favor of the collective defense pact. A SDBPA opinion analysis reported that "The overwhelming majority of Congressmen and press of all political shadings agree that it is of the greatest urgency that the Western powers proceed with SEATO."[73]

The SDBPA also reported that according to a nationwide survey in July 1954, 90% of the respondents approved of the idea of a Southeast Asia Defense Treaty. Furthermore, approximately three fifths of Americans interviewed (60%) gave affirmative answers to the question of whether "our government did everything it could to reach a satisfactory settlement" at Geneva, 17% took negative positions and 23% had no opinion.

---

[70] "Public Reaction to Geneva Conference", July 1954, DOS, AI568J, box 1, NAII.

[71] "Southeast Asia Collective Defence Agreement Concluded", *DSB*, 30, August 1, 1954, 854–856.

[72] Administration's Speeches and Press Conferences Between June and July 1954, *DBS*, 30, 750–946.

[73] Monthly Survey of Public Opinion on US Foreign Policy, DOS, AI568N, box 13, NAII.

On another question, the respondents approved, by a margin of 5 to 2 to "the way our government has handled the Indochina problem." In general, the SDBPA found that despite the year's critical developments in the Far East, US foreign policy actions continued to command majority support and the administration's position on Communist China continued to receive general approbation. Of the Americans interviewed, 56% approved of "the way present officials in Washington are handling our foreign affairs," 31% disapproved, and 1% had no opinion. With regard to Dulles, 66% approved of "the way he is handling his job as Secretary of State," 10% disapproved, and 24% had no opinion.[74]

In the end, although popular support had not always been consistent, Eisenhower and Dulles managed to come out of the crisis with their hardline policy toward Beijing still intact and most of the public behind them. Their national security strategy had to adjust to international circumstances as their public relations program needed to be constantly reviewed to guarantee public support, but the President and the Secretary of State obtained what they wanted: no US ground troops or unilateral intervention in Indochina and a collective security pact which they both believed could act as the best deterrent against the PRC. The United States, Great Britain, France, Australia, New Zealand, Pakistan, the Philippines, and Thailand finally signed the treaty in Manila on September 8, 1954.

REFERENCES

Adams, Sherman. *First Hand Report: The Story of the Eisenhower Administration.* New York: Harper, 1961.
Ambrose, Stephen. *Eisenhower: The President.* New York: Simon & Schuster, 1983.
———. *Eisenhower: Soldier and President.* New York: Simon and Schuster Paperbacks, 1990.
Billings-Yun, Malanie. *Decision Against War: Eisenhower and Dien Bien Phu, 1954.* New York: Columbia University Press, 1988.
Burke, John and Fred I. Greenstein. *How Presidents Test Reality.* New York: Russell Sage Foundation, 1989.
Chang, Gordon. *Friends and Enemies: The United States, China and the Soviet Union, 1948–1972.* Stanford: Stanford University Press, 1990.
Divine, Robert A. *Eisenhower and the Cold War.* New York: Oxford University Press, 1981.

[74] Ibid.

Dumbrell, John. *Vietnam: American Involvement at Home and Abroad*, BAAS Pamphlets in American Studies 22 (British Association of American Studies, 1992).

Eisenhower, Dwight D. *The Eisenhower Diaries*, edited by Robert Ferrell. New York: W.W. Norton & Company, 1981.

Foyle, Douglas C. *Counting the Public In: Presidents, Public Opinion, and Foreign Policy*. New York: Columbia University Press, 1999.

Griffith, Robert. *Ike's Letters to a Friend*. Lawrence: University Press of Kansas, 1984.

Gurtov, Melvin. *The First Vietnam Crisis: Chinese Communist Strategy and United States Involvement, 1953–1954*. New York: Columbia University Press, 1967.

Herring, George C. and Richard H. Immerman. "Eisenhower, Dulles and the Dienbienphu Crisis: "The Day We Didn't Go to War" Revisited." *The Journal of American History* 71 (1984): 343–363.

Immerman, Richard. "Between the Unattainable and the Unacceptable." In *Re-Evaluating Eisenhower: American Foreign Policy in the 1950s*, edited by Richard Melanson and David Mayers. Urbana: University of Illinois Press, 1987.

Lawrence, Mark Atwood and Fredrick Logevall. *The First Vietnam War: Colonial Conflict and Cold War Crisis*. Cambridge, MA: Harvard University Press, 2007.

Rovere, Richard H. *Affairs of State: The Eisenhower Years*. New York: Farrar, Straus & Cudahy, 1956.

White, Mark J. *Against the President, Dissent and Decision Making in the White House: A Historical Perspective*. Chicago: Ivan r. Dee, 2007.

CHAPTER 5

Challenge Two: The First Taiwan Crisis of 1954–1955

Soon after the Indochina crisis, the Eisenhower administration faced its second challenge to its China policy. On September 3rd, 1954, President Dwight D. Eisenhower was vacationing at the Summer White House in Denver. At approximately seven o'clock that evening, he received a message from Deputy Defense Secretary Robert B. Anderson from Washington, DC. He reported that at two o'clock that morning, the Chinese Communists had begun heavy artillery shelling of Jinmen (Quemoy), one of approximately 25 small islands off the Chinese mainland coast held by the Nationalist regime. Two American members of the Military Assistance Advisory Group (MAAG) had been killed and 14 were being evacuated. Anderson's message marked the beginning of a nine-month crisis which carried the country to the brink of nuclear war, almost caused a split between the US and its allies, and seriously tested the administration's ability to uphold its views on national security while preserving domestic consensus for its foreign policy. In the President's own words, "It was the most serious problem of the first eighteen months of my administration."[1]

The vast scholarly literature on United States policy during the crisis has treated the Executive branch's relationship with public opinion, and particularly Congress, as an example of successful public relations management and of Congressional deference to the White House on national security issues during the early decades of the Cold War. Attention has

[1] Dwight D. Eisenhower, *The White House Years: A Mandate for a Change* (New York: Doubleday & Company, 1963), 549–550.

© The Author(s) 2018
M. Oliva, *Eisenhower and American Public Opinion on China*,
https://doi.org/10.1007/978-3-319-76195-4_5

117

focused on the overwhelming approval by Congress on January 28th, 1955 of the Formosa Resolution, granting the President unprecedented authority to employ US armed forces in the Taiwan (Formosa) Straits. A more in-depth analysis, however, shows that the administration's management of public opinion and its relationship with Congress during the crisis are more complex than the lopsided passage of the Formosa Resolution suggests. This chapter analyzes the way which President Eisenhower and Secretary of State John Foster Dulles perceived and handled popular and Congressional feelings throughout the entire crisis and argues that their public relations strategy was not always successful.

In line with the President's and the Secretary of State's realist approach toward public opinion, both men formulated their foreign policy decisions toward the People's Republic of China (PRC) based on US national security interests; then through public information campaigns and consultations with Congress, they tried to generate support for the policy chosen. While that plan worked for the first part of the crisis, the bellicose rhetoric employed in public messages combined with a hostile policy toward Beijing (Peiping) backfired and undercut the fragile consensus fashioned by the Formosa Resolution, leaving Washington with the prospect of fighting a nuclear war without domestic support. Nonetheless, despite failing at generating enough public approval, the administration did not alter its national security strategy. Similarly, to during the Indochina crisis, popular feelings ultimately only narrowed the choice of policy options available but they did not determine Eisenhower's and Dulles's final decision.

A STRATEGY OF AMBIGUITY

During the Sino-Japanese war of 1884–1885, China had lost the island of Taiwan and the nearby Penghu islands (Pescadores) to Japan. In 1943, the Cairo Declaration had established that the jurisdiction over those islands would revert to China at the end of World War II. The Japanese Peace Treaty of 1951 had officially ended the Japanese sovereignty over the islands, but because of the ongoing civil war in China, the ultimate disposition of those territories had remained unsettled. On the other hand, the offshore islands had always remained under the control of China mainland, until Jiang Jieshi (Chiang Kai-shek) and his Nationalist army had fled to the island of Taiwan in 1949.[2]

---

[2] See Chap. 2 for details on the Cairo Declaration; Gordon, Chang, "To the Nuclear Brink, Eisenhower, Dulles and the Quemoy-Matsu," *International Security* 12 (1988): 98–99; Eisenhower, *Mandate for a Change*, 551.

Considering Taiwan to be a vital link in the American security chain in the Western Pacific, the Eisenhower administration had given Jiang Jieshi's Republic of China (ROC) increasingly generous diplomatic, economic, and military help to buttress its territorial security. In 1954, economic aid amounted to $527 million and military aid could be valued at $940 million. Although Washington had never officially stated its position regarding the offshore islands, privately it had instructed the Nationalists to retain control of those territories for action in the defense of Taiwan and for raids against the Communist mainland to obtain prisoners, make the PRC feel insecure about its coastal defenses, and disrupt seaborne commerce. By the start of the 1954 crisis, Jiang had transformed those islands into formidable positions. One fifth of his Nationalist forces were stationed there, with more than 50,000 soldiers, comprising 43,000 first line regulars and 11,000 guerrillas on Jinmen alone.[3]

The military buildup had been accompanied by an aggressive propaganda campaign. After Eisenhower had seemingly unleashed Jiang by removing the Seventh Fleet from patrolling the Taiwan Straits in February 1953, the Nationalist leader had increasingly threatened the Chinese Communists with an imminent attack on the mainland. In his 1954 New Year's message, Jiang warned that he had enough military power to return to China in the "near future." In his Easter message a few months later, he called for a "holy war" against the Communists. In May, South Korean President Symgman Rhee joined the bellicose campaign by launching an appeal to the US to team up with him and the ROC in a war against the PRC and called for US air and naval support for his and Jiang's invasion of the mainland.[4]

The Chinese Communists took the increased Nationalist provocations in the area seriously and held Washington responsible for the mounting tensions. Historians Gordon Chang's and He Di's groundbreaking work reveals that Chairman Mao Zedong (Mao Tse tung) was especially worried over rumors that Washington and Taipei were about to sign a Mutual

---

[3] See Chap. 3 for details on US policy toward Taiwan; "United States Objectives and Course of Action with Respect to Formosa and the Chinese Nationalist Government," NSC146, November 6, 1953, *Foreign Relations of the United States*, XIV, 1952–1954 (Washington, DC: US Government Printing Office, 1985), 307–377 (hereafter *FRUS*, followed by volume, date and page number); "Special Intelligence Estimate: the Situation with Respect to Certain Islands off the Coast of Mainland China," September 4, 1954, *FRUS*, XIV, 1952–1954, 563–571.

[4] Eisenhower, *A Mandate for a Change*, 552.

Defense Treaty. Mao was afraid that such a treaty would sanction the division of Taiwan from the mainland, just as the ceasefire in Korea and the Geneva agreements had done for China's neighbors. To disrupt any possible collaboration between the US and the Nationalists, the PRC launched a massive "liberate Taiwan" propaganda campaign in late July 1954. The Communist leadership was under no illusion that it could successfully capture the island in the future. The overall aim of the campaign was to draw world attention to the issue and to what Beijing perceived as an increased American interference in China's ongoing civil war.[5]

As the political temperature rose, at his weekly press conference on August 17th, President Eisenhower was asked by the United Press White House correspondent, Merriman Smith, what would happen if the Communists did attack Taiwan in force. The President answered that any invasion of the island would have to run over the Seventh Fleet. A few days later, on August 24th, Secretary of State John Foster Dulles was asked if he could clarify whether the American obligation to defend Taiwan included the main island only or smaller islands off the coast of the China mainland also held by the Nationalists. Answering in a non-committal and vague way, Dulles declared that the instruction was to defend only Taiwan, but there were many other islands held by the Nationalists which lay between Taiwan and the mainland, "the defense of which may form a military standpoint so intimately connected with the defense of Taiwan."[6]

On August 26th, the Chinese Communist propaganda intensified as 40 raiders struck on Jinmen, killing 10 Nationalists; then on September 3rd, the artillery bombardment began. The administration now faced, in the words of Secretary Dulles, a "horrible dilemma." Previously in 1953, Eisenhower had privately made it clear to Jiang that Washington would participate in the defense of the offshore islands only if Taiwan and the

<hr/>

[5] Gordon Chang and Di He, "The Absence of War in the US-China Confrontation over Quemoy and Matsu in 1954–1955: Contingency, Luck, Deterrence?" *American Historical Review* 98 (1993): 1500–1524. The article is one of the first collaborative efforts between an American historian and a scholar from the People's Republic of China and it draws from a wide documentary base from American and Chinese archives.

[6] Eisenhower's press conference, August 17, 1954, John T. Woolley and Gerhard Peters, *The American Presidency Project* [online], Santa Barbara, CA, http:www.presidency.ucsb.edu/ws/?pid+9987, Retrieved May 9, 2010 (hereafter *The American Presidency Project* followed by retrieved date); Dulles' press conference, August 24, 1954, Records of the State Department Bureau of Public Affairs, 1954, box 5, National Archives II, College Park, Maryland (hereafter DOS, followed by box number and NAII).

Penghus were also being attacked. Was this a prelude to an attack on Taiwan? The President could not know that the Communists had no intention of launching a full assault on the island and that the shelling of Jinmen was only part of a propaganda campaign.[7]

The administration was divided from the start. Believing that after the stalemate in Korea and the collapse of French Indochina, the West needed a victory in Asia, the Chairman of the Joint Chiefs of Staff (JCS), Admiral Arthur W. Radford, advocated an all-out defense of the offshore islands and the use of atomic weapons if the Chinese Communists launched a major assault on Taiwan. Although he conceded that Jinmen and the other offshore islands were not important from a military stand point to the defense of Taiwan, he argued that the loss of those islands would be a considerable psychological blow for the ROC and other countries looking to America for protection. Among the JCS, only General Matthew B. Ridgway, the Army Chief of Staff, disagreed with that view. In his opinion, the JCS should only be weighing military factors rather than psychological ones; because he did not believe that the loss of Jinmen endangered Taiwan's position, he believed that the best course of action was to not intervene.[8]

Secretary Dulles expressed his initial reaction to the crisis from Manila where he was finalizing the establishment of the Southeast Asia Treaty Organization (SEATO). Like Radford, he thought the US should help the Nationalists to hold Jinmen if it was judged defensible, because the loss of the island would have grave psychological repercussions and would lead to mounting Communist action and deteriorating anti-Communist morale. Fearing that would mark the beginning of a chain of events which would gravely jeopardize the entire offshore position, Dulles further argued that much of the Communist prestige stemming from Dien Bien Phu could be cancelled out if Jinmen was held. However, he did not want to duplicate the mistake that the French had made of making a symbol of what could

---

[7] Eisenhower, *Mandate for a Change*, 463; Chang and Di, "The Absence of War in the US-China Confrontation over Quemoy and Matsu in 1954–1955: Contingency, Luck, Deterrence?" 1507.

[8] The Acting Secretary of Defence (Anderson) to the President, September 3, 1954, *FRUS*, XIV, 1952–1954, 556–557; The Acting Secretary of State (Smith) to the Embassy in the Philippines, September 3, 1954, *FRUS*, XIV, 1952–1954, pp. 557–558; H.W., Brands Jr. "Testing Massive Retaliation: Credibility and Crisis Management in the Taiwan Straits," *International Security* 12 (1988): 124–151; Bennett, C. Rushkoff, "Eisenhower, Dulles and the Quemoy-Matsu Crisis," *Political Science Quarterly* 96 (1981): 465–480.

not be held, especially in the face of Communist willingness to accept immense casualties to gain political objectives.[9]

Squaring off against the JCS and Dulles was Secretary of Defense Charles E. Wilson, who was not an admirer of Jiang. In his view, Taiwan and the Penghus were far more significant than the close-in islands. Jinmen also represented a problem because to defend it successfully, the US would have to attack the Chinese mainland.[10]

Acknowledging that Jinmen had considerable psychological value, Eisenhower was inclined to agree with Wilson that the defense of Taiwan would not be endangered by the loss of the island. Furthermore, he believed that the policy proposed by the majority of the JCS could not be limited to only Jinmen. The island lay under the guns of the PRC and within easy aircraft range of the mainland; therefore, there was a serious risk that the situation would progress rather swiftly to general hostilities with Communist China. "We are not talking of a limited brush-fire war," he warned, "We are talking about going to the threshold of World War III. If we attack China we are not going to impose limits on our military actions as in Korea." Furthermore, the President reminded his staff at a National Security Council (NSC) meeting on September 12th that, "When we talk of war with China, what we mean is general war with Russia." President Eisenhower was certain the Soviets would be forced to intervene if a war broke out; if they did not abide by their 1949 treaty with the PRC, their empire would quickly fall into pieces.[11]

The President also noted that the NSC should take into consideration the repercussions outside the immediate area of interest. He was seriously concerned about the possibility of driving a wedge between the US and its principal Allies, especially Britain. Since the Communist takeover of the mainland, British leaders had looked at America's China policy with suspicion. They thought that by intervening in China's internal affairs, Washington had increased anti-Western feelings in Asia and made the British position in Hong Kong and Malaya difficult. Considering Jinmen as neither essential to the safety of Taiwan nor defensible against any invasion, British Foreign Secretary Anthony Eden made it clear to Dulles that

---

[9] Telegram from Secretary of State Dulles to State Department, Manila, September 5, 1954, FRUS, XIV, 1952–1954, 278.

[10] Memorandum of Discussion at the 231 meeting of the NSC, September 9, 1954, FRUS, XIV, 1952–1954, 583–595.

[11] Ibid.; Eisenhower, A Mandate for a Change, 464.

a US commitment to defend the island would create serious problems among the countries in the North Atlantic Treaty Organization.[12] Public opinion at home was another issue that required consideration. The President was certain that the American people overwhelmingly favored any necessary actions to save Taiwan, but judging from the flow of letters and communication to the White House, he strongly doubted they would support a war in defense of the offshore islands. He warned the NSC that his mailbag was constantly saying, "Why do we care what happens to those yellow people out there?" It would, therefore, be a very difficult task to explain to the public the importance of those islands to US security.[13]

A series of State Department Bureau of Public Affairs (SDBPA) reports on public reactions to a possible US involvement in the Taiwan Straits confirmed President Eisenhower's suspicions. In Congress, not surprisingly, only a small pro-Nationalist faction, captained by Senator William F. Knowland (R-CA), advocated for the use of US forces to prevent the Communists from capturing Jinmen and other islands in Jiang's hands. Newspaper editors were divided on which policy the administration should choose. In general, commentators were in favor of a US intervention to protect Taiwan from a Communist attack, but the prevailing trend was against becoming involved in defending the offshore islands where the US would be at a distinct disadvantage so close to the mainland. Most of the eastern dailies such as the *New York Times*, the *New York Herald Tribune*, and the *Washington Post* maintained Jinmen was not essential to the defense of Taiwan and was not worth risking World War III over it. However, long-term Nationalist supporters such as William R. Hearst Jr., the Scripps-Howard Press, and Henry R. Luce strongly objected. "If the US proposes to keep alive an alternative to Communism for China's millions," opined *Time* magazine, "Quemoy must be defended."[14]

[12] Memorandum of Discussion at the 231 meeting of the NSC, September 9, 1954, *FRUS*, XIV, 1952–1954, 583–595; Brands, "Testing Massive Retaliation: Credibility and Crisis Management in the Taiwan Straits,"127–128.

[13] The President to the Acting Secretary of State (Smith), September 8, 1954, *FRUS*, XIV, 1952–1954, 577–579; Memorandum of Discussion at the 231 meeting of the NSC, September 9, 1954, XIV, 1952–1954, 583–595.

[14] "Special Report on the Nation After Chinese Communist Attack on the Offshore Islands," September 15, 1954, Records of the Office of Public Opinion Studies, Department of State, 1943–1975, AI568J, box 1, National Archives II, College Park, Maryland (hereaf-

A September 1954 State Department public opinion poll found that only a small majority (53%) of the respondents supported "giving the Chinese Nationalist government in Taiwan all the help it needs," with 33% disapproving and 14% having no opinion. The 53% who were supporting assistance to the Nationals were then asked what type of assistance the US should give. The poll indicated that only 20% of the respondents favored sending US troops to assist the Nationalists, while 31% opposed sending troops but supported some sort of undefined aid. The remaining 2% had no opinion.[15]

A few days later, a Gallup poll presented even a bleaker picture; only a minority of the public favored the "present US policy to intervene" in case Taiwan was invaded by the PRC. Out of four Gallup-proposed alternatives, only 10% of the respondents chose "US planes should bomb airfields and factories on mainland China," and 31% would "have US planes and ships help protect Taiwan," making a total of 41% in favor of actively intervening in the Straits. Additionally, 28% of those interviewed would have the "US merely supply guns and other materials" and 21% would have the "US keep out of Formosa altogether," making a total of 49% against US active involvement in the Straits. Essentially, the public withheld support not only for active US involvement in the Straits but also in defense of Taiwan, something that President Eisenhower had taken for granted.[16]

In his study of elite beliefs on public opinion and foreign policy, political scientist Douglas C. Foyle argued that those negative SDBPA reports prompted Dulles to draft a memorandum where he dropped his initial position to defend the offshore islands in favor of a more moderate plan to end the crisis through the United Nations (UN). In it, he reasoned that if the administration used President Harry Truman's 1950 order to the Seventh Fleet to defend Taiwan against a Communist Chinese invasion to justify the defense of the offshore islands, it would incur serious attacks by a sharply divided Congress and domestic public opinion because those islands were not "demonstrably essential to the defense of Formosa as

ter survey title followed by date, DOS, file reference, box number, NAII); China Telegram (CT), September 2 through 15, 1954, DOS, AI568P, box 29, NAII.

[15] Ibid.

[16] "Special report on American Public Opinion," September 1954, DOS, AI568N, box 20, NAII; Gallup, George, *The Gallup Poll: 1949–1958*, vol. 2 (New York: Random House, 1972), 1273 (hereafter Gallup poll, followed by page number); CT, September 16 through 22, 1954, DOS, AI568P, box 29, NAII.

shown by the fact that for four years they have not been included in the area the Fleet was ordered to defend."[17]

The imminent Congressional elections and a hostile world opinion further complicated the situation. It would be better, Dulles wrote, to submit the issue to the United Nations Security Council (UNSC) for consideration by a "neutral" but interested nation, such as New Zealand, with a call for preservation of the status quo and a further study of the issue. Although the US would relinquish control over Taiwan to the international body, Dulles found certain advantages to the option; if the Soviets vetoed the resolution, the US would have gained standing in domestic and world opinion and with its Allies, and could claim the moral high ground; if they chose not to veto the resolution, a possible schism between Moscow and Beijing might occur and the PRC would become "an international outcast" if it still chose to act.[18]

Foyle further contends that when Dulles presented his plan to the 214th NSC meeting on September 12th, Eisenhower heartily endorsed it because the apparent public opposition to military action and concern regarding allied reaction led the President to the conclusion that provocative moves in September were not advisable. Essentially, Foyle argues that "When faced with the need to choose a policy, Eisenhower rejected the use of force to defend the offshore islands primarily because he feared public opposition."[19]

Historian Robert Accinelli supports Foyle's conclusions. In his analysis of the relationship between Congress and the administration during the crisis, he argues that both Eisenhower's and Dulles's concerns with Congressional and public opinion accounted for the relative moderate course of action they chose. Dulles was especially worried that because of the imminent midterm elections, Congress would not respond to an all-out appeal by the President for an authorization to intervene in the Straits. As both men valued bipartisan support, Accinelli goes on, "as a means of under girding a domestic foreign policy consensus, presenting a united front to friends and adversaries alike and protecting against

---

[17] Douglas Foyle, "Public Opinion and Foreign Policy: Elite Beliefs as a Mediating Variable," *International Studies Quarterly* 41 (1997), 141–169; and *Counting the Public In: Presidents, Public Opinion and Foreign Policy* (New York: Columbia University Press, 1999), 53; Memorandum prepared by the Secretary of State, September 12, 1954, *FRUS*, XIV, 1952–1954, 611.

[18] Ibid.

[19] Ibid.

Congressional retaliation in the event the policy failed," a perceived lack of it led them to opt for a more moderate solution that would meet with public and Congressional approval.[20]

Both scholars, however, forget a very important element in assessing the influence public opinion and Congress had on the administration at that stage of the crisis. In the memorandum Foyle quotes as proof of Dulles' shift in position, the Secretary of State also wrote that because of adverse weather conditions an escalation of the crisis was unlikely in the immediate future, "probably the Monsoon season will be used for air and land build-ups of such a character that the issue will be formidably and inescapably posed in a few months." That information was confirmed by a Central Intelligence Agency information estimate, a British estimate, and Nationalist Foreign Minister George Yeh. The administration, therefore, knew it did not need to make an immediate decision on the course of action to take because American national security interests were not at risk at the time.[21]

The absence of an immediate emergency gave Eisenhower and Dulles the opportunity to place the administration in a better position with the public and Congress, should a more bellicose policy become necessary. The President and the Secretary of State clearly saw the decision to defend the offshore islands as the beginning of large-scale war in which they would not hold back and would probably use nuclear weapons. Believing that public and Congressional backing was necessary before engaging in military action and knowing that at that moment that the American people were not in favor of that option, the UN approach provided them with the chance to enlist such support should a war break out. By first invoking the intervention of the UN, Washington could show the home public and the world its good intentions of seeking a peaceful solution to the crisis. If the Chinese rejected the offer and went ahead with an invasion of Taiwan, then any US response could be clearly presented as a defensive action.[22]

[20] Robert Accinelli, "Eisenhower, Congress and the 1954–1955 Offshore Islands Crisis," *Presidential Studies Quarterly* 20 (1990), 329–348; and *Crisis and Commitment: United States Policy Toward Taiwan, 1950–1955* (Chapel Hill: University of North Carolina, 1996).

[21] Memorandum prepared by the Secretary of State, September 12, 1954, *FRUS*, XIV, 1952–1954, 611; "Special Intelligence Estimate—the situation with respect to certain islands off the coast of Mainland China," September 4, 1954, *FRUS*, XIV, 563–567.

[22] Memorandum of Discussion at the 213 meeting of the NSC, September 9, 1954, *FRUS*, XIV, 1952–1954, 583–595.

Contrary to what Foyle and Accinelli argue, neither Eisenhower nor Dulles would have compromised national security to appease the public or Congress. As the President repeatedly told his Secretary of State, he was ready to go any length to defend US vital interests even if he were to risk impeachment. It was important, however, as Dulles explained during a NSC meeting on November 2th, to generate public support for a US intervention by making the American people understand that sometimes to defend peace, it is necessary to go to war. "You don't always actually secure peace," he remarked, "by simply being a pacifist or by talking peace." It was a difficult and novel thing to "most people to realize that the will to fight for vital things is really indispensable to the maintenance of peace." Washington therefore chose the UN approach, not because it bowed to popular pressure, but as the first step in leading the public to support what the administration believed to be the right policy, should the crisis escalate.[23]

The President and the Secretary of State had not sanctioned a bellicose policy yet; they hoped to deter a Chinese Communist armed attack by signing a Mutual Defense Treaty with the Nationalist government. Jiang had been pressing the administration for such a treaty for almost one year. Eisenhower was not against it but first the end of the Korean War, then the Indochina crisis, and the creation of SEATO had delayed the negotiations. Dulles now thought the time had come to formalize the alliance between the two countries. Ironically, Mao's plan to block the treaty had sped up its settlement.[24]

Washington, however, wanted to keep its options flexible. Dulles proposed to "fuzz up" the language of the treaty; it would explicitly cover the defense of Taiwan and the Penghus for which US commitment was already on record, but it would be vague on American commitments to protect the islands near the coast. In exchange for that protection and to ensure that it would not be drawn into a war with China, the administration asked Jiang to secretly pledge not to take any offensive actions against the mainland without US approval. For Dulles, that strategy of ambiguity had the double advantage of maintaining doubts in the minds of both the Chinese Communists and domestic public and the world as to how the US

---

[23] Memorandum of Discussion at the 231 meeting of the NSC, November 2, 1954, *FRUS*, XIV, 1952–1954, 827–893.
[24] Brands, "Testing Massive Retaliation: Credibility and Crisis Management in the Taiwan Straits", 133–134.

would react to an attack on the offshore islands. Believing this uncertainty would deter the PRC and would avoid alienating the public and the Allies, he laughingly remarked at the official signing of the treaty, "Its aim [of the treaty] is to keep both the Communists and the public guessing."[25]

The SDBPA reported that the treaty had been greeted favorably by the entire spectrum of public opinion. Its bipartisan endorsement in Congress was not just the consequence of its vague language, but the result of a careful preparatory work. Before beginning the negotiations, Dulles had consulted key Congressional leaders such as Senate majority leader Knowland and Senator Walter George (D-GA), the ranking Democrat on the Foreign Relations Committee. Among the press, not surprisingly, only the isolationist *Chicago Tribune* saw "no necessity for such a treaty," but both pro-Nationalists and more moderate commentators welcomed the new development. *Time* magazine underscored the unequivocal warning to Beijing, while an editorial in the *New York Herald Tribune* declared, "The treaty makes clear beyond doubt that Formosa and the Pescadores are not up for bargain." Finally, a National Opinion Research Center (NORC) poll revealed that 75% of the respondents approved of the new pact, 10% did not, and the remaining 15% did not know.[26]

A PUBLIC RELATIONS CHAOS

If the administration thought the worst was over and it had succeeded in containing the situation, it was soon disappointed. Throughout the latter part of 1954 and early 1955, its public relations strategy was plagued by domestic controversies, PRC propaganda tricks, and press leaks that seriously tested its ability to preserve public and bipartisan Congressional support. On November 23rd, Beijing announced the espionage conviction of 13 American fliers who had been shot down over China during the Korean War. Predictably, the sentencing provoked cries of outrage in the US. Senator Knowland went as far as to demand a naval blockade of the Chinese mainland unless the PRC released the American prisoners immediately. Considering a blockade as an act of war, a furious Eisenhower told

[25] Memorandum of Discussion at the 231 meeting of the NSC, November 2, 1954, *FRUS*, XIV, 1952–1954, pp. 827–893; Dulles' press conference, December 2, 1954, DOS, 1954, box 5, NAII.

[26] CT, December 2 through 9, 1954, DOS, AI568P, box 29, NAII; "Public Reaction to Mutual Defence Treaty," December 1954, AI568J, box 1, NAII.

Press Secretary James C. Hagerty, "I am completely beginning to lose my patience with Bill Knowland. He has made the most irresponsible statements of late which are hurting us very much with our Allies."[27]

Hagerty suggested that the President should make a strong public statement against Knowland and those within the Republican Party who were engaging in the saber-rattling talk. Eisenhower did not disagree, but fearing he might get involved in a party row that would damage his popularity with the public, he decided to have Dulles take the lead. On the President's instructions, the Secretary of State included a clear and strong condemnation of a blockade as an act of war in a speech he was giving the same night in Chicago. In the meantime, Hagerty canceled the President's press conference scheduled for the following day and arranged instead for Dulles to have his press conference before Eisenhower's "to fend off dangerous questions."[28]

Almost a week later, the President finally took up the issue in public. Without mentioning Knowland directly, he clearly referred to him when declaring that it was an irresponsible thing for people who held public office to express freely their opinions without thinking of the result of their actions because careless statements inflamed public opinion, and once public opinion was in favor of war there no stopping until the war was won. "We owe to ourselves and the world", the President declared, "to explore every possible peaceable means of settling differences before we can think of such a thing as war." Ignoring such criticism, Knowland repeated his demand for a blockade immediately after UN Secretary General Dag Hammarskjold publicly offered to travel to Beijing to discuss the issue of the prisoners with the Communist leadership.[29]

To make things worse, on that same day, Representative Thomas J. Lane (D-Mass.) filed a resolution demanding the release of the 13 Americans "before 60 days have passed" and warning the Chinese Reds and the world that if they were not "free by that time we shall be obliged to adopt more positive measures to effect their release."[30] Two days later,

[27] James C. Hagerty, *The Diary of James C. Hagerty*, ed. Ferrell Robert (Bloomington: Indiana University Press, 1983), 117–118 (hereafter Hagerty's Diaries followed by page number).

[28] Ibid.

[29] Ibid.; Eisenhower's press conference December 13, 1954, *The American Presidency Project* [retrieved May 10, 2010].

[30] Memorandum of Discussion at the 331 meeting of the NSC, January 13, 1955, *FRUS*, II, 1955–1957, 17–30; Daily Summaries of Public Opinion, January 13, 1955, DOS, AI568K, box 7, NAII.

on January 12th, a story in *the New York Times* by James Reston reported that a private memorandum, which had been circulated to members of Congress by the Democratic National Committee, questioned the wisdom of the Senate's ratification of the Mutual Defense Treaty with Taiwan. The document did not dispute the vital importance of Taiwan and the Penghus to the US, but contended that such formal recognition of those islands as territories of the ROC gave substance to the Communists' claim that an attack on them would be part of a civil war and not international aggression. It also doubted the value of Nationalist China's reassurances that it would not provoke a Communist attack.[31]

Eisenhower was furious and wanted an immediate release of a White House statement denouncing "the activities of this cabal at a time when we most desperately need bipartisan support for our foreign policy." Declaring that in his opinion the activities of that group bordered on the traitorous, Dulles was particularly afraid the memorandum would spearhead organized opposition to ratification of the Mutual Defense Treaty in the US Senate. Both the President and the Secretary of State thought of denouncing its authors in a public meeting of the Senate Foreign Relations Committee, but they opted for a softer approach and decided that Dulles should have a private conversation with Walter George. The Democrats had regained control of Congress following the 1954 mid-term elections. The Senator was the Chairman of the Foreign Relations Committee, dean of the Senate Democrats, and de facto spokesman on world affairs for his party in Congress. Accordingly, his collaboration was vital if the administration wanted to preserve bipartisanship in Congress.[32]

Fearing the Republican right might endanger their strategy by making inconsiderate public statements and thus driving some Democrats unwillingly to support the action of the National Committee, Dulles, before meeting with George, personally urged Knowland to refrain from commenting on the issue. Then on January 16th, he received the Georgia Senator at the State Department. Explaining that at that time, the international situation was too dangerous to let partisan policy get into foreign affairs and offering reassurance that he had urged a more responsible GOP attitude, Dulles promised that in exchange for a withdrawal of the

---

[31] Ibid.
[32] Memorandum of Discussion at the 331 meeting of the NSC, January 13, 1955, *FRUS*, II, 1955–1957, 17–30.

Democratic National Committee (DNC) document, he would personally make sure that when it came to the political elections of 1956, George would get his fair share of credit. Acknowledging that the matter had not been handled in the best way, the Senator admitted having read the memorandum but that at the time he had not thought it raised any serious points. He then realized how dangerous such documents could be and agreed to talk to his party members to have it withdrawn.[33]

In the meantime, UN Secretary General Dag Hammarskjold had returned from his trip to China and informed the US Ambassador to the UN, Henry Cabot Lodge, that Zhou En-Lai (Chou En-lai) had offered to grant visas to the families of the US airmen to permit them to travel to the PRC and "see how well we are taking care of the prisoners." Both Eisenhower and Dulles were against that suggestion. It was a neat publicity stunt that would play into the Communists' hands, especially after Hammarskjold added that the airmen had been moved to better quarters only two or three days before his arrival in China and that he had been given some photographs and other documentary material about the prisoners for public release to show "what good conditions they were in."[34]

On the administration's instructions, Lodge met with Hammarskjold a second time to talk him into a plan to minimize the effect of the PRC propaganda maneuver by releasing the offer of the passports first and then a few days later the footage on the fliers to blanket the news stories about the visas. The Secretary General agreed to the plan and released the news about the offer of the visas and the footage of the prisoners in two stages. As expected, the prisoners' images had the desired effect of side-lining the offer of the visas.[35]

Hammarskjold was no puppet though; he regarded his assignment as a chance not only to plead his case for the innocence of the airmen, but to expand the role of his UN office and to contribute to a reduction of tensions between the Chinese Communists and the Americans. The well-schooled Swedish diplomat was on record as favoring the PRC participation in the UN and wanted to use the incident with the prisoners to promote the cause. After making the photographs of the prisoners public,

[33] Memorandum of Conversation with Senator Knowland, January 15, 1955, JFD Papers, General Correspondence Series, box 1, DDEL; Memorandum of Conversation with Senator Walter F. George, January 16, 1955, JFD Papers, Subject Series, box 5, DDEL.

[34] Hagerty's Diaries, 161–162.

[35] Telegram from Representative at the UN (Lodge) to the Department of State, January 17, 1955, *FRUS*, II, 1955–1957, 35–36; Hagerty's Diaries, 161–163.

he made a shocking declaration, "To facilitate the release of the 13 US airmen it would be very useful if the PRC was directly represented in the UN." The following day a story by Thomas Hamilton in the *New York Times*, with UN headquarters dateline stated that according to "reliable sources," the Secretary General believed that the chances for the airmen to be released would improve if the US clarified the defensive nature of its treaty with the ROC.[36]

The pro-Nationalist faction was outraged; to Eisenhower's dismay, Knowland once again went against the President's warning for restraint and lashed out against Hammarskjold in a speech before the Newspaper Advertising Executives Association in Chicago. He called the Secretary General's mission a failure and threatened that the US might consider withdrawing from the UN if the PRC was ever given a seat. Similarly, Henry Luce questioned the role of the international body in a *Time* magazine editorial; "It must be accounted extraordinary that responsible officials of the American executive departments delegate their diplomatic prerogatives to an outsider and that this great nation of ours says it will depend on the UN which has proven so feeble."[37]

The increasing talk about admitting the PRC into the UN prompted the re-organization of the Committee for One Million Against the Admission of the People's Republic of China in the United Nations (Committee of One Million or COOM). Having reached its target of One Million signatures, COOM had gone into a "hibernation phase", but Hammarskjold's declarations triggered a new intense propaganda campaign against the establishment of diplomatic relations with Beijing. In early February, that body began to publish its views in all the major dailies and magazines throughout the country.[38] Five themes dominated: (1) the Committee's bipartisan composition; (2) the appeasement of the Chinese Reds by other Free world governments and organizations; (3) Chinese

---

[36] Ibid. "Public Opinion Reaction to PRC's visas offer and prisoners' photographs," February 1955, DOS, AI568J, box I, NAII.

[37] Memorandum of Conversation between the President and the Secretary of State at the White House, January 17, 1955, *FRUS*, II, 1955–1957, 34; CT, January 13 through 20, DOS, AI568P, box 29, NAII.

[38] The Committee *for* One Million also changed name into The Committee *of* One Million, here still abbreviated as COOM; Publications relating to the Committee of One Million Against Admission of Red China to the United Nations, 1954–1966, Tamiment Library, New York University, New York (NYU); Stanley, Bachrack, *The Committee of One Million, "China Lobby" Politics* (New York: Columbia University Press, 1976), 102–111.

Communist direct and indirect aggression in Korea, Vietnam, Malaya, and Tibet; (4) the importance of preventing the aggressor from entering the UN; and (5) the cause organized in 1953 to collect the one million signatures was in danger.[39]

In early February, the SDBPA reported that "The UN press leaks combined with the pro-Nationalist reaction" and "COOM's new propaganda campaign" were creating doubts among the public about the administration's ability to resist international pressure to establish diplomatic relations with Beijing and consequently, its ability to play a leading role in international affairs. A White House and State Department joint press release denied that their China policy was under review. Eisenhower then dispatched Lodge to see Hammarskjold to impress on him the gravity of the situation. Expressing concern about the reaction in Washington to the newspaper stories which had occurred since the Secretary General's return from China, the Ambassador warned that such negative publicity could have profound consequences in Congress that would endanger the very existence of the UN itself. He then urged him to make his staff understand the vital importance of not leaking sensitive information.[40]

THE FORMOSA RESOLUTION: A CALCULATED IMPRECISION

Through consultations and back channel maneuvers, Eisenhower and Dulles had tried to contain the domestic situation, avoid public confrontation with the Democrats, and limit the damage caused by the PRC propaganda and the UN press leaks. However, the strategy was not working and the administration was beginning to lose the public's support. To make things worse, on January 18th, the crisis in the Straits intensified when the Chinese Communist forces overwhelmed 1000 Nationalist guerrillas on Yijing (Ichiang) Island, just north of the Dechens (Techens) group.[41]

Believing that the PRC intended to overrun the Dechens along with the rest of the offshore islands and eventually try to make good on its pledge to liberate Taiwan, Eisenhower and Dulles concluded their policy of ambiguity had begun to backfire. "Keeping the Communists and the public

<hr/>

[39] Ibid.
[40] "Public Opinion Survey," February 1955, AI568J, box I, NAII; Telegram from the Representative at the UN (Lodge) to the Department of State, January 17, 1955, *FRUS*, II, 1955–1957, 35–36.
[41] Memorandum of phone conversation between the President and Dulles, January 18, 1955, *FRUS*, II, 1955–1957, 37.

guessing," as the Secretary of State had joked in Manila in September 1954, had projected an image of American insecurity to the enemy and had created confusion among the public, leaving the administration exposed to international and domestic attacks. The time had come to make US intentions clear and stick to them. While still hoping to deter a PRC attack, Eisenhower and Dulles devised a four-part plan aimed at presenting a strong and firm declaration of American intent to protect its national security interests in the Straits and generating domestic public support should the situation escalate.[42]

Accordingly, their first task would be to persuade the Nationalists to evacuate the Dechens; which were insignificant from a military point of view. As Eisenhower remarked "The decision would have at least the merit to show the public we are trying to maintain a decent posture." Second, the President and the Secretary of State would ask the British to resume the UN initiative, which had been temporarily shelved. Third, they would push the Senate to speed the ratification of the Mutual Defense Treaty. Finally, and most importantly, they would ask Congress for explicit authority to use US military forces to defend Taiwan and the Penghus, but also Jinmen and the Matzu (Matsu) group.[43]

By making their intention to defend these offshore islands clear, Eisenhower and Dulles hoped to boost the Nationalists' morale and perhaps mollify resentment at being asked to evacuate the Dechens, as well as dissuade the Chinese Communists from any further advances. If deterrence failed, the Congressional resolution would at least remove any uncertainty about the President's authority to use armed forces as he saw fit in the Taiwan Straits and would not leave him vulnerable to criticism as Truman had been dispatching forces in Korea.[44]

To guarantee the success of the plan, it was first necessary to calm an increasingly heated pro-Nationalist faction. After the attack on Yijing Island, the administration had tried to minimize the significance of the event by declaring in public speeches and press conferences that the island in question lay at such a distance from Taiwan as to be of little strategic importance. Both Eisenhower and Dulles had also publicly stated that the

---

[42] Memorandum of Luncheon Conversation with the President, January 19, 1955, JFD Papers, White House Memoranda Series, box 3, DDEL.
[43] Ibid.
[44] Ibid.

US would have no objection if the UN undertook to arrange a ceasefire in the Taiwan Straits.[45]

The SDBPA reported that while the public and most of the press commentators had welcomed that statement, Jiang's supporters had reacted by accusing the administration of abandoning a valuable ally instead of waging war against the PRC to restore the Nationalists on the mainland. Even Henry Luce, who thus far had faithfully supported the administration's foreign policy, spoke out against a UN ceasefire. In a *Life* editorial, he opined that a ceasefire was the first step toward neutralization of Taiwan, which ultimately put an end to any opportunities the Nationalists might have to re-conquer the mainland. "The Formosa Government", Luce went on, "is one of the few obstacles to the Communist drive in Asia precisely because it intends their ultimate downfall. Unless we are willing to support it [the Formosa Government], as Chiang does, then the Formosa alliance is a fraud and the Reds are on the march again."[46]

Luce also wrote Eisenhower a long and emotional letter. Attaching a dispatch from John Osborne, *Time* magazine's Far Eastern correspondent, which detailed the demoralized public reaction in Asia about the ceasefire proposal, he explained that the administration's policy was having a "devastating effect" not only on free China friends in the US but also "among the friends of freedom" in the Far East.[47]

Trying to reassure Luce, Eisenhower replied "There was a great deal of misunderstanding about the ceasefire." It was not meant to prevent the Nationalists from ever returning to the mainland, but to protect them because Beijing had a tremendous military advantage on the small offshore islands. The President was, however, increasingly worried that the heated front-page headlines continuously generated by Jiang's supporters combined with some Democrats' desire to exploit the issue for partisan

[45] Memorandum of Phone Conversation Between the President and Dulles, January 18, 1955, *FRUS*, II, 1955–1957, 37; Eisenhower's press conference, January 19, 1955, *The American Presidency Project* [retrieved May 9, 2010]; JFD's press conference, January 18, 1955, State Department press release 32, JFD Papers, box 90, Seely G. Mudd Manuscripts Library, Princeton University, New Jersey (hereafter JFD Papers, followed by record reference, box number, ML).

[46] CT, January 19 through 25, DOS, AI568P, box 29, NAII; *Life*, January 27, 1955, 21.

[47] Luce to Eisenhower, January 22, 1955, DDE Papers, Central Files, Official Files, box 866, DDEL.

advantage would eventually inflame public opinion and force the administration to act imprudently.[48]

Although Eisenhower and Dulles were trying to generate public support for US armed intervention in the Straits should the crisis escalate, they wanted to do so in a way that would leave their options flexible. They still hoped to deter the Chinese Communists from any further advance, but if that did not work, they wanted to make sure that American actions were perceived domestically and internationally as a defensive reaction. Talks of war, as Eisenhower had already remarked with reference to Knowland in his December 1954 press conference, would not facilitate that but could instead influence public opinion to support a more aggressive policy and thus push Washington to take military risks in the Straits.

The President and the Secretary of State therefore set out to "educate Congress, and in particular the Republican right-wingers" on the requirements of the current situation. Hoping that such a clarification would calm them down and thereby generate the unreserved bipartisan support necessary to obtain a swift and overwhelming mandate from the legislative branch, Eisenhower instructed Dulles to meet with the Congressional leaders on January 21, 1955.[49]

The Secretary of State opened the two-hour meeting by describing the Nationalist position on the Dechens as "hopeless." With the islands too far from Taiwan and too close to the mainland, he declared that the recent "public fuss" about them had been detrimental to American security. Jinmen instead had very important strategic and psychological values because if captured it could be used as a staging point for an attack on Taiwan; Washington therefore should focus on it rather than wasting time arguing about "insignificant positions."[50]

Radford, also attending the meeting, stressed the psychological importance of the whole issue. Believing that if Jiang thought instead of believed he could not rely on the US, he might give up altogether, the Chairman of the JCS predicted that this would force the US to go in to keep Taiwan out of Communist hands. The Secretary then informed the group that the administration was considering a parallel move involving a call for ceasefire.

[48] Eisenhower to Luce, January 24, 1955, DDE Papers, Diary Series, box 9, DDEL.

[49] Memorandum of Phone Conversation Between the President and Dulles, January 18, 1955, *FRUS*, II, 1955–1957, 37.

[50] Memorandum of Conversation with Congressional leaders, January 21, 1955, *FRUS*, II, 1955–1957, 55–68.

If the program was adopted, he continued, the President wanted to have some authority from Congress to use armed forces in the area for the protection of Taiwan and the Penghus. Dulles also urged the prompt approval of the Mutual Defense Treaty. Explaining that one reason why the Chinese were making a move against the Dechens was to frighten the US so that the pact would remain un-ratified, he stated that its quick endorsement by the Senate might therefore cause them to back off in the offshore islands. He concluded that the plan would have a stabilizing effect in persuading the enemy the US was not going to retreat further.[51]

At the end of the meeting, both the Secretary of State and Radford felt that the issue had been fully explored. The Congressional leaders had asked many questions and they understood the dangers inherent to the situation and the immense importance of an unequivocal statement of the US position. Despite his conviction that Congress would promptly give the President the powers he needed to meet the situation, Dulles still suggested it might be necessary for him to appear personally before a joint session of the two Houses. However, Eisenhower expressed doubts about a personal appearance before Congress lest it overdramatize the situation, thereby precipitating a war scare among the public. "What we want to stress," he said, "is the continuity of our policy."[52]

While the Nationalist government communicated its acceptance of the plan, Great Britain forced a major change in its prerequisites. The British Ambassador to the US, Sir Roger Makins, reported that London did not like the idea of a commitment to defend Jinmen. It believed that if the Nationalists continued to hold Jinmen, the minimum cooperation necessary to the success of the UN initiative could never be secured. Further reluctance stemmed from fear that to hold Jinmen and Matzu, the US might be obliged to use nuclear weapons. Accordingly, it would go along with the UN plan only if the US withheld its proposed guarantee to defend Jinmen. Dulles' negative reaction prompted the Ambassador to propose an alternative whereby London would inform Moscow and Beijing privately through diplomatic channels of US intention to support of Jinmen. Dulles answered that this would put Washington in a "tricky position;" if

[51] Ibid.
[52] Transcript of background news conference, January 24, 1955, JFD papers, box 10, ML; Memorandum of Discussion at the 223 meeting of the NSC, January 20, 1955, *FRUS*, II, 1955–1957, 69–82.

the private warnings were successful, the public impression would be one of Communist restraint rather than resolution on the part of the US.[53]

Although some members of the JCS protested, particularly Radford, Eisenhower decided to accept the British ultimatum. Considering the US alliance with Great Britain to be far more important than "some little off-shore islands," on January 24th, the President sent his message to Congress, its last version did not mention Jinmen and Matzu. To avoid public attack from the pro-Nationalists, however, Dulles privately reassured Knowland that Eisenhower was ready to defend Jinmen and Matzu if an attack on them seemed to be a prelude to an invasion of Taiwan.[54]

Declaring the seizure of Taiwan by an unfriendly power would "seriously dislocate" the Western position in the Pacific, the Presidential message asserted the necessity of taking firm measures "designed to improve the prospects of peace," including preparations for the use of military power. It requested special Congressional authorization to commit American forces in the Straits "but only in the situations which are recognizable parts of, or definite preliminaries to, an attack the main position of Formosa and the Pescadores." It then urged quick ratification of the Mutual Defense Treaty and welcomed UN Action to contain the situation.[55]

The SDBPA reported that "the overwhelming majority of the press from California to the East Coast" approved of the President's message as a move toward peace and called upon Congress to give him "the show of national unity he needs and he is entitled to." James Reston of the *New York Times* called the Formosa resolution "a calculated imprecision" because its broad language guaranteed freedom of maneuver but did not tie down the administration to one fixed option that made it vulnerable to attacks from all parties involved. The Pro-Nationalist Scripps-Howard press depicted it as "an expression of unified purpose of the American Government, the Congress and the people which will lessen the likelihood of Chinese Communist miscalculation possibly leading to war." Some sceptics, such as journalist Walter Lippmann, wanted the President's

---

[53] Memorandum of Conversation, January 22, 1955, II, 1955–1957, 106–107.

[54] Memorandum of Discussion at the 233 Meeting of the NSC, January 21, 1955, *FRUS*, II, 1955–1957, 89–96.

[55] Message from the President to Congress, January 24, 1955, *FRUS*, II, 1955–1957, 115–119.

authority explicitly restricted to Taiwan and the Penghus, but overall, the SDBPA concluded, press reaction had been very positive.[56]

Similarly, according to a State Department opinion poll taken the day after the message was delivered, most respondents, 58%, approved of the President's action and believed that his message to Congress had clarified the US stand and lessened the risk of stumbling into a third world war. Only 19% of those interviewed disapproved.[57]

The administration now needed and wanted a swift passage of the Formosa Resolution, which was introduced immediately after the President's message was received on January 24th. The longer the debate stretched out, the greater the opportunity for divisiveness and partisanship that would detract from the resolution's usefulness as a consensus builder and deterrent. On January 26th, after an abbreviated debate and operating under the tight rule of prohibiting any amendments, the House of Representatives gave consent by a whopping 409 to 3 margin.[58]

The Senate was more deliberate in its pace but the administration smoothed the resolution's path by cooperating with Congressional leaders and trying to allay doubts and anxiety. In executive sessions over three days, a joint session of the Foreign Relations and Armed Forces committees presided over by Senator George, heard testimonies from Dulles and Radford. The Secretary of State reassured the joint committee that the President did not consider the resolution a predated declaration of war, that he did not contemplate using American ground forces in the Formosa Straits, and did not harbor plans to restore Jiang on the mainland. He also guaranteed that the US would have full British support for the plan.[59]

Senator Wayne Morse (I-OR) was, however, not reassured by Dulles' and Radford's testimonies and requested that General Ridgway be allowed to testify as an unscheduled witness. In answering a question submitted by Morse, Ridgeway stated that the President and the Secretary of State had not asked for his opinion on the resolution, thus indicating that it lacked the unanimous endorsement of the JCS.[60]

---

[56] CT, January 19 through 25, 1955, DOS, AI568P, NAII; James, Reston, "The Formosa Resolution: A Calculated Imprecision," the *New York Times*, April 7, 1955, 13.

[57] "Public Opinion Reaction to Formosa Resolution," January 25, 1955, DOS, AI568J, box 1, NAII.

[58] Philip J. Briggs, "Congress and the Cold War: US-China Policy, 1955," *The China Quarterly* 85 (1981): 80–95.

[59] Hearings on Senate Joint Report, January 24, 1955, JFD Papers, box 17, ML.

[60] The *New York Times*, January 25, 1955, 3.

Ridgeway's declarations were a blow to the administration's attempt at generating public and bipartisan support for its policy. While the press began speculating on why the General's opinion had not been sought, Senator Hubert Humphrey (D-MN) proposed an amendment to the resolution and Senator Easter Kefauver (D-TN) introduced a substitute for it, with its purpose being to limit the geographic scope of the President's authority to defend Taiwan and the Penghus.[61]

Both were rejected by identical votes, 20 to 8, and on January 27th, the joint committee voted 26 to 2 to report the resolution favorably without amendments. However, the debate did not subside, and when the resolution went to the Senate floor, Morse attacked it again in a two-hour speech that concluded with the statement "its passage would legalize the position of the proponents of preventive war." Knowland immediately denounced him as having endangered the security of the US by allowing the Communists to understand or pretend that the nation was ready to provoke war.[62]

The Senate hearings followed by the heated Senate debate had a very negative impact on the press and public opinion and the initially unanimous endorsement of the resolution faded quickly. Editors and columnists began questioning the extent of the President's power. Leading off such criticism, the *Christian Science Monitor* and Walter Lippmann, already on record for having withdrawn support for the administration's hardline policy toward the PRC, now asserted that the ambiguity of the language of the resolution could only lead to an escalation of the crisis. They also claimed that the establishment of diplomatic relations with Beijing would have averted the danger. The White House recorded an increase of almost 50% in the number of letters that were received against military intervention because of Taiwan.[63]

Eisenhower issued a statement to further clarify and reassure the public of the peaceful scope of the resolution. That categorically declared that the deployment of US naval and air forces in the Taiwan Straits were solely for defensive purposes. Only the President would decide whether they should be used other than in immediate defense of Taiwan and the Penghus.

---

[61] Eisenhower to Senator George, January 27, 1955, DDE Papers, Diary Series, box 9, DDEL.

[62] Briggs, "Congress and the Cold War: US-China Policy, 1955," 90–95.

[63] Meeting with the President, January 28, 1955, JFD Papers, White House Memoranda Series, box 3, DDEL.

Eisenhower's military background and the general esteem in which he was held gave his reassuring statement more weight. Following his announcement, Senator George spoke on behalf of the resolution. Claiming that if a line were drawn in the Taiwan Straits beyond which the US was not obliged to defend, the result would be an enemy "sanctuary," he reassured the public of America's peaceful intentions but concluded that the language of the document had to remain vague to protect American national security interests.[64]

George's remarks in conjunction with Eisenhower's statement succeeded in eliminating opposition to the resolution. The SDBPA reported that despite a decrease in approval during the Senate hearings and debate, most of the press and public, 73% of the national sampling, now supported the resolution. "Among the significant press commentators," only the *Christian Science Monitor* and Walter Lippmann remained opposed.[65]

On January 28, the Upper Chamber approved the Resolution by a vote of 85 to 3, with only Wayne Morse, William Langer (R-ND), and Herbert Lehman (D-NY) opposed to it. On February 9, 1955, less than two weeks after the passing of the Formosa Resolution, the Senate ratified to the Mutual Defense Treaty by a margin of 65 to 6. In conjunction with the Democratic and Republican hierarchy on Capitol Hill, the administration had successfully forged a bipartisan front, kept the right-wing Republicans on its side, and made Congress an accomplice to its policy.[66]

A SHORT-LIVED SUCCESS

Eisenhower's and Dulles' success in generating public and bipartisan Congressional support for the resolution was short-lived, however. The failure to implement the fourth and final part of their strategy, the UN initiative, and Jiang's reaction to the refusal of the US to publicly declare its intention to defend the offshore islands seriously eroded popular support and eventually forced a change in the administration's plan.

Expecting that the PRC or the Soviets would proscribe such an arrangement, Washington continued to view the UN initiative not as a key to a

---

[64] The *New York Times*, January 27, 1955, 1–5.

[65] "Public Opinion Survey on Formosa Resolution," February 15, 1955, DOS, AI568J, box I, NAII.

[66] CT, February 3 through 16, 1955, DOS, AI568P, box 29, NAII; "Recent Opinion Polling Results on US-Chinese Relations," August 5, 1955, DOS, AI568J, box I, NAII.

prospective diplomatic solution, but as a deterrent against further Chinese encroachment on the islands and as a moral cover for possible American intervention. Even in the absence of such intervention, by supporting the UN action, the administration could generate favorable domestic and international publicity for its handling of the crisis.

On January 26th, the New Zealand government submitted a plan to the UNSC, code-named Oracle, but two days later in a surprise move, the Soviets inserted themselves into the diplomatic maneuvering by officially requesting that the Security Council meet to consider "acts of aggression" against the PRC by the US and demanding withdrawal of American forces in the Straits and other territories belonging to China. Placing both the New Zealand and the Soviet items on its agenda, the Council then invited a Chinese Communist representative to participate in its discussion regarding the issue. Zhou En-lai categorically rejected the invitation, because the New Zealand proposal was a "cover up for American aggression."[67]

The refusal by the PRC to participate in the meeting further raised the level of anxiety among the Allies. Eden immediately lost interest in moving to the next stage of Oracle because any expectation that the UN venture might incite a peaceful settlement had disappeared. A disappointed Dulles agreed to put the exercise on hold.[68]

Meanwhile, Jiang was furious. He had understood that immediately following the passing of the resolution by the Senate, statements would be issued by his government and the US announcing a withdrawal from the Dechens for strategic reasons and the redeployment of forces and American intention to defend Jinmen and Matzu, respectively. The US Ambassador to Taipei, Karl Lott Rankin, sent a telegram to the State Department describing Jiang as very upset, "He seems more nervous...than I remember seeing him before." The Generalissimo resolved that if Washington did not live up to its commitment, then he would not announce the evacuation of the Dechens.[69]

Jiang's reaction placed the administration in a tight spot. Broadcasting the existence of the commitment would violate the presumed understanding with Britain because it was wholly at odds with the ambiguous language

---

[67] Editorial note, *FRUS*, II, 1955–1957, 178–179.

[68] Memorandum of Conversation with Sir Roger Makins, February 2, 1955, *FRUS*, II, 1955–1957, 195–197.

[69] Telegram from Ambassador Rankin in the Republic of China to Department of State, February 1955, *FRUS*, II, 1955–1957, 193–195; Editorial Note, *FRUS*, II, 1955–1957, 199.

utilized in the Formosa Resolution to shroud American intentions toward Jinmen and Matzu, and could disrupt the delicate popular and political consensus that had formed around the President's leadership. On the other hand, the evacuation of the Dechens would remain suspended until Taipei formally asked for American assistance.

Finally, on February 5th, under heavy pressure from Washington, Jiang announced the evacuation of the Dechens islands without disclosing US commitment. Feeling he had been let down however, he resolved to try and get the word out in his own manner. On February 11th, a *New York Times* front page article broke the story that Chinese Nationalist Foreign Minister George Yeh had told a newsman that the US had pledged to defend Jinmen and Matzu. Administration officials immediately moved to deny the existence of such a commitment and dismissed Yeh's declarations "as pure home consumption." Yeh was forced to retreat and state that the journalist had misquoted him.[70]

A few days later, quoting a "high authority" in Taiwan as his source, journalist Joseph Alsop, wrote in his regular *New York Herald Tribune* column "A Matter of Fact" that Dulles had promised Foreign Minister Yeh that after Congressional action, President Eisenhower would issue a statement guaranteeing defense of Jinmen and Matzu. Then on March 1st, during an interview for *CBS*'s "See it Now", Jiang reminded Ed Murrow and his audience that his goal was to free the mainland by means of counterattack for which he expected the full support of his American Allies.[71]

The following day, Eisenhower categorically denied such a plan, "The United States is not going to be part of an aggressive war." But the news stories reignited the Senate debate over the extent of the President's authority and caused the first cracks in bipartisanship. Representative James Richards (D-SC) accused the administration of a lack of clarity; his understanding when the resolution came to Congress was that the US would defend Jinmen and Matzu, a recollection that House majority leader John W. McCormack (D-Mass.) confirmed. Richards' outburst was far from being spontaneous. An ardent pro-Nationalist, he had learned firsthand from Yeh that Washington had refused to permit an announcement of the defensive commitment. Consequently, he himself attempted to tear

---

[70] "Dulles did pledge defence of Quemoy and Matsu," the *New York Times*, February 11, 1955, 1–6.

[71] Alsop, Joseph, "A Matter of Fact," the *New York Herald Tribune*, February 14, 1955, 3; CT, February 25 through March 2, 1955, AI568N, box 29, NAII.

off the veil of mystery from the administration's Jinmen-Matzu policy. Representative Clement J. Zablocki (D-WI), also a Nationalist supporter, also called on Dulles for "a definite statement of our policy regarding Quemoy and Matsu" in front of the House of Foreign Affairs Committee. Senator Knowland responded that such a statement was not necessary because both the President and the Secretary of State had already made clear that they would fight for the defense of all the offshore islands.[72]

Senators Humphrey and John Sparkman (D-AL) counter-charged, however, that in their understanding, the resolution had not authorized President Eisenhower to use US armed forces to defend the offshore islands. Finally, questioning whether the defense of Jinmen and Matzu were necessary, Senator Kefauver declared that the US ought to refrain from speaking about defending them and stop pretending that Jiang was the key to blocking the spread of Communism in Asia.[73]

The SDBPA reported that the heated Congressional debate raised levels of fear of an imminent war among the public. A NORC opinion poll revealed that 85% of the respondents feared another world war would break out within a year because of US-PRC hostility. Gallup reported that "an overwhelming majority of the nation-wide sample," 90%, opposed US involvement in the Straits to defend the offshore islands, and 58% were also opposed to sending "American boys to defend Taiwan."[74]

The State Department and White House mail bags were soon filled with letters from a distraught public. Eisenhower was particularly touched by a petition sent by the Tennessee Save Our Sons (SOS) Committee. SOS had been founded by the wives, parents, and relatives of US soldiers during the dark days of the Korean War. The increased talks of war prompted the committee to re-group and initiate a nationwide "Stay out of Asia" petition against sending American soldiers to defend "the despicable and corrupt Chiang Kai-shek" and in favor of withdrawing "US troops, planes and ships from Formosa and all Chinese territories." In addition to collecting and sending more than a million signatures to the President, SOS also urged American citizens to write to their two senators, their

---

[72] Eisenhower's press conference, March 2, 1955, *The American Presidency Project* [retrieved: May 24, 2010].
[73] CT, February 25 through March 2, 1955, DOS, AI568N, box 29, NAII.
[74] "Special Public Opinion Survey," February 1955, DOS, AI568J, box 1, NAII.

representatives, and newspapers editors to deter any involvement in war with China.[75]

The administration was backing itself into a corner. With peacetime war making power granted by the Formosa Resolution, Eisenhower had staked his personal reputation and US prestige on the defense of the Nationalist cause, now centered on the offshore islands. Their loss to a Communist assault would be humiliating and devastating to American credibility and would likely result in a collapse of the Nationalist government, but on the other, hand public opinion was clearly against a commitment to the offshore islands. The administration was in a deadlock.[76]

The President clearly did not relish a military encounter with the PRC and its accompanying undesirable repercussions at home and with the Allies, but neither was he willing to give up American national security interests to appease the public. A compromise could, however, be reached if Jiang agreed to remove, or at least substantially scale down, his forces on the coastal islands. If he were not to invest so much military and symbolic importance in his forward positions, their loss would be considerably less costly to the Nationalists. Consequently, their occupation by the Communists would be unlikely to undermine the political stability of the GMD government or the fighting spirit of its armed forces, nor would it reflect on American credibility. Under those circumstances, the administration would have much less cause to concern itself with the defense of the islands because their intrinsic military value was insufficient to justify intervention.[77]

Eisenhower, however, wanted to avoid a forced retreat that would tarnish American credibility in Asia, demoralize the Nationalists, leave Taiwan more susceptible to a Communist attack, and incite criticism at home. He decided that Dulles should have a stop in Taipei during his forthcoming trip to Bangkok and try to plant the idea of voluntary withdrawal in Jiang's mind while simultaneously avoiding any hint of compulsion. To facilitate the Secretary of State's task, he also asked his friend and newspaper czar Roy Howard, who was in the process of leaving for Taiwan for a private visit with Jiang, to try to discreetly redirect the Generalissimo's attention

---

[75] Save Our Sons Committee to Eisenhower, February 20, 1955, DDE Papers as a President, Central Files, General Files, box 802, DDEL.

[76] Memorandum of Discussion at the 237 meeting of the NSC, February 17, 1955, *FRUS*, II, 1955–1957, 279–286.

[77] Memorandum of Conversation with the President, February 24, 1955, JFD Papers, White House Memoranda Series, box 3, DDEL.

from his forward bases. If he could make the Nationalist leader understand that in "holding Formosa and the Pescadores for the free world, he must not permit his position to become a fixed one, one which is closely linked to those offshore islands," then, the President concluded, Howard would be doing a service to the free world.[78]

TO THE BRINK OF NUCLEAR WAR

Public opposition to the defense of the offshore islands had forced the administration to adjust its strategy. Eisenhower now seemed ready to compromise on those positions to appease popular discontent. But Dulles' tour of Asia convinced him of the existence of an elevated Chinese Communist threat that required a strong US counteraction, and led him to opt for a bolder and more aggressive alternative.

Reporting to the President and the NSC about his trip, Dulles explained that he had not advanced the idea of voluntary withdrawal to Jiang because he was now convinced that the PRC had serious intentions to conquer all the islands and ultimately Taiwan. He had further communicated his sense that there could be "much subversive activity" in Taipei if the US pressed Jiang too hard, which could lead to the loss of the island. Based on conversations with military people in the area, he concluded that an effective defense required the use of nuclear weapons.[79]

Agreeing that the US should help defend the coastal islands, Eisenhower, however, decided to give deterrence a final try. First, he instructed Dulles to resume talks about Oracle with the British; he felt a real responsibility in line with his message to Congress to push the plan as far as possible in the UN and did not believe that they had exhausted that possibility. Second, Washington should take advantage of the approaching Bandung Conference of Asian and African nations, including the PRC, to work the diplomatic back channels. Accordingly, the State Department should conduct a campaign of persuasion and education among the pro-American Governments invited to the conference to sensitize them to Washington's viewpoint and to enlist their collaboration in urging a peaceful accommodation. If those attempts at deterrence failed, then Eisenhower and the

---

[78] Ibid.; Hagerty's Diaries, 201–203.

[79] Memorandum of Conversation with the President, March 6, 1955, JFD Papers, White House Memoranda Series, box 3, DDEL; Memorandum of Discussion at the 240 NSC meeting, March 10, 1955, *FRUS*, II, 1955–1957, 345–350.

NSC agreed that the US should be ready to use its military might, including nuclear weapons.[80]

The strategy had clearly been formulated based on American national security interests. The threat of losing Taiwan had forced the President and the Secretary of State to abandon their original plan to minimize the importance of the offshore islands. However, both men knew that to implement it, they had to bring on board a public who was staunchly opposed to the use of nuclear weapons. Eisenhower and Dulles were confident enough to sway public opinion through an effective information campaign.[81]

Justifying the use of nuclear weapons first required intensifying public hatred and fear of the enemy. In public statements over the ensuing weeks, the administration increasingly portrayed Red China as an imminent and real peril and deliberately introduced specific comments about utilizing tactical nuclear weapons if war broke out in Taiwan. Accordingly, during his radio and TV report to the nation about his Asian trip, Dulles depicted Beijing as a mortal danger to all humankind that could only be defeated with the use of atomic weapons. During his March 15th press conference, he then openly described the situation in the Taiwan Straits as extremely dangerous because of "Chinese recklessness." Adding that America could not stand by and watch such a terrible enemy threaten its national security, he concluded that the US would fight for freedom with all its might, including nuclear weapons.[82]

The following day, Eisenhower caused a furor when at his news conference, he declared that he saw no reason why "nuclear weapons should not be used just exactly as you would use a bullet or anything else." On March 17th in Chicago, Vice-President Richard M. Nixon echoed the President's and the Secretary of State's statements by stating that "tactical atomic weapons are now conventional and will be used against targets of any aggressive force," and warning China against any belligerent moves. The sharpest attack came on March 21st, when Dulles accused Beijing of "being dizzy with success" and an "acute and immediate threat." Adding that in the short-term the PRC "may prove more dangerous and

[80] Ibid.
[81] Ibid.
[82] "Secretary of State's report to the Nation on Asian trip," *Department of State Bulletin*, 25, March 23, 1955, 34–38 (hereafter *DSB* followed by issue number, date and page reference); Dulles' press conference, March 15, 1955, JFD Papers, box 90, ML.

provocative of war" than the Soviet Union, he concluded that "the aggressive fanaticism of the Chinese Communist leaders presents a certain parallelism with that of Hitler."[83]

The information campaign, however, suffered from a lack of coordination among the federal departments. Eisenhower had to meet with Defense Secretary Wilson several times to urge caution because the casual statements he was constantly making in press conferences and elsewhere caused serious embarrassment to the administration. One example was his declaration that the loss or retention of Jinmen and Matzu would make slight difference in the long term. "While I think he considers himself a master of public relations," the President told Hagerty, "he seems to have no comprehension at all of what embarrassment such remarks can cause the Secretary of State and me in our efforts to keep the tangled international situation from becoming completely impossible."[84]

On March 26th, a rash of front page newspaper stories reported that the administration expected a showdown over Jinmen and Matzu soon after April 15th and that militants among the President's advisors, including the military, were urging him to defend the islands even at cost of war with the PRC. It soon emerged that those stories were the consequence of a dinner that had been arranged by journalist Marquis Childs at Chief of Naval Operations Admiral Robert B. Carney's request. The Admiral had made it clear to the invited newsmen that he was speaking with the full concurrence and support from Radford, and did not disguise the fact that he and Radford believed the moment had arrived for a showdown with Beijing. Childs believed that the main purpose of Carney's briefing was to push Eisenhower to authorize American intervention if the Communists attacked the offshore islands.[85]

The President immediately moved to muzzle the Admiral and correct the impression of an impending showdown. Instructing Hagerty to talk to the journalists, he declared "You should tell the reporters that of course the Chinese Reds are fanatical Communists and have publicly stated that they are going to take Formosa, but we are trying to keep peace. We are

---

[83] Eisenhower's press conference, March 16, 1955, *The American Presidency Project* [retrieved: May 27, 2010]; the *New York Times*, March 16, 1955, 1–8; and March 18, 1955, 1; and March 22, 1955, 1–5.

[84] Memorandum for the files, March 10, 1955, DDE Papers, Ann Whitman Diary Series, box 4, DDEL.

[85] CT, March 2 through 30, 1955, *DOS*, AI568P, box 29. NAII; Harkness, Richard (*CBS*) to Eisenhower, March 31, 1955, DDE Papers, Central files, Official Files, box 856, DDEL.

Public opinion opposition to US
intervention in the Taiwan Straits

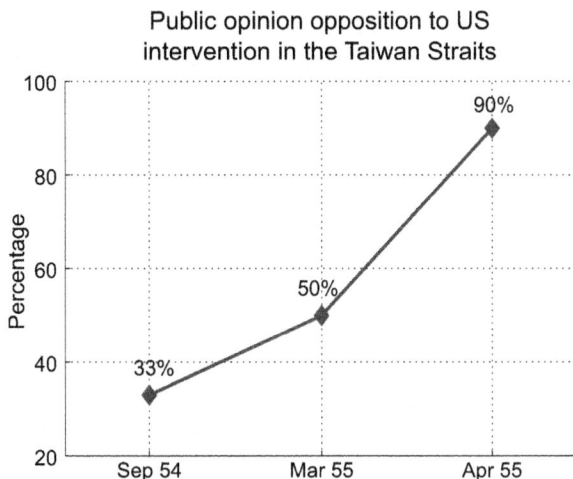

Fig. 5.1   US public opposition to American intervention in the Taiwan Straits crisis increased from 33% at the beginning of the crisis to 90% in April when the Eisenhower administration announced its intention to use nuclear weapons to end the crisis. Source: Records of the Department of State Office of Public Opinion Studies, 1954–1955, NAII

not looking for war and I think stories like the ones they get from Carney, when published, are a great disservice to the US. They are going to look awfully silly when 15 April comes and there is no incident."[86]

Although Hagerty noted in his diary that his discussion with the newsmen had been accurately reflected in articles in the *New York Times*, the *Washington Post* and other major US dailies, the Carney-inspired stories threw a new fright into the country that failed to subside. Gallup reported that support for the Nationalists was at an all-time low; only 1 out of 10 Americans interviewed said the US should help the Generalissimo. A SDBPA poll revealed that 90% of the respondents feared a nuclear war would break out within 6 months because of the situation in the Straits; and 93% of those interviewed believed that the way to avoid such a catastrophe was for the US to withdraw completely and turn the issue over to the UN (Fig. 5.1).[87]

[86] Hagerty's Diaries, 218–219.
[87] Special Opinion Survey, April 1955, DOS, AI568J, box 1, NAII.

Reports that Senator Knowland and Styles Bridges (R-NH) wanted Eisenhower to pledge a no-holds-barred defense of Jinmen and Matzu added fuel to the fire. Highly placed Congressional Democrats, deeply critical of what they termed as "irresponsible" war talks, urged the President to put a stop to it. Senator Sparkman declared that Eisenhower and Dulles were joining the Senate Republican leaders in turning the GOP into the "war party." In a heated exchange with Knowland on the floor of the Senate, Majority Leader Lyndon B. Johnson (D-TX) accused the right-wing Republicans of "talking of war." At a luncheon with the Congressional leaders, the President and the Secretary of State tried to patch up the splintering bipartisan front, but the apparent drift toward war disturbed even those who had rooted for the administration, including Senator George. He lamented to Dulles that Jinmen and Matzu had become a political football game and cause for division.[88]

The Carney incident had proved a complete boomerang. As journalist Stewart Alsop privately observed, "Radford-Carney planned to wake up the country. The net effect was to scare everybody." The war scare combined with the administration's nuclear bravado undercut the fragile domestic popular and political consensus fashioned by Eisenhower and Dulles. The President and the Secretary similarly realized that the use of nuclear weapons would shock much of the domestic and world public and they would not be able to count on a unified Congress or public in the event of hostilities over Jinmen and Matzu, the Formosa Resolution notwithstanding. Dulles speculated that the Soviets might welcome a US resort to such weapons for the propaganda bonanza it would give them.[89]

Faced with such a strong opposition, Eisenhower decided once more to adjust his to still be able to protect US vital interests and meet with domestic and world opinion approval. The President sent Assistant Secretary of State for the Far East Walter Robertson and Admiral Redford, the Generalissimo's two staunchest supporters in the administration, on a secret mission to Taiwan to convince Jiang to withdraw from all the offshore islands, including Jinmen and Matzu, in exchange for a "maritime interdiction," in other words a sea blockade. For

[88] Memorandum of Breakfast Conversation with Senator George, March 24, 1955, JFD Papers, Subject Series, box 5, DDEL; Bipartisan Meeting with Congressional Leaders, March 30, 1955, Hagerty Papers, box 2, DDEL.
[89] Diary Entry, April 5, 1955, Alsop Stewart's Papers, box 7, Library of Congress Manuscript Division, Washington, DC (hereafter LoC).

Eisenhower and Dulles, the purpose of the evacuation/blockade proposal was to get the administration off the hook in the offshore islands under conditions that would save face for Jiang and the US and bolster security for Taiwan. By letting the islands fall under Communist control and inscribing a clear-cut divide line between Taiwan and the mainland, the US would appease its concerned Allies and define a policy that was much more acceptable to American and world opinion. Morally, legally, and politically a defensive policy that encompassed only Taiwan and the Penghus was far easier to justify. Furthermore, Eisenhower and Dulles realized that a line of demarcation between the GMD and the Communist-controlled territories running through the Taiwan Straits rather than just off the coast of China was conducive to stabilization of the area through a *de facto* two-China policy.[90]

Eisenhower did not anticipate an unmanageable Congressional or public outcry against the proposal if it were implemented. He believed that once the Nationalists had retreated from the offshore islands, the US could more readily garner domestic and international support for a bold measure whose avowed purpose was to protect only Taiwan and the Penghus and to pressure the Communists into pursuing their claims to those territories by non-violent means. He and Dulles were certain that the plan "would immeasurably serve to consolidate public opinion."[91]

That a Nationalist pull-out from the offshore islands would have generated support from most of the world community and united the American public and Congress behind the administration was certain. That American participation in a blockade of Southeast China would have met similar approbation was highly questionable. Whatever euphemism was substituted for the term "blockade," Eisenhower could hardly conceal the reality of what it was doing or avoid accusations that it was legally an act of war. The previous autumn, the President himself had scorned Knowland's suggestion of a blockade to compel the release of the imprisoned American airmen.

Fortunately, neither the rest of the world nor the Chinese Communists were ever required to respond to the Dulles-Eisenhower ultimatum. Despite several days of talks, Jiang refused to entertain any idea of reducing his forces on the islands, let alone abandoning them to the Communists.

---

[90] Memorandum of Conversation with the President, April 17, 1955, JFD Papers, White House Memoranda Series, box 9, DDEL.

[91] Ibid.

It was Zhou En-lai who offered the Eisenhower administration an escape from the dilemma when he announced on April 23rd at the Bandung Conference that China was willing to begin direct discussion with the United States on the situation in the Taiwan Straits.[92]

The conclusion of the crisis highlighted the administration's flawed public relations strategy. Had not Jiang rejected Washington's proposal or Zhou En-lai offered to begin negotiations on the situation in the Straits, Eisenhower and Dulles would have been left with the prospect of going to war without the nation's support. Their propaganda campaign against Communist China had certainly reinforced public hatred toward the enemy, but instead of increasing the people's will to fight, it had backfired and generated fear of an imminent nuclear war. Faced with the proposition of another conflict, the public had decided that the US should withdraw entirely from the Straits and leave the issue to the UN.

Nonetheless, considering Taiwan a vital link in the Western Pacific, neither Eisenhower nor Dulles was willing to give up the island to appease the public. Although ready to adjust their strategy and give up the offshore positions, that was as far as they would go. As in the Indochina crisis, therefore, the influence of public opinion on the administration's foreign policy toward the PRC in the first Taiwan crisis was only limited to narrowing the choice of policy options available. Despite strong popular beliefs against US intervention in the Straits, those did not affect Washington's decision to pursue its China policy and defense of the island.

References

Accinelli, Robert. "Eisenhower, Congress and the 1954–1955 Offshore Islands Crisis." *Presidential Studies Quarterly* 20 (1990): 329–348.

———. *Crisis and Commitment: United States Policy Toward Taiwan, 1950–1955.* Chapel Hill: University of North Carolina, 1996.

Bachrack, Stanley. *The Committee of One Million, "China Lobby" Politics.* New York: Columbia University Press, 1976.

Brands, H.W., Jr. "Testing Massive Retaliation: Credibility and Crisis Management in the Taiwan Straits." *International Security* 12 (1988): 124–151.

Briggs, Philip J. "Congress and the Cold War: US-China Policy, 1955." *The China Quarterly* 85 (1981): 80–95.

Chang, Gordon. "To the Nuclear Brink, Eisenhower, Dulles and the Quemoy-Matsu." *International Security* 12 (1988): 98–99.

[92] Taipei US Embassy to State Department, April 23, 1955, *FRUS*, II, 1955–1957, 509.

Chang, Gordon and He Di. "The Absence of War in the US-China Confrontation over Quemoy and Matsu in 1954–1955: Contingency, Luck, Deterrence?" *American Historical Review* 98 (1993): 1500–1524.

Eisenhower, Dwight D. *The White House Years: A Mandate for a Change.* New York: Doubleday & Company, 1963.

Foyle, Douglas C. "Public Opinion and Foreign Policy: Elite Beliefs as a Mediating Variable." *International Studies Quarterly* 41 (1997): 141–169.

———. *Counting the Public In: Presidents, Public Opinion and Foreign Policy.* New York: Columbia University Press, 1999.

Hagerty, James C. *The Diary of James C. Hagerty*, edited by Ferrell Robert. Bloomington: Indiana University Press, 1983.

Rushkoff, Bennett C. "Eisenhower, Dulles and the Quemoy-Matsu Crisis." *Political Science Quarterly* 96 (1981): 465–480.

CHAPTER 6

A Missed Opportunity

Following Premier Zhou En-lai's (Chou En-lai) dramatic offer at the Bandung conference in April 1955, the US government agreed to enter talks with the People's Republic of China (PRC) to defuse the tensions that had arisen over the Chinese Communists' attempts to recapture the offshore islands of Jinmen (Quemoy) and Matzu (Matsu), and settle other unresolved issues between the two countries. The negotiations took place in Geneva and lasted two years and proved to be inconclusive. The inflexibility of the US and its refusal to relax the total trade embargo implemented in 1951 and allow free travel and cultural exchange with Beijing (Peiping) were the main reasons for the lack of progress.

Scholars have explained the Eisenhower administration's hard line policy toward Communist China in two ways. Historian Nancy Bernkopf Tucker and political scientist Leonard A. Kusnitz have argued that while both President Dwight D. Eisenhower and Secretary of State John Foster Dulles privately realized the need to be more flexible toward the PRC and to accept the reality of "two Chinas," they would not risk their relationship with the right wing in Congress to openly pursue such a possibility. Others such as Gordon H. Chang and David A. Mayers have claimed that

Parts of this chapter were originally published in Mara Oliva, "Beaten at Their Own Game: Eisenhower, Dulles, US Public Opinion and the Sino-American Ambassadorial Talks of 1955–1957," *Journal of Cold War Studies* 20 (2018): forthcoming.

the administration's strategy of driving a wedge between Moscow and Beijing required a policy of isolating Communist China so that Mao would quickly learn the drawbacks of its alliance with the Soviet Union.[1]

More recently, historian Rosemary Foot has put forward a third explanation. As a result of the Korean War and because of the new Soviet leadership's willingness to put its relationship with Beijing on a more equal basis, the PRC had begun to enjoy increased status within the Communist bloc. Those developments, along with the French defeat at Dien Bien Phu in May 1954, helped to convince the Eisenhower administration that conciliatory gestures from Washington could empower Beijing with fatal consequences for US interests in Asia.[2]

The purpose of this chapter is to understand the often-underestimated role of American public opinion in influencing the ambassadorial talks. Contrary to traditional scholarly literature which dismisses American public opinion rigidly against any improvement of Sino-US relations, an accurate analysis of popular feelings during those two years clearly shows that the American people were far more inclined than was the Eisenhower administration toward establishing some sort of contacts with Communist China. How then did the administration sell its hard line policy? Did it succeed in making the public accept its hostile stance? And what consequences did its domestic public rhetoric ultimately have on Sino-US relations?[3]

THE GENEVA NEGOTIATIONS

Against the background of deep anxiety over the possibility of war in Taiwan (Formosa), the American people warmly welcomed Premier Zhou En-lai's offer to negotiate directly with the US. A Gallup poll taken a few

---

[1] Nancy, Bernkopf Tucker, "Cold War Contacts: America and China, 1952–1956" in *Sino-American Relations, 1945–1955: A Joint Reassessment of a Critical Decade*, ed. Harding Harry et al. (Wilmington: Scholarly Resources, Inc., 1989); Leonard Kusnitz, *Public Opinion and Foreign Policy: America's China Policy, 1949–1979* (Westport: Greenwood Press, 1984); Gordon Chang, *Friends and Enemies: The United States, China and the Soviet Union, 1948–1972* (Stanford: Stanford University Press, 1990); David Mayers, *Cracking the Monolith: US Policy Against the Sino-Soviet Alliance, 1949–1955* (London: Louisiana State University Press, 1986).

[2] Rosemary Foot "The Eisenhower Administration's Fear of Empowering the Chinese," *Political Science Quarterly* 111 (1996): 505–521.

[3] Hans J. Morgenthau, "John Foster Dulles," in *An Uncertain Tradition: American Secretaries of State in the Twentieth Century*, ed. Norman A. Graebner (New York: McGraw Hill, 1996).

days after the Bandung conference announcement indicated a strong popular approval for negotiating with Communist China in a larger conference. According to that survey, three out of four Americans interviewed
thought that the US should ask Russia, the PRC, and all other interested
nations to meet to see whether a peaceful solution could be worked out in
the Taiwan Straits. Only 16% of respondents opposed such a conference
and 10% had no opinion.[4] A nationwide survey carried out by the State
Department Bureau of Public Affairs (SDBPA) confirmed those findings.
When asked "Whether it would be a good or a bad idea for US representatives to meet with the Chinese Communists to try to reach an agreement
on some of the problems on Asia," 70% of those interviewed said "it
would be a good idea" and only 21% thought "it would be a bad idea."[5]
    That staunch support from the public for the talks was clearly the result
of the recent scare of war over Taiwan. Americans had not come to regard
the Chinese Communists as friends. On the contrary, because of the
Taiwan crisis, the US public considered China more dangerous than the
Soviet Union. According to one State Department poll, six out of 10
Americans interviewed thought that World War III would break out "fairly
soon" because of Communist China. The fear of another global conflict
therefore pushed the public to favor direct diplomatic negotiations with
Beijing.[6]
    The public's less negative attitude toward the eventual PRC admission
into the United Nations (UN) corroborates that point. The Indochina
crisis had strengthened public hostility toward Beijing's recognition by the
world organization. In August 1954, a Gallup poll found that it had
reached an all-time high of 79%. Following the Taiwan crisis, however, the
Gallup poll recorded only 67% opposition in July 1955, with only 11% of
the respondents wanting the US to withdraw from the UN in the event of
PRC recognition compared with 25% a year earlier.[7]
    The administration found considerable support for the talks among the
press as well as in Congress. The SDBPA conducted a series of interviews
among publishers and editors of prominent newspapers and magazines

[4] Monthly Survey of Public Opinion, May 1955, Records of the Office of Public Opinion
Studies, State Department, 1943–1975, AI568L, box 12, National Archives II, College
Park, Maryland (hereafter DOS, file reference, box number and NAII).
[5] Monthly Survey of Public Opinion, June 1955, DOS, AI568L, box 12, NAII.
[6] Ibid.
[7] Monthly Survey of Public Opinion, August 1954 and July 1955, DOS, AI568L, box 12,
NAII.

around the country. Apart from the Luce publications and a few minor daily newspapers, all those contacted agreed that, in the interest of world peace, it was time to sit down and talk to the Chinese Communists.[8]

In Congress, not surprisingly only Jiang Jieshi's (Chiang Kai-shek) supporters, headed by Senator William F. Knowland (R-CA), were against establishing any form of contact with the PRC. The Senate Minority Leader clearly worried about the effect that the talks would have on the Republic of China, gave a dramatic interview to the press, calling Beijing's proposal "unacceptable" and another "invitation to Munich." His charges were supported by the newly reorganized Committee of One Million. The Committee had originally been established in 1953 with the goal of collecting one million signatures to present as a petition to President Eisenhower to ensure that he continued his policy of non-recognition. After a period of hibernation, "sentiment for a softer policy toward Communist China...among liberal and international-minded Republicans and Democrats" prompted its reorganization. In response to Zhou's offer, the Committee issued a statement to Eisenhower, Dulles, and the press repeating its slogan that "the Chinese Communists should not be permitted to shoot their way into the UN." The Committee also mobilized its supporters in the religious community, releasing an open letter to the President signed by clergymen representing all major faiths and urging a stop to any further appeasement of the Chinese Communists.[9]

In contrast, a majority in Congress viewed Zhou's bid with an open mind. Senator Walter F. George (D-GA) was certainly enthusiastic about the opportunity. To the administration's dismay, the Chairman of the Senate Foreign Relations Committee publicly expressed the belief that such a meeting could "lead to some accommodation" of the war threat in the Taiwan area. On CBS's "See it Now," he called for a meeting before the end of the year between Dulles and Zhou. Dulles believed that George's public statements had been influenced by the New York Times correspondent James Reston. Reston was not a friend of the administra-

[8] "Special Press Review on Talks with the PRC," May 25, 1955, DOS, AI568K, box 7, NAII.

[9] Daily Summary of Public Opinion, April 28 and May 2, 1955, DOS, AI568K, box 7, NAII; Stanley Bachrack, *The Committee of One Million: "China Lobby" Politics, 1953–1971* (New York: Columbia University Press, 1976), 106–107, 118–119.

Table 6.1 Special press review on talks with the PRC

	In favor of talks with the PRC	Against talks with the PRC
Publications	Baltimore Sun, Boston Herald, Chicago Sun Times, Christian Science Monitor, Dayton News, Des Moines Register, Houston Post, Kansas City Star, Louisville Courier Journal, Milwaukee Journal, New York Herald Tribune, New York Journal American, New York Mirror, New York News, New York Post, New York News, Philadelphia Bulletin, Philadelphia Inquirer, Providence Journal, Richmond Times Dispatch, Salt Lake City Tribune, San Francisco Chronicle, St Louis Globe Democrat, St Louis Post Dispatch, Wall Street Journal, Watertown Times, Washington News, Washington Post, Washington Star	Chicago Tribune, Human Events Letter, Luce's publications
Congressmen	Senators Aiken (R-VT), Allot (R-CO), Beal (R-MD), Bush (R-CT), Capehart (R-IN), Carlson (R-KS), Case (R-NJ), Cotton (R-NH), Duff (R-PA), Flanders (R-VT), George (D-GA), Fulbright (D-AR), Humphrey (D-MN), Johnson (D-TX), Mansfield (D-MT), Payne (R-ME), Russell (D-GA), Saltonstall (R-MASS), Smith (R-NJ), Sparkman (Ala), Thurmond (D-SC), Representatives Judd (R-MN), Powell (D-NY)	Senators Bridges (R-NH), Knowland (R-CA), Jenner (R-IN), McCarthy (R-Wis), Representative Hale (R-ME)

The list refers only to those with explicit editorial policy and publicly stated opinion. The list is meant to be representative, not exhaustive

Source: "Special Press Review on Talks with the PRC," May 25, 1955; Daily Summaries of Public Opinion, April 28 and May 2, 1955, DOS, AI568K, box 7, NAII

tion and had recently been "playing up" George in his articles to back his opposition to Eisenhower's China policy (Table 6.1).[10]

Despite such strong popular support, the administration's public stance toward any possible contact with the PRC was very cautious. Both Eisenhower and Dulles privately acknowledged that the talks could turn out to be useful because they could help in defusing the war prospect in the Far East. They could get jailed Americans in China released and block the Soviet efforts at including Beijing as a member of the "Big Five" at an

[10] Daily Summary of Public Opinion, April 28 and May 2, 1955, DOS, AI568K, box 7, NAII; Dulles call to Hagerty, July 27, 1955, JFD Papers, Subject Series, box 5, Dwight D. Eisenhower Library, Abilene, Kansas (hereafter DDEL).

upcoming international conference. Publicly however, the White House and the Department of State put up a coordinated effort to play down the importance of those talks.[11]

The language that the President and Secretary of State used to refer to the PRC during the press conferences and public speeches in the months leading up to the beginning of the negotiations was far from encouraging and always aimed at portraying the Communist leaders as lawless and aggressive dictators. When James Reston asked the President about the progress in establishing contacts with Communist China, Eisenhower replied he was not even sure the talks were going to take place. Privately, however, through the British and Indian governments, the administration was finalizing the details of its first meeting with the Communists.[12]

The hostile rhetoric did not change even when the talks finally opened on August 1, 1955. The negotiations were led by Ambassador to Czechoslovakia, U. Alexis Johnson for the US and by Ambassador to Poland, Wang Bingnan for the Chinese. They quickly agreed on a two-point agenda: (1) the return of US and Chinese citizens detained in each other's countries, and (2) the settlement of other practical matters at issue between the two governments.[13] On the eve of the talks, the Chinese released 11 Air Force personnel shot down over PRC territories during the Korean War. Through the Indian government, they privately informed Washington of their hope that such a gesture could lead to a relaxation of the strict trade embargo that had been in force against the PRC since 1951, a suggestion that clearly did not correspond with US intentions. In response, the administration increased its hostile public portrayal of the Communists.[14]

Why did Eisenhower and Dulles decide to adopt such a hostile rhetoric? The President and the Secretary of State wanted to restrain public enthusiasm to retain negotiating flexibility. Because of the war scare over Taiwan and

[11] Estimate of Prospects of Soviet Union Achieving its Goals, Paper IV, July 1, 1955, John Foster Dulles Papers, box 90, Seely, G. Mudd Library, University of Princeton, New Jersey (hereafter JFD papers followed by box number and ML).

[12] Eisenhower's press conferences May 18 and May 31, 1955, John T. Woolley and Gerhard Peters, *The American Presidency Project*, http://www.presidency.ucsb.edu [retrieved May 2, 2010] (hereafter the *American Presidency Project* followed by retrieved date).

[13] Foot, "The Eisenhower Administration's Fear of Empowering the Chinese."

[14] Telegram from Ambassador Johnson to the State Department, August 2, 1955, *Foreign Relations of the United States*, III, 1955–1957 (Washington, DC: US Government Printing Office, 1986), 3 (hereafter *FRUS* followed by volume, year, and page).

the Chinese Communists' apparent attempts at showing good faith, popular feelings were clearly in favor of a softer policy toward Beijing. Eisenhower was afraid that public opinion might be carried away and force the administration into making decisions that strategic conditions did not allow. As he told Dulles: "We need to keep public enthusiasm under control, we don't want to be forced into a position that might endanger our security in Asia."[15]

The main problem was still the situation of the offshore islands. Jiang would not give them up, and they were untenable by the Nationalists without assistance from the US on a large scale. The US did not have a desire to enter into a major war with Communist China for which it would lack allied and domestic support, but to allow Jinmen and Matzu to be taken by the PRC and many Nationalist forces to be destroyed would have a grave effect upon morale not only in Taiwan, but also in Korea, Japan, the Philippines, and the whole of Southeast Asia.[16]

In that sense, the Geneva negotiations were the perfect opportunity to undermine a Chinese renewal of hostilities in the Straits. Eisenhower hoped that if the talks forestalled a Communist attack on the offshore islands, he could use the time to build up domestic and world opinion to force the Chinese Communists into accepting the status quo in the Straits. He was, therefore, not anxious to push talks in Geneva to a conclusion except for getting American civilians out. Domestic public support for a softer policy toward Beijing had to be kept under control.[17]

Wang Bingnan wrote in his memoirs that the American plan differed significantly from Chinese objectives. Beijing's main goal was to undermine the status quo in the Straits and to make the international community accept that Taiwan was part of the mainland. By establishing diplomatic ties between the US and China, the PRC also wanted to lay the groundwork for direct talks between Dulles and Zhou, which in turn would increase Chinese prestige in Asia. Those two differing agendas led to a quick deterioration in the talks with the only successful outcome being the agreement regarding the return of civilians, signed on September 10, 1955. Following that, the negotiations turned into a public relations battleground.[18]

---

[15] Memorandum of Conversation Between the President and the Secretary of State, August 5, *FRUS*, III, 1955–1957, 15–17.

[16] Ibid.

[17] Ibid.

[18] Zhang, Baijia and Jia, Quingguo, "Steering Wheel, Shock Absorber, and Diplomatic Probe in Confrontation: Sino-American Ambassadorial Talks Seen from a Chinese

On September 13th, Dulles sent Ambassador Johnson new instructions on President Eisenhower's orders. While bearing in mind the necessity of avoiding a breakdown in the talks, he wanted the discussions regarding item two to be postponed until all the prisoners had been released. As instructed, the following day Johnson informed Wang and the press of the decision.[19] Angered by Washington's decision, Beijing made two public announcements condemning the US position. On September 14th, Wang leaked a detailed but biased account of his bargaining position to the press, contrary to the initial agreement regarding confidentiality. Beijing also began to release propaganda alleging that the US government was harassing and intimidating Chinese students who wished to return to Communist China.[20]

The American public was also quite disappointed. A State Department nationwide survey carried out in September 1955 found that 85% of the respondents thought that the decision "was a mistake," 82% of the respondents were ready to take the negotiations to the next level and would support a meeting between Dulles and Zhou. Even more surprisingly, the October poll found that for the first time since the end of the Korean War, most of the public, 55% of those interviewed, was in favor of a relaxation of the US trade embargo against Communist China if the trade did not include war material, because an economic relationship might help promote peaceful conditions.[21]

Support for a continuation of the talks and a relaxation of the trade embargo also came also Britain and France. London was particularly eager to find a solution regarding Taiwan. The crisis had complicated British-Chinese relations over Hong Kong. Since the end of the Korean War, the two allies had also been putting considerable pressure on Washington to

Perspective," in *Re-Examining the Cold War: US-China Diplomacy, 1954–1973*, ed. Robert Ross et al. (Cambridge: Harvard University Press, 2011).

[19] Telegram from the Acting Secretary of State to Ambassador Johnson at Geneva, September 13, 1955, *FRUS*, III, 1955–1957, 87–88.

[20] Goldstein, Steven, "Dialogue of the Deaf? The Sino-Ambassadorial Level Talks, 1955–1970," in *Re-Examining the Cold War: US-China Diplomacy, 1954–1973*, ed. Robert Ross et al. (Cambridge: Harvard University Press, 2011) 209; Alexis U. Johnson, *The Right Hand of Power: The Memoirs of an American Diplomat* (Englewood Cliffs: Prentice-Hall, 1984), 251; Telegram from Johnson to Department of State, September 14, 1955, *FRUS*, III, 1955–1957, 88–90.

[21] CT September 20 through October 15, 1955, DOS, AI568P, box 29, NAII; Monthly Survey of Public Opinion, October 1955, DOS, AI568K, box 7, NAII.

remove the China differential altogether and adopt the same trade controls for Red China as for the Soviet bloc.[22]

In discussing Beijing's smear campaign in the press and the public reaction to it, the administration concluded that the PRC was "deliberately" and successfully "misleading the public as to its obligations and actions related to the Agreed Announcement." Reports from Geneva also showed that Johnson's position had become quite difficult as the Chinese Ambassador repeatedly cited US favorable popular feelings for the expansion of the talks and condemned the administration's "stubborn" position.[23]

Under such pressure, Dulles announced to the press on October 18th that while the US reserved the right to reopen item one at any time, if it did not seem that the agreement was being carried out in good faith, Ambassadors Johnson and Wang had begun substantive discussion of agenda item two. Furthermore, the question of the renunciation of force in the Taiwan Straits was being discussed and the issue of the trade embargo was next.[24] However, to foreclose any possibility of progress in the negotiations, as well as contain the increasing public support for a relaxation in Sino-American relations, Washington decided to adopt a strategy of total inflexibility toward the PRC and increase its rhetorical thoroughness. The administration demanded that Beijing accept what amounted to a "two-China" policy; Communist China had to renounce the use of force in the Taiwan Straits except for defense purposes, and accept US presence in the area. The PRC initially refused but then softened the negotiating terms and repeatedly offered to declare that China would settle the dispute with the US peacefully "without resorting to the threat or the use of force." Upon further elaboration of those points, Beijing declared that "it was willing to settle the question by peaceful means."[25]

Dulles was not satisfied however. He believed that the position of the PRC still evaded a "clear cut renunciation of force" in the Taiwan Straits. The US requirement for absolute explicit phrasing on the issue set the negotiations back. Chinese attempts to shift the negotiations to the trade embargo were also blocked because Johnson argued that such an item

[22] Shu Guang, Zhang, *Economic Cold War: America's Embargo Against China and the Sino-Soviet Alliance, 1949–1963* (Stanford, CA: Stanford University Press, 2001), 17–49.

[23] Telegram from Dulles to Johnson, *FRUS*, III, 1955–1957, 125–126.

[24] Dulles' press conference, October 18, 1955, DOS, box 8, NAII.

[25] Telegram from Secretary of State to Ambassador Johnson, December 6, 1955, *FRUS*, 1955–1957, 206–207; Foot, "The Eisenhower Administration's Fear of Empowering the Chinese," 509–510.

could not be negotiated before solving the Taiwan problem. Even if the two parties were to reach an agreement over Taiwan, trade discussions would still be subject to release of all US detained civilians.[26]

According to the September text, Johnson continued to press for the immediate release of the remaining 19 Americans throughout October and November 1955. Beijing angrily began to blame the US for stalling the talks and mounted a range of offensive propaganda claiming that the treatment of Chinese aliens in the US violated the agreement.[27] The US responded with a coordinated public relations effort to instead portray the Chinese Communists as being responsible for the lack of progress in Geneva and convince the US public that the enemy had not changed other than to become more dangerous. Between October 1955 and July 1956, the President, the Secretary of State, and other members of the State Department gave more than 80 speeches, press conferences, and interviews concerning Asia, and particularly Communist China. All the administration's public statements focused on four main themes: (1) what America considered the foot-dragging by the PRC in carrying out the September repatriation agreements; (2) its aggressive record in Korea, Indochina, and Taiwan; (3) the US historical friendship with the Chinese people; and (4) the suffering and starvation that the Communist dictatorship had brought to China.[28]

From a public point of view, the administration's policy of rhetorical toughness succeeded in strengthening Americans' hostility toward the PRC, but that was not an arduous task. After all, the public's support for diplomatic contacts with Beijing was born out of the desire to avoid World War III, not because it believed that the Chinese had suddenly changed. On the contrary, a February 1956 State Department survey found that eight out of 10 Americans who were interviewed believed that the Chinese held "peculiar attitudes toward human life" and valued it less than Westerners, including the Soviets.[29]

The main effect was to heighten fear of an imminent military conflict. As negative reports about Communist China increased, so did apprehension regarding threats to peace. Influential columnists such as Hanson

[26] Ibid.

[27] Johnson, *The Right Hand of Power: The Memoirs of an American Diplomat*, 228–266.

[28] *Department of State Bulletin*, October 1955 through March 1956 (hereafter *DSB*, followed by issue number, date and page reference).

[29] Monthly Survey of Public Opinion, January, February, and March 1956, DOS, AI568L, box 13, NAII).

Baldwin of the *New York Times* and the Alsop brothers wrote that the likelihood of a new Far Eastern crisis in February or March 1956 was already being discussed nervously in the State Department.[30]

Dulles' controversial interview with James Shepley, published in *Life* magazine in January 1956, sent a chill throughout the nation. Reviewing the administration's policy on Korea, Indochina, and Taiwan, the Secretary claimed that the US had gone to the brink of war three times to keep the peace. "You have to take chances for peace, just as you take chances in war," Dulles told Shepley. He went on to declare, "the ability to get on the verge without getting into war is a necessary art, if you cannot master it, you inevitably get into war. If you try to run away from it, if you are scared to go to the brink, you are lost." *Life* headlined the story "Three Times at the Brink of War: How Dulles Gambled and Won."[31]

The article began a furious debate. Democratic Presidential hopeful Adlai Stevenson led the charge, saying, "I am shocked that the Secretary of State is willing to play Russian roulette with the life of our nation." Editorialists and columnists condemned Dulles for his arrogance as well as his foolhardiness. Dulles' declarations that the US had been on the verge of unleashing atomic war against China on three occasions gave Wang the perfect rationale to contest US requests for a PRC renunciation of use of force in the Straits. The virulent criticism finally led *Life* publisher, Henry Luce, to publicly state that Dulles had not approved the article nor had he read it in advance. He apologized for the lurid headline and argued that most of the comments centered on one paragraph on the original story that had been taken out of context.[32]

China still took advantage of that public relations nightmare to push its agenda. Beijing charged that the US was deliberately dragging out the ambassadorial talks, had refused to come to an agreement on the means for relaxation of tensions in the Taiwan area, and had demanded Chinese acceptance of the "status quo of US armed occupation of Taiwan." It declared that given the gravity of American conduct, the only practical and feasible means of settling disputes between the PRC and the US would be a meeting between Foreign Ministers.[33]

[30] CT, November 10 through 16, 1955, DOS, AI568P, box 29, NAII.
[31] James Shepley, "How Dulles Averted War," *Life*, XL, January 16, 1956, 70–80.
[32] Telegram from Johnson to Department of State, *FRUS*, III, 1955–1957, 271–273; *Time*, January 23, 1956, 15; January 30, 1956, 30.
[33] The *New York Times*, January 19, 1956.

As US acrimony toward the PRC and talks of war increased, so did the public's fear and its desire to find a diplomatic solution to avoid war. A mid-year Gallup poll in 1956 found a majority of 80% in favor of continuing the Geneva talks. According to a State Department special review of public attitudes toward US recognition of the PRC, popular sentiment had kept moving in the direction of approving Beijing's seating. In the summer of 1956, disapproval had decreased to 55% and approval had reached 35% of those surveyed. An even larger proportion, 80% of those interviewed, thought that the US should continue to belong to the UN even if Communist China were admitted, which constituted a massive 49% increase from October 1955.[34]

The SDBPA also reported that, "criticism of Washington's inflexible policy towards the PRC had become more and more frequent in the press." In March 1956, *Newsweek* opined that the need for a change in relations with Beijing had become "essential if Washington wanted to avoid World War III." A *New York Times* editorial asked if keeping "Red China out of the UN was still a wise choice." The *Denver Post* wondered, "is the American position realistic and tenable or should this government reappraise and revise its policy?"[35]

More and more prominent Americans began to call for a reexamination of the US-China policy. Testifying before the Senate Subcommittee on Disarmament, Arthur Dean, former Special Ambassador on Korean armistice talks, said that US refusal to recognize Red China made a "workable" disarmament agreement impossible. Likewise, the Chairman of the Senate Foreign Relations Committee Theodore F. Green (D-RI), who had replaced Senator George, declared during a *CBS* interview that US-China policy had simply become absurd. Although he did not like Beijing's form of government, the US could not continue to ignore the most populous country in the world.[36]

Pressure to admit Communist China to the UN came from the Americans for Democratic Action, the American Association for the UN, and the Quaker movement. Scholars advocating a Far Eastern policy change also began to find a wider audience for their views. In an article for

[34] Monthly Survey of Public Opinion, June 1956, DOS, AI568L, box 13, NAII; "Special Report on American Opinion," August 1954, DOS, AI568K, box 13, NAII.
[35] *Newsweek*, March 23, 1956, 23–24; CT April 9 through 16, 1956 and June 7 through 14, 1956, DOS AI568P, box 30, NAII.
[36] CT January 9 through 16 and February 20 through 27, 1957, DOS, AI568P, box 30, NAII.

the April 1957 issue of *Atlantic*, Harvard professor and China expert John K. Fairbank argued that US "revulsion toward Communist China is an attitude rather than a policy" and there was an urgent need to formulate a proper and real policy. "Our present posture toward China is isolated and negative. Our defense of Taiwan seems to have no future," Fairbank wrote. He favored an independent republic in Taiwan, guaranteed as such by the UN and Red China's admission to the UN.[37]

The business community, meanwhile, also called for a revision of the trade embargo. On November 18, 1956, John S. Coleman, President of the US Chamber of Commerce advocated resumption of trade in non-strategic goods between the US and the PRC. On the same day, at the tenth annual session of the American Assembly, a group of business, community, and government leaders sponsored by Columbia University published a report on the US and East Asia. The report argued that present US policy on Communist China tied the hands of US trade not only in regard to China but also in the Far East in general. It recommended that measures be taken to liberalize such trade with Communist China as that would not impair the security position of the non-Communist countries. On the contrary, according to the authors of the report, trade with Beijing, its admission to the UN, and US recognition of its government would result in a peaceful settlement and might also permit "substantial" cuts in US military aid programs for South Korea, Taiwan, South Vietnam, and Thailand.[38]

Henry Ford II's address in San Francisco urging a reexamination of US trade relations with Communist China in the interest of US surplus production generated the strongest approval among the press. The SDBPA reported, "From the East to the West coast an overwhelming majority of publications calls for a relaxation of the restrictions" in the hope of reducing American stockpiles of surplus commodities and promoting peaceful world conditions. As the *San Francisco Chronicle* pointed out, "Ford could not have picked up a more appropriate city than San Francisco in which to raise the Red China trade question because our docks are losing business in consequence of the China trade ban." The *Washington Post* declared, "Mr. Ford's comments are the more impressive coming from a

---

[37] "Special Report on American Opinion," April 3, 1957, DOS, AI568K, box 13, NAII.

[38] Daily Summary of Public Opinion, November 19, 1956, DOS, AI568K, box 8, NAII; Monthly Survey of Public Opinion, December 1956, DOS, AI568L, box 13, NAII; Telegram from Ambassador U. Alexis Johnson to the Department of State, December 13, 1956, *FRUS*, III, 1955–1957, 451–452.

man of impeccable Republican background who cannot be accused of being soft on Communism, and the administration as well as Congress would do well to heed them." In an attempt to promote better understanding of Communist China and facilitate contacts between Beijing and Washington, DC, the Ford Foundation also invested $420,000 in a 5-year study of "Men and Politics in Modern China."[39]

Statements by those industrial leaders were in line with increasing acceptance by the public of a relaxation of non-strategic trade with Communist China. In March 1957, the State's opinion analysts found that 58% of Americans who were interviewed were now in favor of reviewing the trade embargo policy.[40]

The only support for the administration's hard line policy came from the Committee of One Million which since the beginning of the ambassadorial talks had used Beijing's complicity in the international narcotics smuggling as the main reason to oppose recognition of Communist China. To revamp Jiang Jieshi's image as one of America's most loyal and oldest allies in the Far East and thus deserving US protection from the evil Communists, the White House tried to persuade Henry Luce to run a series of special features on the Generalissimo in *Life* magazine. But even Luce refused on the basis that it would make a poor sale for his magazine.[41]

The administration did not budge from its inflexible position however, and carried on with its hostile rhetoric. As Dulles explained in a statement on China policy issued from Canberra, Australia, where he was attending the third meeting of the Council of the South East Asia Treaty Organization in March 1957, "The United States adheres steadfastly to three main aspects of its China policy which is to recognize the Republic of China; not to recognize the so-called People's Republic of China; and to oppose the seating of the People's Republic in the United Nations." He then further explained during a press conference that the policy was not merely "an expression of emotional dislike of Chinese Communism, although this was repugnant to us." Rather, it was based on consider-

[39] CT February 6 through 13, 1957, DOS, AI568P, box 30, NAII; Monthly Survey of Public Opinion, March 1957, DOS, AI568L, box 13, NAII; letter from Alfred Kohlberg to Rowan Gaither Jr. President of Ford Foundation, November 4, 1955, CD Jacksons Papers, box 70, DDEL.

[40] "Special Report on American Attitudes Towards Trade with Communist Countries," March 1957, DOS, AI568K, box 13, NAII.

[41] Thompson to Jackson, August 8, 1956, CD Jackson Papers, box 69, DDEL; Bachrack, *The Committee of One Million, "China Lobby" Politics 1953–1971*, 121–123.

ations of both national and international interest. Diplomatic recognition of the Chinese Communist regime would serve no national purpose but would strengthen and encourage influences hostile to the US and their allies, and further imperil lands whose independence was related to America's own peace and security.[42]

In short, the China issue had become a vicious circle. The more the public expressed support for a review in policy, the more Washington increased its rhetorical attacks on China, and the less the public approved of the hard line policy. More importantly, that lack of support for Eisenhower's policy undermined the American position in Geneva to give the Chinese Communists the initiative in the talks. Since the beginning of the negotiations, US strategy had aimed at dragging the talks for as long as possible to buy time in the Taiwan Straits and frustrate the Chinese Communists. Dulles wrote to Johnson in the summer of 1955, "the more time we buy, the better, if the Communists become impatient and want to break off the talks even better, it would make them look bad in the eyes of the world and improve our position."[43]

The Chinese did not fall for the US trap, however. As the ambassadorial talks went on, they developed a better understanding of US intentions. Zhou realized that Washington was using the Taiwan declaration "to deliberately prolong the talks in order to freeze the status quo" and push Beijing to call off the talks and thus look as the unreasonable party. Although frustrated by Washington's strategy, they did not call off the talks. On the contrary, they used the situation to their advantage and turned directly to the American public in the hope it might pressure the US government to make some negotiations. At the opportune moment for them, they kept making and publicizing proposal after proposal of seemingly praiseworthy character, such as trade and free travel and cultural exchange, which the US rejected every time but most of the American and international public approved of.[44]

---

[42] *DSB*, 32, April 24, 1957, 132–134.

[43] Telegram from Secretary of State to Ambassador Alexis U. Johnson, August 1, 1955, *FRUS*, III, 1955–1957, 213–214.

[44] Baijia and Quinnguo, "Steering Wheel, Shock Absorber, and Diplomatic Probe in Confrontation: Sino-American Ambassadorial Talks Seen from a Chinese Perspective," 180.

NEWSPAPERMEN TRAVEL BAN

The most important of those, the one that certainly had the most impact on Eisenhower's strategy, was an invitation to American reporters to visit China. In August 1956, the PRC issued 18 visas to American reporters, representing major newspapers, wire services, magazines, and television networks for a month-long visit to China. The State Department immediately reiterated its determination to maintain the ban on travel to the PRC because, in its rationale, the reporters' visit would jeopardize the conduct of US foreign relations and undermine efforts to negotiate the release of American citizens held as political hostages in Beijing. Naturally, the decision to maintain the travel ban came under heavy fire from media executives and editors across the country for its position, but the issue somehow subsided for a few months.[45]

It made headlines again when on December 24, 1956, William Worthy, a correspondent for the *Baltimore Afro-American* newspaper, entered the PRC in violation of the ban. Worthy was soon followed by Edmund Stevens and Philip Harrington, a reporter-photographer team for *Look* magazine. In response, on December 28th the State Department issued a statement indicating that because of the violation of passport regulations, the three journalists' passports would be valid only for their return to the U.S. and that any unlicensed financial transactions by American citizens with Communist China including purchase of any goods or services while in Communist China, constituted a violation of the Foreign Assets Control Regulation Act of 1950.[46]

The decision triggered a ferocious public attack on the administration. "American reporters go many places where Americans and other free men are mistreated," stated the *New York Post*. The *Boston Herald* pointed out that correspondents had recently visited North Vietnam and Bulgaria, both unrecognized by the US, while American newsmen were stationed in Moscow for a quarter of a century before the US established diplomatic relations with the Communists. On that point, the *Washington Post* declared, "If mere reporting from foreign countries constituted moral approval of the Governments concerned, many areas of the world would be a prohibited list. The administration's policy amounts to censorship."[47]

---

[45] *DSB*, 32, September 23, 1956, 55.
[46] Ibid.
[47] CT, December 30, 1956 through February 7, 1957, DOS, AI568P, box 30, NAII.

The State Department's arguments were rejected one by one by press observers as they advanced strong counter arguments to show that the US position had become untenable. "If Communist China, as Secretary Dulles implies, is trying to make a deal by which it would release 10 American prisoners if the US would permit its newsmen to visit Red China, it is the best reason yet proffered for lifting the ban," a *New York Times* editorial argued. By May 1957, the administration had received more than one hundred ninety letters from editors and publishers all over the country against the travel ban.[48]

Congressional interest in the problem grew exponentially. Senator Ralph E. Flanders (R-VT) declared that the State Department's position seemed "too drastic" and would be debated in the Senate. Senator Hubert H. Humphrey (D-MN) commented that the Department "had made a mistake in its whole approach to the problem." Senator Thomas C. Hennings (D-MO) wrote an open letter to Dulles expressing doubts about whether the imprisoned Americans and their families and friends "will be grateful to you, nor will they understand your curious claim that rulers of Red China were trying to blackmail the US by making the release of prisoners conditional on your helping the American free press to exercise its constitutional responsibilities for benefit of our country." He also announced that his Judiciary Subcommittee on constitutional rights would investigate the State Department's travel restrictions.[49]

Senator Green was also critical of State Department policy, declaring US news gatherers should be encouraged "to go anywhere." On a *NBC* program, Representative Emmanuel Celler (D-NY) expressed the view that the issue of prisoners and the right of the newsmen to travel could not be put in juxtaposition because they had nothing to do with the other. "It is essential to find out what is going on in Red China," he declared, "So we can forearm against machinations of Red Chinese."[50]

In the meantime, William Worthy appeared on Eric Sevareid's nationwide newscast on Sunday afternoon and managed to evoke sympathy for his position. A State Department nationwide poll taken on the evening of the broadcast showed that 78% of those interviewed considered the gov-

---

[48] The *New York Times*, January 20, 1957, 22; "Review of State Department Mail," May 13, 1957, DDE Records as a President, White House Central Files, General Files, box 802, DDEL.

[49] "Congressional Reaction to Newspapermen Travel Ban," February 1957, DOS, AI568K, box 13, NAII.

[50] Ibid.

ernment's decision to withdraw Worthy's passport too hard and a massive 87% thought the administration should allow US journalists to travel to Communist China.[51]

A furious Eisenhower called Dulles at his home at 9.30 p.m. demanding an explanation for the public relations disaster. He blamed the State Department, and implicitly Dulles, for not having adequately explained the full story to the American people. He was convinced that if the full story had gotten across, the public's reaction "would have been supportive of the government's decision." Faced with flat public defiance and the President's fury, Dulles decided to hold a meeting with a small group representing the press.[52]

The meeting took place on February 18, 1957. Present at the meeting were Robert Hurleigh, president of the American Association of Radio Television correspondents; William Dwight, president of the Newspapers and Publishers Association; Jenkins Jones, president of the American Society of Newspapers and Editors; and Henry Luce, president of Time Inc. The Secretary welcomed the group saying that he was appreciative of the opportunity of frankly discussing with them US policy on travel of Americans in Communist China. He recognized that the government had perhaps not put forward as convincing a case as it should, in part because not all of it could be made public, and in part perhaps because the State Department may have not considered all the elements. In that latter respect he looked for the meeting to be helpful, and hoped it might come to some agreement.[53]

The Secretary then outlined the factors underlying US policy. He began by saying that the US was in a state of semi-war with Communist China resulting from the Korean hostilities and technically at war in the sense of still-existing orders and regulations. He touched upon the continuing threat of warfare and the violation of the armistice by the Chinese Communists.[54]

Dulles also tried to impress the importance of two other factors. First was the effect upon other countries, notably the anti-Communist states of the Pacific and Southeast Asia, of any policy of permitting US

---

[51] "The People Speak on Red China," *Editor & Publisher*, February 1957, 6, Library of Congress Washington, DC (hereafter LoC).

[52] Memorandum of Telephone Conversation Between the President and the Secretary of State, February 13, 1957, *FRUS*, III, 1955–1957, 478–479.

[53] Memorandum of Conversation, February 18, 1957, *FRUS*, III, 1955–1957, 481–487.

[54] Ibid.

citizens to go to Communist China apparently with the US government's blessings. Second was that cultural exchanges and travel by Americans into Communist China were of such importance because the Chinese Communists sought more than anything else to give themselves a sense of respectability. Washington could deny this if they were on the US forbidden list. Even more importantly, if they achieved culture exchanges with the US, then they could use it most effectively with the less strong neighboring countries. The US could presumably trust in the Americans who would participate in a cultural exchange, particularly reporters, but representatives of the weaker countries were far more vulnerable. Thus, the Secretary said, if the US changed its position and treated the Chinese Communists as respectable members of the international community, even though they had done nothing to earn it, the net effect in his view would be to weaken the US overall anti-Communist position.[55]

To corroborate that point, Dulles also described the difficulty that the government had experienced on the trade issue because of the pressure exerted by other governments for a relaxation of trade controls. After full and careful thought, the US had decided not to agree to liberalization even though bootlegging activity would increase, simply because of the political impact on the important anti-communist countries close to Communist China. The Secretary feared that along the same lines of erosion, with the inevitable passing of the elder, strong anti-communists such as Jiang, successors motivated by less deep conviction might permit a weakening which could lead to the loss of the countries without fighting.[56]

Dulles then pointed out that he did not believe any policy revision could be limited to newspapermen, whose admission would soon lead to the entry of missionaries, educators, businessmen, and others in the area of cultural exchange. Finally, addressing the problem of the prisoners held by the Chinese, the Secretary asserted that Ambassador Wang had made clear to Ambassador Johnson that Beijing would release the remaining prisoners only when US attitude on cultural exchanges was revised. The administration could not operate under threat of blackmail.[57]

Only Hurleigh responded positively to Dulles' explanations in declaring that his network would try to clarify the position to the American people.

[55] Ibid.
[56] Ibid.
[57] Ibid.

He saw American newsmen simply as Americans in this proposition. All the other press representatives flatly rejected Dulles' arguments.[58]

Having made no progress during the meeting, on March 3rd, 1957, Dulles had dinner with Frank Bartholomew, head of United Press. Bartholomew told Dulles that the administration had to meet the press half way if it wanted the public attacks to subside. He suggested the possibility that some arrangement might be made whereby one or possibly three persons would be agreed upon by all the news media to go to China on a reporting mission and that if it could be handled in that way, that would get away from the concept of general breakdown of ostracism of the Chinese Communists and a beginning of "cultural exchange."[59]

Dulles responded positively to the suggestion. If the news media would agree on one person or not more than three to travel to China on such a mission, he believed that they might be able to set it up on a framework which would be free of the difficulties that he had foreseen in any general relaxation of restriction. He likened the situation to wartime when under special conditions the news agencies agreed on pooling their resources through one or a very limited number of people. Although he questioned whether the Chinese would accept this recommendation, he thought it was worth trying.[60]

During that time the administration's public position was not improving. The Senate Foreign Relations Committee voted on the motion proposed by Alexander Smith (R-NJ), Hubert Humphrey (D-MN), Mike Mansfield (D-Mont), and William Fulbright (D-AR) to hold public hearings on news bans within two weeks, with Secretary Dulles testifying. The Committee also decided to study a variety of connected queries, including whether the State Department should permit engineers, scientists, and other specialists to conduct studies in Communist China.[61] Worthy's reports on his six-week sojourn in Communist China were carried serially by the *New York Post,* and the *New Republic* published an article by him on "reporting in Communist China." His testimony before the Senate Subcommittee on Constitutional Rights received extensive press coverage, as did Under-Secretary Murphy's testimony before the Foreign Relations

[58] Ibid.

[59] Memorandum of Conversation Between the Secretary of State and Frank Bartholomew, March 3, 1957, *FRUS*, III, 1955–1957, 492–493.

[60] Ibid.

[61] CT, March 20 through 27, 1957, DOS, AI568P, box 30, NAII.

Committee in defense of State Department policy.[62] Murphy received heavy Congressional criticism. Senator Humphrey took sharp issue with his explanation that to allow newsmen to travel to Red China before all American prisoners are freed would be yielding to blackmail: "This is a nonsense argument that cannot be validated," Senator Fulbright pointedly remarked "You seem to feel we would be conferring favor on Red China to let newsmen go there. I think it would be to our benefit not theirs."[63]

Look magazine reported on the Stevens-Harrington visit to Communist China in a pictorial special issue. The image it portrayed of China contrasted with the one that was presented by the administration. First, he was very impressed by the friendliness of the people and found the officials far more "relaxed and agreeable than Russians." Many had been educated in America, therefore, communication was not a problem. Despite the close political and economic ties between the Soviet Union and China, it did not take long to discover that in temperament, culture, and approach to human problems, the Chinese had little in common with Russia, except Communism. China was not a Soviet satellite and its government had a far broader basis of popular support that any other Communist government, including the USSR. Finally, with the reality of China's steadily growing industrial capability and its burgeoning population meant that "This awakening giant of a country was not getting the intention it deserved from the West."[64]

Holiday magazine's June issue had a special feature on Communist China by the well-known novelist Han Suying, author of the best-seller *A Many-Splendored Thing*. She reported about the accomplishments she saw on a return visit to her native Beijing: "China under the Communists is making stupendous progress, its people are happy, crime's non-existent, vast public works are underway, universities are multiplying and there is a growing spirit of free discussion." The article ended with an editorial note by the editors of the *Holiday* that it had been written "by a foreigner because the State Department has foolishly barred American writers and photographers from Red China."[65]

In trying to stem the wave of positive publicity, the administration put out a rumor to undermine William Worthy's reputation. Acting Director of the Bureau of Security and Consular Affairs Robert Cartwright reported

---

[62] Ibid.
[63] Ibid.
[64] CT, April 4 through 11, 1957, DOS, AI568P, box 30, NAII.
[65] DDE Papers, Diary Series, box 24, DDEL.

during his testimony to the Senate Foreign Relations Committee that he had been found guilty of defying the draft law in 1944. However, Worthy's clarification of the issue prompted Senator Joseph O'Mahoney (D-WY) to call for an apology from the Department.[66] As the situation continued to get out of hand, the administration had cause to regret its decision to prosecute the journalists. To conclude the matter quickly, passport officials spent nearly 6 hours behind closed doors trying to make a deal with Worthy. They asked him repeatedly to promise that he would not travel to off-limit Communist countries in the future should his passport be renewed. Worthy reportedly promised to use his passport in countries where it should be used, but gave no further assurance. As soon as he exited the hearings room, he gave a press conference explaining in detail what the administration had tried to do.[67]

The Chinese government followed Americans' reaction to the newspapermen ban closely and Wang skillfully exploited the issue in Geneva. Essentially, what the Chinese did was to beat the Americans at their own game. They used the issue to buy time and force Washington to break off the talks. Ambassador Johnson found it increasingly difficult to juggle the administration's strategy. Officially, he insisted that Communist China must release all American civilians who were detained there before any cultural exchanges could take place. However, in his daily correspondence with Dulles, he lamented several times that his position "had been severely weakened." Wang had repeatedly mocked him by asking how China could take any US government proposals seriously when they did not represent the American people's wishes. Beijing also made sure that the entire world was aware that the deadlock in the talks was the fault of those in Washington. In statements and press conferences, the Chinese Ambassador stressed how "ridiculous" and "hypocritical" the US position was and openly questioned the "values of American democracy" because Washington did not follow the public's desires.[68]

The upsurge in public criticism against the administration combined with the increasing calls for a review of US-China policy and a relaxation of the trade embargo put Washington in an awkward situation. An angry President Eisenhower told Dulles that the lack of support for the govern-

[66] CT, April 4 through 11, 1957, DOS, AI568P, box 30, NAII.

[67] The *New York Times*, April 25, 1957, 1.

[68] Memorandum of Conversation Between the President and the Secretary of State, June 3, 1957; Robertson to Dulles, June 1957, JFD Papers, box 121, ML.

ment's foreign policy was unacceptable and extremely dangerous. The administration could not be pushed around by the press and the public, so it had to regain the lead and it had to do it quickly. The perceived necessity to control the volume of public discussion was evident from a memo Robertson sent Dulles in May 1957. In it, he asserted, "Recent statements by notable public figures and increased press and public opinion support for a review of our China policy have caused speculation throughout Asia as to our China policy and given particular concern to our Asia Allies. It is necessary to clarify our position."[69]

With that in mind, on June 28th, 1957 Dulles gave his harshest speech up until that time against the PRC. Commencing with the familiar theme of American historical friendship with the Chinese people, he then stated that the Chinese Communist party "came to power by violence" and "have lived by violence" in subjecting the people to "massive forcible repression." Unlike the Soviet Union at the time, the US recognized that the PRC's record was one of "armed aggression." Citing the experience of Sino-American negotiations, Dulles castigated Beijing's leaders for their refusal to rule out force in their dealings with Taiwan and failure to live up to the terms of the September 1955 agreement.[70]

Referring to the assertion that "If we assist the Chinese Communists to wax strong, then they eventually break with Soviet Russia and this is our best hope for the future," he argued that if one harbored that belief, the same error of appeasing the Axis of powers might be repeated. "Perhaps too if the Axis of powers had won World War II, they would have fallen out among themselves, but no one suggested that we should tolerate and assist on Axis victory because in the end they would quarrel."[71]

Dulles insisted that "Neither recognition, trade or any form of cultural relations would favorably influence the evolution of the affairs in China." Regardless of what other countries did, the heavy security commitment from the US in the China area ruled against it helping to "build up the military power of its potential enemy by trading with it."[72]

Despite the strong reaffirmation of the government's policy, the attacks on the administration did not subside. Under pressure from news organi-

---

[69] Memorandum of Conversation Between the President and the Secretary of State, June 3, 1957; Memorandum from Robertson to Dulles, June 1957, JFD papers, box 121, ML.
[70] Address by the Secretary of State, June 28, 1957, *FRUS*, III, 1955–1957, 558–566.
[71] Ibid.
[72] Ibid.

zations, Congress, and the public, the State Department finally gave approval to 24 American reporters to travel to China "in order to permit direct reporting by them to the American people about conditions in the area under Chinese Communist control." The permission, however, was limited to a 7-month trial period, and the policy of change was unilateral. The State Department still refused to offer reciprocal visas for Chinese reporters "bearing passports issued by the Chinese Communist regime" to visit the United States.[73]

On August 26th, the PRC responded to the US announcement in an article in the *People's Daily*. The Department of State's decision to permit a limited number of American correspondents to travel to China was rejected as completely unacceptable. With the injection of the reciprocity issue into the controversy, the frustrated press leveled a blast of criticism not only at Beijing for "reneging" on its original invitation, but more so at the State Department for "bungling" the China news coverage problem from the start and attaching "provocative conditions" to its relaxation of the news ban "which practically guaranteed" a rejection by Red China. Again, under attack, the State Department publicly declared its willingness to make "new efforts to set up an exchange of correspondents."[74]

During that time, just as Dulles had feared, other groups of citizens began pressuring for permission to travel to Communist China. On November 16th, Robertson received a letter from Mrs. Mary Downey renewing an earlier request that she be permitted to visit her son John Downey, one of six remaining American prisoners, who was under sentence of life imprisonment. Robertson forwarded the letter to Dulles with a note: "Given the public relations nightmare we are in this might be an appropriate occasion to renew US policy with respect to travel of relatives of Americans imprisoned in China." It seemed to him that a visit of relatives was unlikely to damage the prospect of the prisoners for release at that point and withdrawal of US objection to such visits would serve to demonstrate to relatives and others that the government had taken every possible step to promote the release of the prisoners.[75]

Dulles approved the plan and on December 6th the State Department issued a press release stating, "Following consideration of renewed requests

---

[73] The *New York Times*, August 23, 1957, 2.
[74] The *New York Times*, August 26, 1957, 1.
[75] Memorandum from Robertson to Dulles, November 16, 1957, *FRUS*, III, 1955–1957, 635–636.

from certain relatives of Americans imprisoned in Communist China for passports in order to visit them, the Department of State has decided to issue passports not restricted as regard to travel to Communist China."[76]

The administration's policy of rhetorical toughness had clearly backfired. By portraying Communist China as a dangerous and belligerent enemy to rally support for their inflexible foreign policy, Eisenhower and Dulles had frightened the public. Fearing Washington's intolerant attitude toward the PRC might trigger a new global war, a significant segment of American public, press, and Congress was asking for a review of US-China policy. That climate of opinion undermined the administration's position domestically and internationally and gave a tremendous political advantage to Communist China.

Dulles was particularly struck by the fact that no one in Congress had supported the government's policy on the newspapermen travel ban. Speaking with his senior advisors on August 20, 1957, he openly admitted that their management of public opinion had failed and anticipated the time was approaching when the US must treat Communist China on the same basis as the Soviet Union, a situation reached with regard with trade.[77]

The American public's support for a review of US-China policy aroused great antipathy and misgivings in Taiwan. In May 1957, savage anti-American riots took place in Taipei. The US Embassy was thoroughly demolished by a large mob, which then destroyed the United States Information Service headquarters and the Military Assistance Advisory Group building. There was a feeling among other Asian allies that domestic pressure would soon force Washington to negotiate a deal with Beijing, which would leave those Asian allies in the lurch who had been following its lead on China policy.[78]

Even worse, the public's lack of support for the administration's policy undermined the American position in Geneva to give the Chinese Communists the initiative in the talks. Since the beginning of the negotiations, US strategy had aimed at dragging the talks for as long as possible to buy time in the Taiwan Straits and frustrate the Chinese Communists. As Dulles wrote Johnson back in the summer 1955, "The more time we buy the better. If the Communists become impatient and want to break

[76] Ibid.

[77] Memorandum of Conversation, August 20, 1957, JFD papers, box 301, ML.

[78] Telegram from the Ambassador in the Republic of China (Rankin) to the Department of State, May 23, 1957, *FRUS*, III, 1955–1957, 535–537.

off the talks even better, it would make them look bad in the eyes of the world and improve our position."[79]

The Chinese did not fall for the US trap however. They were clearly eager to establish some sort of contact with the US and although frustrated by Washington's strategy, they did not call off the talks. On the contrary, they turned it to their advantage. They kept making and publicizing proposal after proposal of seemingly praiseworthy character, such as trade and free travel and cultural exchange which the US rejected every time but most of the American and international public approved of.

Consequently, the Geneva talks were no longer an effective instrument for securing the release of the imprisoned citizens. They had the opposite effect in fact. The administration reasoned that because the Chinese Communists considered the negotiations of value for them, they would continue to hold some American hostages to ensure that the talks continued. They might project that if all the Americans were freed, then the US would have attained their objective and immediately terminate the talks. In August 1958, realizing their position had become untenable, Washington decided to downgrade the talks from an ambassadorial level to a consular level and move them to Warsaw.

REFERENCES

Bachrack, Stanley. *The Committee of One Million: "China Lobby" Politics, 1953–1971.* New York: Columbia University Press, 1976.

Bernkopf Tucker, Nancy. "Cold War Contacts: America and China, 1952–1956." In *Sino-American Relations, 1945–1955: A Joint Reassessment of a Critical Decade,* edited by Harding Harry and Ming Yuant. Wilmington: Scholarly Resources, Inc., 1989.

Chang, Gordon. *Friends and Enemies: The United States, China and the Soviet Union, 1948–1972.* Stanford: Stanford University Press, 1990.

Foot, Rosemary. "The Eisenhower Administration's Fear of Empowering the Chinese." *Political Science Quarterly* 111 (1996): 505–521.

Goldstein, Steven. "Dialogue of the Deaf? The Sino-Ambassadorial Level Talks, 1955–1970." In *Re-Examining the Cold War: US-China Diplomacy, 1954–1973,* ed. Robert Ross and Jiang Changbin. Cambridge: Harvard University Press, 2011.

[79] Telegram from the Secretary of State to Ambassador U. Alexis Johnson, August 1, 1955, *FRUS,* III, 1955–1957, 213–214.

Johnson, Alexis U. *The Right Hand of Power: The Memoirs of an American Diplomat*. Englewood Cliffs: Prentice-Hall, 1984.

Kusntiz, Leonard. *Public Opinion and Foreign Policy: America's China Policy, 1949–1979*. Westport: Greenwood Press, 1984.

Mayers, David. *Cracking the Monolith: US Policy Against the Sino-Soviet Alliance, 1949–1955*. London: Louisiana State University Press, 1986.

Morgenthau, Hans J. "John Foster Dulles." In *An Uncertain Tradition: American Secretaries of State in the Twentieth Century*, edited by Norman A. Graebner. New York: McGraw Hill, 1996.

Shu Guang, Zhang. *Economic Cold War: America's Embargo Against China and the Sino-Soviet Alliance, 1949–1963*. Stanford, CA: Stanford University Press, 2001.

Zhang, Baijia and Quingguo Jia. "Steering Wheel, Shock Absorber, and Diplomatic Probe in Confrontation: Sino-American Ambassadorial Talks Seen from a Chinese Perspective." In *Re-Examining the Cold War: US-China Diplomacy, 1954–1973*, edited by Robert Ross and Jiang Changbin. Cambridge: Harvard University Press, 2011.

CHAPTER 7

Hard Line Until the End

In September 1958, the British Ambassador to the US, Sir Harold Caccia, reported to the Foreign Office in London that the American public was getting increasingly frustrated with the difficult state of Sino-American relations. "Dissatisfaction is nothing new, but it is being expressed more openly now," he wrote. The American public particularly blamed Jiang Jieshi (Chiang Kei-shek) and his associates in Washington for the dangerous situation in the Taiwan Straits. A large portion of the public was now willing to abandon Eisenhower's hard line policy and implement a softer approach if it could avoid another military crisis or worse, nuclear war.[1]

The purpose of this chapter is to analyze the public discontent that plagued the last years of the Eisenhower administration. The calls for a reassessment of Sino-American relations, which had begun at the end of the first Taiwan (Formosa) crisis, intensified through 1958 and reached a peak when the Chinese Communists began shelling the offshore islands for a second time in the autumn of that year. While support for establishing diplomatic relations with Beijing (Peiping) and its admission into the United Nations (UN) never reached an overall national majority, removal of the trade embargo and negotiations to minimize tensions and lower the risk of a nuclear conflict were advocated for by an overwhelming majority of Congressmen, press, and the public. Only a few diehard Nationalist supporters continued to argue that hostility was the only correct policy

[1] De la Mare to Dalton, September 26, 1958, FO 371/133535, National Archives, Kew, London.

© The Author(s) 2018   183
M. Oliva, *Eisenhower and American Public Opinion on China*,
https://doi.org/10.1007/978-3-319-76195-4_7

toward the Communist regime. However, President Dwight D. Eisenhower and Secretary of State John Foster Dulles refused to acquiesce to popular demand. They remained convinced that their hard line policy was the best way to protect American national security interests.

CONTINUING CRITICISM

The Eisenhower administration remained under fire for its China policy at the beginning of 1958. A State Department Bureau of Public Affairs (SDBPA) public opinion review reported that although the public and the media commended the State Department for its "humane and worthwhile gesture" in allowing the mothers of those prisoners still held by the People's Republic of China (PRC) to visit their sons, criticism of Washington's rigid China policy persisted. Among the press, only the Luce publications, the *Manchester Union Leader*, the *Chicago Tribune,* and the *Oakland Tribune* still advocated a hard line policy in favor of the total trade embargo against Beijing and opposition to its recognition and admission by the UN. Most of the press supported a policy review. Of those, the SDBPA continued, a considerable group, including the *New York Herald Tribune*, and even the pro-Nationalist Scripps-Howard and Hearst chains, believed that although it might be too soon for recognition, the US must constantly show its willingness to participate in any talks with the Chinese Communists which offered any promise of reducing world tensions. A smaller group, including C.L. Sulzberger of the *New York Times*, the *Washington Post*, the *Wall Street Journal*, the *Christian Science Monitor*, columnist Walter Lippmann and the entire spectrum of religious press openly advocated recognition, relaxation of trade restrictions, and Beijing's seating in the UN as the only "realist policy available" to solve East-West tensions.[2]

In Congress, support for the administration's inflexible policy came only from the pro-Nationalist wing. Senators William F. Knowland (R-CA), H. Alexander Smith (R-NJ), and Styles Bridges (R-NH) and Representative Walter H. Judd (R-MN), among others, had teamed up with the Committee of One Million against the Admission of Communist China into the UN

---

[2] "Public Opinion on US Foreign Policy", January 1958, Records of the Office of Public Opinion Studies, Department of State, 1943–1975, AI568J, box 1, National Archives II, College Park, Maryland (hereafter survey title followed by date, DOS, file reference, box number, NAII).

(Committee of One Million or COOM), the SDBPA reported, "to stem the increasing flow of public requests" for a review of China policy. Three themes became the focus of their propaganda campaign in early 1958: (1) the increased use of opium and other drugs by American teenagers which would follow US recognition of Beijing or establishment of normal trade relations; (2) call for immediate and further US action to determine the fate of 450 Americans still unaccounted for since the Korean War; and (3) an appeal to the Japanese people and government to reconsider their recent trade agreements between Japanese private firms and Communist China.[3]

Congressional advocates of a review of US-China policy, the SDBPA stated, "are more and more vocal however," particularly after a summit conference on disarmament between East and West became a concrete possibility. In view of worldwide apprehensions on the effects of radioactive fallout from nuclear tests, President Eisenhower had proposed to the Soviet Union and other nuclear nations to negotiate a ban on all testing of atomic weapons and the creation of an international control system. Although negotiations with the Russians had initially proved difficult, at the beginning of 1958 a common understanding seemed closer.[4]

Senator Hubert Humphrey (D-MN) pointed out in an interview for the *New York Times* that "Red China could scarcely be excluded from a summit conference on disarmament. If we except to achieve any disarmament among powers, some settlement of the China issue must take place, otherwise this would be an invitation for the Soviet evasion of the disarmament agreement by collusion with Red China." Similarly, Senator William Fulbright (D-AR) commented in the *New Republic* that the Soviet Union had already staged a nuclear explosion in the 9-kiloton range within Chinese territory and could continue to conduct such tests even after agreeing to test suspension, if China was outside the international inspection agreement.[5]

---

[3] On February 27, 1958, a trade agreement had been signed between the China Committee for the Promotion of International Trade and several Japanese business groups; Publications relating to the Committee of One Million Against Admission of Red China to the United Nations, 1954–1966, Tamiment Library, New York University, New York (hereafter NYU); Stanley Bachrack, *The Committee of One Million, "China Lobby" Politics* (New York: Columbia University Press, 1976), 143.

[4] Dwight D. Eisenhower, *The White House Years: Waging Peace* (London: William Heinemann LTD, 1965), 467–477.

[5] China Telegram (hereafter CT), February 4 through April 29, 1958, DOS, AI568P, box 30, NAII.

The public continued to show a majority opposition to admitting the PRC into the UN, but that had decreased to 58% of the Gallup poll respondents. Furthermore, according to a Roper poll, 53% of the national sample believed that the US should follow its allies and remove the trade differential against Communist China. A more detailed regional analysis of popular feelings toward Beijing, however, revealed that sharp differences existed among the US states on those issues. The debate on US-China policy was included for the first time among the eight topics discussed by the Foreign Policy Association Great Decisions Program. The exercise showed that West Coast states such as California and Oregon were far more inclined than Midwestern states to review Washington's stance toward the PRC.[6]

The *San Francisco Chronicle*, which sponsored the discussion group for North California and published the balloting results stated, "The majority of Northern Californians thinks our China policy is wrong." It also revealed that 85% of the survey participants favored recognition of Beijing and 78% would admit it into the UN, while 82% favored removing special restrictions to liberalize trade with the PRC. Similarly, Oregon State College, which tabulated Oregon ballots, indicated "a growing sentiment for easing foreign policy and trade relations with Red China." According to the survey, 64% of the group discussion participants declared that the US should extend full or partial diplomatic recognition to Beijing and 75% would ease the embargo and apply the same restrictions to Red China that applied to other Communist countries.[7]

[6] In relations to the Great Decisions Program, the Foreign Policy Association (FPA) produces a National Opinion Ballot Report each year based on the tabulation of opinion ballots submitted by the participants in the Great Decisions Program. Since 1955, opinion ballots have been included in the Great Decisions Briefing Book and have been sent to the White House, the State Department, the Department of Defense, members of Congress, educational institutions, media, and concerned citizens. A full copy of the 1958 Briefing Book is currently unavailable. The FPA is unable to provide one because of repository laws. One copy is stored at the British Library in London; however, at the time this research thesis was being completed the British Library was relocating some of its collections and therefore could not provide the document. The data mentioned in this chapter are from extracts of the 1958 Briefing Book that had been included in the State Department daily, weekly, and monthly reports on US public opinion or are among Press Secretary James C. Hagerty Papers (hereafter Hagerty Papers) at the Dwight D. Eisenhower Presidential Library in Abilene, Kansas (hereafter DDEL).

[7] CT, March 25 through May 27, 1958, DOS, AI568P, box 30, NAII; Hagerty Papers, box 45, DDEL.

Although a full list of the participants of those discussions is unfortunately unavailable, it is no surprise that those West Coast states, which in
the past had greatly benefited from East-West trade, were so overwhelmingly in favor of a policy review. Midwest States such as Kansas and
Missouri, however, were still strongly opposed to any relaxation of Sino-
American relations. The *Kansas City Star* showed that 87% of the participants did not support establishing diplomatic relations with the PRC and
93% were in favor of the total trade embargo. Popular feelings in Missouri
were in line with those in Kansas.[8]

While those states represented the two extremes of the opinion spectrum, the administration seemingly perceived the balloting in Chicago as
more representative of the average nationwide popular feelings. Answering
to questions by the Chicago Council on Foreign Relations and the Junior
Association of Commerce and Industry posed in the *Chicago News*, 55%
of the respondents favored easing trade relations with the PRC. Of those,
35% said there "should be as much trade as possible," and the remaining
20% said there "should be only as much as US principal Allies conduct,"
while 45% opposed any trade with Communist China. On the question of
admitting the PRC into the UN, 35% of those voting urged continuance
of Nationalist membership and all possible help to Taiwan short of military intervention; but the same proportion favored seating Beijing in the
UN as the real government of China.[9]

The trade issue became a sore point for the administration when in May
1958 press observers across the nation subjected the State Department to
a merciless ribbing over the decision to bar the importation of a giant
panda from Communist China for a US zoo. Still bitter because of
Secretary Dulles' refusal to renew William Worthy's passport and allow US
journalists to travel to the PRC, newspapers throughout the country
laughed at the official explanation by the State Department that "acquir-
ing the panda would violate the trade ban against Communist China."
Commenting on the "subversive panda" the *Wall Street Journal* mocked,
"We have got to understand the reasoning of diplomats in this matter. If
they allow the panda in this country, the security of the entire nation
would be in danger." In the opinion of the *Des Moines Register*, "The
wooden rigidity of the State Department on having anything to do with
Red China has never been quite ridiculous as in the panda case. Shame on

---

[8] Ibid.
[9] Ibid.

you Mr. Dulles and all your little dullards for denying us this fuzzy-wuzzy animal." "No doubt," scoffed the *Washington Post*, "this bold, decisive and impressive action which the State Department is credited with will shatter Red Chinese economy." "How silly can we be? What happened to our sense of proportion?" asked the *Milwaukee Journal*.[10]

Mockery, however, turned into fury when *New York Times* reporter Murray Schumach revealed that earlier that year a pair of dogs from Chinese-controlled Tibet had been imported by way of Nepal, via London for Thomas Stephens, a former secretary to the President. "Has this administration no decency?" the *Wall Street Journal* questioned. "Our China policy is a farce" quipped the *Christian Science Monitor*. "How can the State Department forbid import of the giant panda on grounds of national security and allow instead two Chinese dogs to enter the country? It is about time we end this absurd China policy," Walter Lippmann stated.[11]

Although the administration did not respond to public criticism, some serious reassessment of the effectiveness of the China differential was taking place beyond closed doors. In a lengthy document, the State Department reported that because the US was the only country that insisted on a total trade embargo toward China, it was damaging US policy and economy and its relationships with the allies, particularly Britain and Japan. Without the rest of the international community, the US looked like an inflexible power heading toward isolation. The Department argued that admitting the Communist giant into the UN and finally establishing trade and diplomatic relation would benefit the US immensely. Those developments would not only please the allies, but they would also go a long way on improving Washington's standing among the public at home and abroad. Finally, relaxing tensions with the PRC would "likely cause concern in the Kremlin over the possibility of a crack in the Communist monolith," which, after all, was one of the original goals of NSC166.[12]

---

[10] CT, May 3 through May 16, 1958, DOS, AI568P, box 30, NAII; Monthly Review of Public Opinion, June 1958, DOS, AI568K, box 13, NAII.

[11] Ibid.; Schumach, Murray, "Zoo Bound Panda from Red China Is a Trade Risk," The *New York Times*, May 7, 1958, 1.

[12] K.G. Ritchie, British Embassy in Beijing to Foreign Office, January 31, 1958, Foreign Office Records, FO371/13341 (1958), National Archives, Kew; Shu Guang, Zhang, *Economic Cold War, America's Embargo Against China and the Sino-Soviet Alliance, 1949–1963* (Stanford: Stanford University Press, 2001), 174–198.

Eisenhower and Dulles refused to approve those changes in the US-China policy. Although increasingly concerned about the strain on the relationship with the allies and the state of domestic and international public opinion, they feared a softer approach would project an image of a weak United States throughout Southeast Asia. That would force those neutral nonaligned countries to turn to Beijing for guidance and protection, thus effectively putting an end to American authority in the area.[13]

Eisenhower was concerned about the lack of public support for the administration's position however. As he explained to Dulles and Press Secretary James C. Hagerty, he genuinely believed that it was Washington's fault. Convinced that his policy was the right one but that he had somehow been unable to make the public understand that, he urged both men "to come up with some ideas" before the administration lost control of the agenda. The President also turned to the business world for help, in the person of Eric A. Johnston, former Chairman of the International Development Advisory Board. Without public support, he told Johnson, it was very difficult for the "Nation to put forward maximum effort to obtain maximum results." To counter this, the President declared, "It would be highly gratifying for me and a great service to the Nation if you'd be willing to call in Washington a conference of business and organizations leaders, bipartisan in character, to explore means of conveying to our citizens a fuller flow of information on the foreign aspects of our national security."[14]

The one-day event took place on February 25th with both Eisenhower and Dulles in attendance. Presentations by communication experts, advertising executives from Madison Avenue, and business leaders conveyed two messages. First, the necessity for a company, or in that case a government, to be in control of the output of information rather than letting public opinion and the media rule the news agenda. Second, and consequently, the importance of "singing from the same tune sheet." To

---

[13] Minutes of the 356 NSC meeting, February 27, 1958, *FRUS*, IV, 1958–1960, 703–706; Briefing notes, drafted by Robert Cutler and Robert H. Johnson, February 27, 1958, *FRUS*, IV, 1958–1960, 710–712; Minutes of the 364 NSC meeting, May 2, 1958, *FRUS*, IV, 1958–1960, 713; Philip, Funigiello, *American-Soviet Trade in the Cold War* (Chapel Hill: University of North Carolina Press, 1988), 11–17.

[14] Letter to Eric A. Johnston on the Need for Public Information as to the Foreign Aspects of National Security, January 11, 1958, Eisenhower, Dwight D. *The Presidential Papers of Dwight D. Eisenhower*, ed. Galambos Louis and D. van Ee (Baltimore: John Hopkins University Press, 1996), 16–17 (hereafter EPP followed by page number).

avoid public confusion and exposure of the administration to partisan attacks, the President's message should not be undermined by a lack of coordination among the different competing federal agencies, as had occurred during the first Taiwan crisis, but should be supported and spread by all government officials.[15]

Following the conference, the White House issued a top-secret memorandum to all federal departments stressing the importance of adequate public information, particularly in foreign policy, to facilitate the government's job and present a united and bipartisan front. A lengthier version of the paper was sent to the State and Defense Departments. Among the guidelines listed was the necessity of avoiding press leaks, unless authorized by the President or the Secretary of State, and of coordinating the administration's public message, particularly in the area of China policy which, the document stated, "has recently suffered from a serious lack of domestic support." For that reason, all public statements and speeches on that issue needed to be cleared with the Secretary of State or senior members within the department.[16]

THE SECOND TAIWAN CRISIS: PHASE ONE

The administration did not need to wait long to test those new guidelines. In August 1958, the Central Intelligence Agency (CIA) informed the President that the PRC was planning to resume its "liberate Taiwan" campaign. Washington's management of that new crisis failed to take into consideration the lessons learned in 1955. As during the first Taiwan crisis, the decision to protect US national security interests at any costs, including the use of nuclear weapons, combined with Eisenhower's belief in his ability to sway public opinion in favor of his policy backfired and triggered a war scare among the public. Despite the wide-ranging opposition, popular feelings only restrained the administration by limiting the choice of policy options available, but it did not influence its overall China policy. The crisis, however, further widened the gap between policy makers and the people and eroded the public's confidence in the administration.

[15] "Notes on one-day conference on public opinion" February 25, 1958, Hagerty Papers, box 10, DDEL.
[16] "Improving Public Opinion Management," Memorandum to Federal Agencies, May 1958, Hagerty Papers, box 10, DDEL; "Public Opinion and Foreign Policy," Memorandum to State and Defense Department, May 1958, Hagerty Papers, box 10, DDEL.

The crisis was the inevitable consequence of the administration's inability to deal with Jiang Jieshi. In April 1955, Washington tried to convince the Nationalist leader to abandon the offshore islands for good but failed to achieve any substantial results. Instead, the Generalissimo decided to reinforce his position by moving one third of his army to these little territories. He used those to conduct propaganda and reconnaissance raids to mainland China. In response, Beijing moved planes to its bases in nearby Jinmen (Quemoy). Allen Dulles, Director of the CIA and brother of the Secretary of State, reported that he did not expect an immediate Communist invasion of the islands but that the situation was certainly "heating up."[17]

Washington was faced once again with the familiar problem of having to decide whether the psychological value of those small territories justified US intervention or not. As Eisenhower told the Chairman of the Joint Chiefs of Staff (JCS), General Nathan Twining, "There are good reasons for taking the view that these islands should be abandoned. However, a great part of the Chinese Nationalist forces is now deployed on the islands and their removal or loss would be a signal to all Asia that there is no hope that can be held out against the Communists in China."[18]

Dulles, also present at the meeting, concurred with the President that the positions were insignificant in military terms but psychologically they had acquired even more importance over the past three years. Elaborating on his thoughts regarding the danger of abandoning Jinmen and Matzu, the following day the Secretary of State also stated his conviction that the Chinese Communists were testing and probing America's will: "The Communists bloc might now be pushing all around the perimeter to see whether our resolution is weakened by the Soviet possession of nuclear missiles." Believing the Communists would retreat in the face of American resolve, Dulles believed that the United States had to take a strong stand; "If it appeared that we are standing firm, then they would not take action that would risk precipitating a large-scale war." Those two fundamental assumptions about the increased psychological importance of the islands and the Chinese intention to probe the American will entered into every

---

[17]A.J. Goodpastor, Memorandum of Conference with the President, August 25, 1958, Dwight D. Eisenhower Papers (hereafter DDE Papers), Ann Whitman File, International Series, box 10, DDEL; Discussion at the 375 meeting of the National Security Council, August 7, 1958, DDE Papers, NSC Series, box 10, DDEL.
[18]Memorandum of Conference with the President, August 11, 1958, JFD Papers, Chronological Series, box 16, DDEL.

assessment of defending Jinmen and Matzu and shaped the administration's strategy throughout the entire crisis.[19]

To deter a Communist attack, Eisenhower and Dulles agreed to publicly announce that the ties between Taiwan and the offshore islands had now grown so close that the United States could not treat those positions as detached from Taiwan. To that end, on August 23rd, 1958, the administration released a letter to the press from the Secretary of State to the Chairman of the House Foreign Affairs Committee asserting that "Ties between Taiwan and the offshore islands have increased in the last three years." It also warned that "It would be highly hazardous" for anyone to assume that a Communist attempt to change the situation by seeking to conquer those islands could be held to a "limited operation."[20]

The same day that the letter was published, the PRC began shelling the Jinmen and Matzu groups and implemented a naval blockade. Eisenhower's response to Beijing's move was to issue a statement reinforcing US commitment to defend its Nationalist ally. It declared: "The ties between these islands and Formosa had become closer and their interdependence has increased." Therefore, any "attempt to conquer them would, I fear constitute a threat to the peace of the area."[21]

On August 25th, Allen Dulles reported that the situation was still contained because the Communists had not yet gathered enough ground and amphibious forces that would allow them to invade the islands. Eisenhower thought it was important to send a message about American resolve to the PRC through a "show of force." He decided the US warships would escort Nationalist supply ships trying to make their way to the islands, although those were to stay in international waters.[22]

A few days later, Washington sent some units of the Composite Air Strike Force, a specialized attack group that possessed atomic capability, to the Straits. It also moved a US Air Force fighter squadron from Okinawa to Taiwan. Altogether, the Pacific command had over "200 atomic air-

[19] Ibid.; Memorandum of Conference with the President, August 12, 1958, JFD Papers, Chronological Series, box 16, DDEL.

[20] Eisenhower, *Waging Peace*, 256.

[21] Memorandum of Conference with the President, August 23, 1958, JFD Papers, White House Memoranda Series, box 7, DDEL.

[22] Memorandum of Conference, August 25, 1958, DDE Papers, Ann Whitman File, International Series, box 10, DDEL; Special Watch Report of the Intelligence Advisory Committee, August 29, 1958, DDE Papers, Ann Whitman File, International Series, box 10, DDEL.

craft" at its disposal. Those moves were not kept a secret, quite the contrary. Eisenhower ordered the Defense Department "to leak a few revealing words to the press so that these would not escape the notice of the Communists."[23]

The President refused, however, to authorize the possible use of tactical atomic weapons against the mainland and specifically reserved judgment to see how events developed. His view had changed considerably since the 1955 crisis, when he had tried to prepare the world for atomic war by comparing an atomic bomb to a bullet. In 1958, Eisenhower was more apprehensive of the backlash from world opinion if the weapons were used. As he told the National Security Council (NSC), sanctioning the use of nuclear weapons at that early stage of the crisis would "cause public outrage" by creating the impression that a nuclear conflict could break out soon. Precipitating a war scare among the public, as he well knew, would only make the crisis more difficult to manage.[24]

But world and domestic public opinion were already showing signs of opposition to Washington's tough stance. Among the Allies, Japan and Britain were the most vocal in supporting a negotiated settlement, rather than risking war over insignificant military territories. The British even volunteered to act as intermediary and approach the Soviets to restrain the Chinese Communists. Similarly, the SDBPA reported that the American public did not see the administration's warnings and military moves favorably. In Congress, only Walter Judd publicly declared his full support for the defense of the offshore islands: "The Red Chinese have been warned of deep concern which the US feels over any threat to the offshore islands. The Seventh Fleet is not a paper-tiger and an attack on Quemoy would certainly draw heavy retribution." However, most of the Congressmen opposed getting "embroiled in a war over wholly insignificant pieces of real estate." Senator Morse (D-OR) reasserted his belief that the Formosa Resolution had not authorized the US to assist Taipei in the defense of Jinmen and Matzu and declared, "If we attempt to defend them, then we will be branded an aggressor nation."[25]

---

[23] Ibid.; Eisenhower, *Waging Peace*, 297.

[24] Memorandum of Conference with the President, August 29, 1958, DDE Papers, Diary Series, box 35, DDEL.

[25] Review of World Opinion on the Formosan Straits Situation, August/September 1958, DOS, AI568J, box 1, NAII; "Special Opinion Review on Formosa Straits Situation" August 1958, DOS, AI568J, box 1, NAII; CT, August 26 through September 3, 1958, DOS, AI568P, box 30, NAII.

A few newspapers, such as the *New York Times* and the *New York Herald Tribune*, approved of Washington's warnings as a tactic to deter the Chinese Communists' attempt at renewing tensions in the Straits. Nevertheless, a substantial segment of opinion was critical of US policy and convinced that the islands were not worth "shedding any American blood." Those publications also argued that the US would not receive any support from the Allies if it decided to intervene, that Washington fundamentally had no legal claim on those territories, and that a war over them could not be justified.[26]

Even worse, the SDPBA's opinion analysis stated that "Newspapers and magazines throughout the country" believed it was Washington's fault should the US be faced once again with the dilemma of defending (or not) those positions because the Eisenhower administration had done nothing to solve the problem, "despite numerous calls for a review of its China policy." The *Washington Post* declared, "US policymakers must face the fact that the basic problem of American China policy will continue as long as we fail to grapple with the essential problem of Formosa. Some long-range planning must be done to our entire, unrealistic policy in that area." Likewise, a *Wall Street Journal* editorial stated, "It is nonsense to pretend that the Nationalist Government is the Government of China. The sooner we face the fact, the sooner we will be able to extricate ourselves from the explosive situation in the Taiwan Straits." "The importance of Quemoy and Matzu may be described as hand-made," Joseph Alsop contended, "to give some color of reality to the administration's unleashing of Chiang Kai-shek."[27]

Finally, a SDBPA opinion poll revealed that 85% of the respondents believed that the US should not get involved and should turn the issue over to the UN. Of those interviewed, 40% also declared that Washington could have avoided the crisis if it had relaxed its hard line policy against the PRC.[28]

However, the Chinese Communists continued to shell Jinmen heavily throughout August and September and managed to isolate the islands. In early September, the JCS informed the President that as the crisis escalated, "conventional weapons" would not be enough to destroy the

[26] Ibid.
[27] Ibid.
[28] Ibid.

Communist installations. The US would need to use tactical nuclear weapons. The question, as Admiral Arleigh Burke said, was:

> Are we to risk loss of prestige and influence in the world, through the loss of the offshore islands occasioned by the failure to exert a maximum defense; or are we to risk loss of prestige and influence, through limited use of nuclear weapons to hold the islands?[29]

The JCS agreed unanimously that the US should use nuclear weapons. Failure to do so would project an image of US weakness across the world. More importantly, the entire administration's national security policy would need to be revised.[30]

Dulles, who had not approved of Eisenhower's August 29th decision to refuse authorization of possible use of tactical nuclear weapons, fully supported the assessment of the JCS. As he told General Twining, "There is no use in having a lot of stuff and never being able to use it." However, he was also aware that it would be a difficult pill to swallow for the American public. It was necessary to create an adequate information program to bring the American people on board. First, however, he had to persuade the President of the necessity to change the plan to defend US national security.[31]

On September 4th, Dulles met with Eisenhower in Newport, Rhode Island, where the President was vacationing. In making his case, he openly told him that his decision not to approve use of tactical nuclear weapons was fundamentally a rejection of US national security policy. "We had acknowledged the risk of political and psychological dangers of the use of these weapons when we decided to include them in our arsenal. If we will not use them when the chips are down because of public opinion, we must revise our defense set up." Eisenhower still worried that a Communist response might not be limited to Jinmen but it would extend to Taiwan and could quickly escalate into a world war. The US could not expect to fight and win a war without its people's support. Dulles did not give up and in the end, the President conceded that national security interests were a far higher priority than public approval. He agreed to authorize use of tactical nuclear weapons.[32]

---

[29] "Taiwan Straits: Issues Developed in Discussions with the JCS," September 2, 1958, DDE Papers, International Series, box 10, DDEL.

[30] Ibid.

[31] Ibid.

[32] Memorandum of Conversation with the President, September 4, 1958, JFD papers, White House Memo Series, box 7, DDEL.

Having swayed the President, it was now time to turn to the public. Before leaving Newport, to raise public awareness of the situation in the Straits and at the same time deter the Chinese Communists from any further moves, Dulles read a very strong statement to the press. He reiterated "The President is authorized by the Joint Congressional Resolution of Congress to employ the armed forced of the United States for securing and protecting...Quemoy and Matsu." Moreover, "We have recognized that the securing and protecting of Quemoy and Matsu have increasingly become related to the defense of Taiwan." Dulles concluded that statement by extending the possibility of resuming the ambassadorial talks with the PRC to achieve a settlement, however, in a question-and-answer session after reading the speech he clarified that if Jinmen was threatened, the United States might bomb mainland China. "If I were on the Chinese side," he declared, "I would certainly think very hard before I went ahead in the face of this statement."[33]

In the first phase of the crisis, the administration clearly opted for a hard line policy which included the possible use of tactical nuclear weapons with the hope of deterring the Chinese Communists from attacking the offshore islands. Although the President had initially been reluctant to authorize their use because of fear of a public outcry, ultimately American national security interests prevailed and he agreed to step up US commitment in the Straits. He also felt confident that having made the right decision for the country, he would eventually be able to sway the public to support his views. In congratulating Dulles on his September 4th Newport speech, Eisenhower remarked that although the American people might not welcome Washington's position at the moment, he was sure, "There is no question that they will be for defending Quemoy and Matsu because of their belief in me and in the administration." Dulles' statement had already "done a good deal to this end."[34]

[33] "Authorised Statement by the Secretary of State following his review with the President on the situation in the Formosa Straits area," September 4, 1958, JFD papers, White House Memoranda Series, box 7, DDEL. Transcript of News Conference, September 4, 1958, JFD papers, White House Memoranda Series, box 7, DDEL.
[34] Telephone call to the President in Newport, September 8, 1958, JFD papers, Telephone Calles Series, box 13, DDEL.

THE SECOND TAIWAN CRISIS: PHASE TWO

The President proved himself to be seriously mistaken in his assessment of public opinion. Popular reaction at home and across the world to Dulles' speech showed clear opposition to any US involvement in the Straits. Between September 5th and 9th, 1958, the White House received 640 letters regarding the Taiwan Straits crisis. Of those, 470 wanted to avoid war at all costs. 89 believed that referring the issue to the UN was the only way forward. And only 39 supported the administration's stance of defending the islands. Correspondence received by the State Department was even more negative. Eighty percent of the letters received showed the individuals were opposed to Washington's policy. A Gallup poll showed that 62% of Americans opposed aiding the Nationalists to hold the islands if that meant all-out war and the use of nuclear weapons. Only 18% supported such aid even if it involved all-out war and atomic weapons, while 82% of the respondents wanted the issue to be discussed at the UN before resorting to military force.[35]

The SDBPA reported that the editorial opinion of major papers criticized the US policy of making the islands the first line of defense. The *New York Times* called the domino theory "too naive" and thought the administration's reasoning that the Chinese Communists never had authority over those islands made no sense. In a letter to President Eisenhower, Senator Theodore F. Green (D-RI), chairman of the Senate Foreign Relations Committee, declared that Jinmen was not vital to the defense of either Taiwan or the United States and that he opposed "military involvement at the wrong time, in the wrong place, and on issues not of vital concern to our own security, and all this without Allies." Senator John F. Kennedy (D-Mass.) gave a public speech against a policy of intervention. Democratic Congressional leaders Sam Rayburn (TX) and Lyndon Johnson (TX), who just a few weeks earlier had championed US intervention in Lebanon, now condemned the President's decision.[36]

---

[35] Letters and Telegrams regarding the Formosa and the Offshore Islands as of September 9, 1958, DDE Papers, International Series, box 10, DDEL; quoted in George Eliades C. "Once More Unto the Breach: Eisenhower, Dulles, and Public Opinion During the Offshore Islands Crisis of 1958," *Journal of American-East Asian Relations* 4 (1993): 68–87.

[36] "Press Reaction to Secretary Dulles 4 September speech," DOS, AI568J, box 1, NAII; Green to Eisenhower, September 29, 1958, JFD Papers, White House Memorandum Series, box 7, DDEL.

In summarizing the state of American public opinion, the Deputy Director of the United States Information Agency (USIA), Abbott Washburn, wrote, "Unless there is some tragic triggering incident, I don't believe that American public opinion can be brought to support our going to war, with the attendant risk of nuclear involvement over Quemoy and Matsu." He also sketched a very bleak outline of world reaction to a US intervention to defend the offshore islands. According to a USIA analysis, only the governments of Nationalist China, South Korea, South Vietnam, Thailand, and the Philippines might approve of such action and the use of nuclear weapons. Even in those countries the people had mixed feelings. "In brief," the report concluded, "the governments and the peoples of every country in the world would condemn us and see us as aggressors."[37]

Historians George C. Eliades and Appu K. Soman have argued that those public opinion data brought about a major shift in American policy and forced the Eisenhower administration to abandon the offshore islands. "Every principal actor on the American side of the crisis altered his stance within a one-week period. Public opinion caused this change," the former wrote.[38] However, while it is true that the JCS reassessed the importance of Jinmen and Matsu to the defense of Taiwan and concluded that because of the hostile international and domestic feelings toward the use of nuclear weapons it would be better "to demilitarize the islands with the Nationalists in control," Eisenhower still resolved to defend those positions.[39]

The President admitted that the "opinion poll data shook him" and that it "would probably be a good thing" to abandon the islands to appease the public. However, once again, the importance of projecting an image of a very strong America that stood by its allies prevailed. As the President told special assistant Gordon Gray, giving up Jinmen and Matsu meant giving up on Southeast Asia entirely. The countries in the area would think the US did not live up to its tough rhetoric and would even-

---

[37] Enclosure to Washburn to Eisenhower, September 9, 1958; World Radio and Press Reaction to President Eisenhower's speech of September 11, Daily Report, Supplement World Series, September 16, 1958, DDE Papers, International Series, box 10, DDEL.

[38] Eliades, "Once More Unto the Breach: Eisenhower, Dulles, and Public Opinion During the Offshore Islands Crisis of 1958," 68–87; Appu K., Soman, "Who's Daddy in the Taiwan Straits? The Offshore Islands Crisis of 1958," *The Journal of American East-Asian Relations* 3 (1994): 373–398.

[39] JCS memorandum to Secretary of Defense, DDE Papers, International Series, box 19, DDEL; Memorandum of Conversation with the President, September 11, 1958, JFD papers, White House Memoranda Series, box 7, DDEL.

tually turn to the Communist sphere for protection and support, which was something the US could definitely not allow.[40]

Eisenhower was still convinced that a strong public message would eventually sway popular feelings to support his position. This time, however, he would not delegate the task to Dulles or any other administration officials. The President staked his personal reputation by directly addressing the nation in a radio and television speech. Comparing Chinese Communist aggression to that of Hitler's Germany, he remarked that allowing the PRC to seize the offshore islands would constitute appeasement on Munich's level. Eisenhower continued, "Let us suppose that the Chinese Communists conquer Quemoy. Would that be the end of the story? We know that it would not be the end of the story. History teaches us when powerful despots can gain something through aggression, they try, by the same methods to gain more and more."[41]

Eisenhower reiterated the constant theme that containment of the threat was essential and deterrence with American military was the best way to achieve it. He then noted that all Chinese propaganda indicated that assault in the islands was a prelude to an attack on Taiwan to assert the validity of the Formosa Resolution.[42] His most forceful passage, which left no doubt as to American resolve, came well before the end of the address:

> There will be no retreat in the face of armed aggression...Some misguided persons have said that Quemoy is nothing to become excited about. They said the same about South Korea, about Vietnam and about Lebanon. Now I assure you that no American boy will be asked by me to fight just for Quemoy. But those who make up the armed force—and I believe the American people as a whole—do stand ready to defend the principle that armed forces shall not be used for aggressive purposes...if we are not ready to defend these principles, then indeed tragedy after tragedy would befall us.[43]

The speech did not achieve the goal desired. The Chinese Communists' blockade remained in place and the CIA reported that without supplies, the situation on the islands was getting more and more critical.

[40] Gordon, Gray, Memorandum of Record, September 12, 1958, DDE Papers, Special Assistant Series, box 3, DDEL.

[41] "Radio and Television Report to the American People Regarding the Situation on the Formosa Straits," September 11, 1958, EPP, 696.

[42] Ibid.

[43] Ibid.

Following Eisenhower's September 11th address to the nation, the administration worked hard to present a strong and coordinated public message on the importance of defending the offshore islands, even if that included the use of nuclear weapons. In the time span of three weeks, Washington presented its case to the American people on 23 occasions. The strongest public statement was delivered by Dulles on September 27th. Speaking before the Far East American Council of Commerce and Industry, he compared Jinmen and Matzu to Berlin. Declaring the fight over those positions as essential to prevent a Communist takeover of Asia as protecting Berlin was to Europe, he reiterated US intentions to defend the islands.[44]

The public reaction to those statements was very negative. The *New York Times* scoffed "Matsu and Quemoy have become Berlin only because Generalissimo Chiang put a third of his forces there." The *San Francisco Chronicle* declared the islands "are no more or less Nationalist Chinese territories than the Techens." The *Wall Street Journal* declared, "The flaws in the analogy are so many and so obvious as hardly to merit discussion...Berlin dense cluster of meanings, lies at the center of world struggle. How close to center geographically, politically, military or morally is Quemoy?"[45]

The SDBPA reported that 95% of the editorial pages of the national press were now against the administration's policy of intervention. Of those, "a considerable amount strongly supports" either neutralization of Taiwan through the UN or US recognition of the Beijing regime as the best way to end the crisis.[46] Similarly, a September 28th Gallup poll revealed that "Public opinion overwhelmingly favors letting the UN trying to handle the perplexing problems of Quemoy and Matsu." Likewise, a SDBPA poll showed that 91% of respondents declared they "would like to see the US work out solution in the UN" and 61% thought it would be a "great idea for Taiwan to be neutralized—that is put under UN protection to avoid any further crisis."[47] Even worse, because of a State Department press leak, a September 28th *New York Times* front page story broke the news that 80% of the 5000 letters and telegrams

[44] CT September 23 through 30, 1958, DOS, AI568P, box 30, NAII.

[45] "Special public review in reaction to Secretary Dulles's 27 September speech," September 28, 1958, DOS, AI568J, box 1, NAII.

[46] Ibid.

[47] Ibid.

Table 7.1   Editorial opinion on US intervention in the Taiwan Straits, September 1958

Opposed to administration policy			In favor of intervening in Taiwan
Against US involvement	US should recognize PRC	Ceasefire— Neutralization UN	
Cleveland Plain Dealer, Marquis Childs, Chicago Daily News, The Washington Evening Star, Chicago Sun-Times, Nashville Tennessean, The Boston Daily Globe, The New York Herald Tribune, Edward R. Murrow—CBS, St Louis Post Dispatch, The Washington Post, The New York Times, Minneapolis Tribune, Philadelphia Inquirer, Courier Journal Kentucky Milwaukee Journal, Kansas City Star, Minneapolis Star, San Francisco Chronicle, Los Angeles Times, The Denver Post, Arthur Krock—NYT	Quincy Howe—NBC, The Casper (Wyoming) Tribune Herald, Christian Science Monitor, Wall Street Journal, St Petersburg Times, St Lake Tribune, New Orleans Times—Picayune, Cleveland Plain Dealer, James Reston—NYT, Capital Times (Madison, Wisconsin), Walter Lippmann, The Chattanooga Times, Sioux Falls (South Dakota) Angus Leader, San Francisco Chronicle	New York World Telegram, Boston Herald, The Hartford Courant, The Evening Star (Washington), Des Moines (Iowa) Register & Tribune, The Chicago Sun-Times, The San Francisco Chronicle	Luce's Publications, The Chicago Tribune, The Manchester Union, Leader, The Oakland Tribune

List is meant to be representative not exhaustive

Source: "Special public review in reaction to Secretary Dulles's 27 September speech," September 28, 1958, DOS, AI568J, box 1, NAII

received by the State Department in the previous three weeks opposed the administration (Table 7.1).[48]

---

[48] "US Public Against Intervention in New Formosa Crisis," The New York Times, September 28, 1958, 1.

A very welcome breakthrough took place on September 29th when the JCS reported that the supply crisis had finally been broken because US "convoys successfully escorted Chinese Nationalist supplies to the beach" on Jinmen. Three days later, Beijing announced a ceasefire effective for one week, if Washington stopped delivering supplies to the islands. That ended on October 8th.[49]

Relieved by the ceasefire news, the press and the public now demanded a settlement of the Taiwan situation. The SDBPA reported that "neutralization of the entire area" was by now the only policy supported by the public but Eisenhower and Dulles refused to acquiesce to popular demand and abandon America's Nationalist ally. While the President agreed that the offshore islands problem had become untenable both domestically and internationally and that those positions had to be evacuated to prevent another crisis, he rejected the idea of turning Taiwan over to the UN.[50]

In what his secretary Ann Whitman called a "strong letter" to Dulles, Eisenhower declared that Jiang be given extensive amphibious lift capability and destroyers to "make him really mobile." After obtaining those, Jiang would not need the offshore islands to defend Taiwan or mount an attack on mainland China and could therefore remove "all or nearly all his garrisons" from those positions. By doing so the President believed that the US would no longer be faced with "the thorny issue" of those insignificant positions and at the same time could still protect its national security interests in the Far East without losing face with Jiang. In a surprising change of direction, Dulles declared during a press conference that Washington was now supporting a reduction of Nationalist troops on the offshore islands.[51]

Beijing was not entirely pleased with Washington's response and on October 20th, it resumed shelling of the offshore islands, which prevented Dulles from persuading Jiang to reduce his forces on those territories. The crisis concluded on October 25th, with the Chinese Communists announc-

[49] Memorandum to President, September 28, 1958, DDE Papers, JCS Series, box 850, DDEL; Memorandum on the Situation in the Formosa Straits, October 9, 1958, DDE Papers, NSC Series, box 815, DDEL.

[50] "Special Review of Public Opinion," October 1958, DOS, AI568J, box 1, NAII.

[51] Eisenhower to Dulles, October 7, 1958, DDE Papers, Ann Whitmann Series, box 13, DDEL; JFD press conference, October 8, 1958, JFD Papers, press conferences 1958, box 17, Seely, G. Mudd Library, University of Princeton, New Jersey (hereafter JFD papers followed by box number and ML).

ing that they will only carry on with the shelling on odd numbered days so that the Nationalists could resupply every other day.[52]

HARD LINE UNTIL THE END

The crisis and its unclear conclusion left the administration's public image scarred. While public opinion rejoiced at the ceasefire news, questions on how the US again got involved in such a dangerous situation, and pressure to put Taiwan under UN protection with a guarantee of neutrality and to review Washington's China policy persisted. Eisenhower and Dulles remained undeterred and carried on with their hard line policy against the PRC.[53]

The first casualty of the administration's China policy was the GOP representation in Congress after the mid-term elections. Of the staunchest Nationalist supporters, only Walter Judd won re-election. The Senator from Formosa and Minority leader, William F. Knowland, decided to run for governor of California but he lost his bid to Edmund G. Brown. At the age of 79 years, Senator H. Alexander Smith decided to retire. Overall, the Democrats won a 283 to 154 majority in the House and a 66 to 34 Senate majority.[54]

Clair Engle (CA) became the spokesperson for the Democratic Party's opposition to the administration's China policy. A few weeks into office, he delivered one of the strongest attacks against the White House to date: "I am convinced that our China policy needs critical re-examination. I am prepared to dispute the premise that our present policy is adequate and that nothing about it should be changed." Of all the mistakes made by Eisenhower and Dulles, he particularly condemned the decision not to respect the principle of reciprocity when exchanging journalists, the refusal to remove the China trade differential, and support for Jiang's unrealistic aspirations of ever returning to the mainland. The time had come, according to Engle, to let the UN take over in solving the Taiwan problem and begin earnest negotiations with the Chinese Communists.[55]

---

[52] Memorandum of Meeting Between Secretary Dulles and Generalissimo Chiang Kai-shek, October 21, 1958, JFD papers, box 67, ML.

[53] CT, October through November 1958, DOS, AI568P, box 30, NAII.

[54] Leonard Kusnitz, *Public Opinion and Foreign Policy: America's China Policy, 1949–1979* (Westport: Greenwood Press, 1984). 81.

[55] "Freshman Engle on China Policy," the *New York Times*, February 6, 1959, 1.

Similarly, in an interview with Chalmers Roberts for the *Washington Post*, the new Chairman of the Senate Foreign Relations Committee, Senator William Fulbright, declared that although he did not "quarrel with administration's non-recognition policy under existing circumstances," the US ought to explore possibilities of some type of over-all Far Eastern settlement involving Korea, Vietnam, and Taiwan. He added that he would let Red China and the world know "we are willing to negotiate. Continued reiteration of our position that we are not going to recognize them now or ever under any circumstances is not quite realistic."[56] Concurring with Fulbright, Senator Kennedy stated on a TV broadcast to New York stations that he was opposed to diplomatic recognition of Red China "under present conditions, but the quicker we could work out an amicable relationship with them, the better off we'd all be." Another prominent Democrat and former Presidential hopeful, Adlai Stevenson, however, openly called for Red China's admission on grounds that current policy of "isolating China" had been a failure.[57]

Launching a lengthy discussion of US-China policy in the House similarly to Senator Engle's, Representative Charles O. Porter (D-OR) criticized "our hopelessly confused and outmoded China policy" and introduced an amendment to deny all military aid to Jiang Jieshi unless he cut his 600,000-man army to 200,000. Adding, "We should actively encourage exchange of newsmen and other measures to develop trade relations," he proposed a trade mission to China as a first step toward ascertaining "recent and reliable facts" on which China policy could be based.[58]

The Democrats were not alone in questioning the administration's China policy. Some Republicans were also beginning to see cracks in Eisenhower's hard line stance. Senator Alexander Wiley (WI), one of the original signatories of the Committee of One Million petition of 1953, reported that he had asked the Foreign Relations Committee "to undertake an examination of current events in Communist China," and possibly come up with a new plan that could lead to an improvement in Sino-American relations.[59]

[56] Roberts, Chalmers, "An Interview with Senator William Fulbright," the *Washington Post*, December 6, 1958, 7.

[57] CT, January 2 through 23, 1959, DOS, AI568P, box 30, NAII.

[58] Ibid.

[59] CT, January 24 through February 23, 1959, DOS, AI568P, box 30, NAII.

Wiley's initiative resulted in the "Conlon report," named that because research for the document had been mainly conducted by Conlon Associates, a San Francisco research firm. The report concluded: "The Chinese Communist Government will have a lengthy tenure." The exception with regard to Taiwan was: "Either Taiwan will be joined with the mainland China or the process of Taiwanization will continue. In the concrete terms of the present, if Taiwan does not go to the Communists, it will go increasingly Taiwanese."[60] The report suggested that the current policy of "containment through isolation" was no longer effective and recommended instead to explore new possibilities for negotiations with Beijing, provided of course, that the PRC was willing "to coexist" with the US.[61]

A few weeks later the Rockefeller Brothers Foundation published a report entitled "The Mid-Century Challenge to US Foreign Policy." The document essentially held the same conclusions and made the same recommendations as the Conlon report. US-China policy needed a radical reassessment and the first step to achieve that was to allow US newsmen to visit Communist China and obtain first-hand information about it. "The need for complete knowledge of what is going on is permanent…that lesser interests or concerns should give way to ensure full reporting by Americans on the spot." While the report did not openly advocate a normalization of Sino-American relations, it did state: "We must not let emotions or difference of ideology close the door to such possibilities of better relations with the Chinese people as they may arise in years to come."[62]

Both reports received wide-spread coverage in the press. The Luce publications, William Knowland's *Oakland Tribune,* and columnist Joseph Alsop were the only strong opponents to any improvement of Sino-US relations. "An attempt to mollify or tame Mao Tse-tung and his colleagues," the latter wrote in his *Washington Post* column, "by exploration and negotiation," or by US recognition, "will convey an impression of American weakness and retreat to millions in Asia who now fear the Chinese Communists."[63] The SDBPA, however, reported that "the overwhelming

---

[60] The Conlon Report, October 31, 1959, Hagerty Papers, box 67, DDEL.

[61] Ibid.

[62] "The Mid-Century Challenge to US Foreign Policy," Rockefeller Brothers Fund Report, November 1959, Hagerty papers, box 67, DDEL.

[63] "Public Reaction to the Conlon Report and Rockefeller Brothers Fund Report," December 1959, DOS, AI568J, box 1, NAII.

majority of the press" urged that "The widest possible distribution to be given to both documents," which "recommend themselves for their responsible and gradual approach to a permanent solution," in the hope that a proper and constructive public debate on China policy would follow.[64]

Of all the recommendations listed by the reports, the media welcomed first and foremost the exchange of newspapermen between the US and the PRC. That possibility was also supported by most of the public. The SDBPA reported that a National Opinion Research Center (NORC) poll revealed that 92% of respondents favored sending American journalists to Communist China in the hope of obtaining more precise information of what was going on in that country. However, 85% of those also expressed doubts that the Beijing regime propaganda machine would allow "honest reporting" to take place. Similarly, removal of the trade differential with the PRC was favored by 75% of the editorial opinion pages and 90% of the public.[65]

Press and popular sentiments about the recognition issue were not, however, so clear. The SDBPA reported that while a clear majority of publications (95%) wanted a review of China policy, only 35% of them openly advocated establishing diplomatic relations with the PRC and its admission into the UN, 50% favored negotiations to relax tensions. Several nationwide NORC and Gallup polls taken throughout 1959 revealed that 65% of the respondents were still against full diplomatic relations with only 35% in support it. Of the national sample, 55% were, however, in favor of considering negotiations with Beijing at a higher level than ambassadorial talks.[66] The religious world also made its reaction to the two reports public. On November 21, 1959 in Cleveland, the World Order Study Conference of the National Council of Churches of Christ in the USA "passed a unanimous resolution in favor of US recognition of the PRC and its admission to the United Nations."[67]

In reaction to the Conlon report, the COOM released a document which recited the history of US public and private opposition to the softening of American policy toward Chinese Communists and expressing doubts about the competence of Conlon associates:

[64] Ibid.
[65] Ibid.
[66] Ibid.
[67] Ibid.; Bachrack, *The Committee of One Million*, 143–151.

To our best knowledge, Conlon Associates conducted no serious investigation of either sentiment of the American people or their leaders, more important, sentiments of our Allies in Asia. The Committee is the one organization in the United States dedicated to the single purpose of opposing recognition and admission in the UN. We were not consulted at any time.[68]

It then orchestrated a poll of Protestant Clergymen and bought a full-page advertisement in the *New York Times* to report that those, 7000 in total, had signed a petition to oppose Sino-American relations normalization. A few weeks later a COOM letter updated the numbers to 9088 clergymen, with 7837 opposed to recognition or Beijing's entry into the UN. At some point one pamphlet claimed that 46,000 Clergymen had been interviewed and all were opposed to any form of relaxing tensions with China whatsoever. From COOM records, it seems that those figures are not reliable, but they are rather the result of fabrication; a hypothesis supported by historian Stanley Bachrack. Because of the inconsistency of those data and the Committee's exaggerated claims, its counter-propaganda did not have much effect on public opinion.[69]

While the issue was picked over and covered by the press, the SDBPA reported that "the effect on the public was again minimal." Those publications and citizens opposed to sitting Communist China in the UN simply saw it as further confirmation of their belief that establishing diplomatic relations with the PRC "would be an affront to international decency." Whereas those in favor argued that "it would be easier to hold the Red Chinese accountable inside the UN."[70]

The public was not alone in asking for a review of China policy. Administration officials had also been discussing the possibility of altering Washington's stance toward the PRC. Mentioning the lack of allied and domestic public support as "a serious impediment to the effective conduct of US-China policy," in October 1958, Assistant Secretary for Policy Planning Smith proposed that Dulles undertake a study of Sino-American

[68] Publications relating to the Committee of One Million Against Admission of Red China to the United Nations, 1954–1966, Tamiment Library, NYU.
[69] Ibid.; Bachrack, Stanley, *The Committee of One Million, "China Lobby" Politics*, 148.
[70] "Public Reaction to COOM's propaganda campaign," May/June 1959, DOS, AI568J, box 1, NAII.

relations from the last 10 years, with the view of "shifting to a softer approach towards Beijing."[71]

A few months later the Regional Planning Adviser in the Bureau of Far Eastern Affairs, Mr. Green, sent a memorandum regarding the offshore islands to Walter Robertson, the Assistant Secretary of State for Far Eastern Affairs. Claiming "US prestige has become closely identified with the maintenance of the Chinese Nationalist position on the offshore islands," the document argued that "in view of the general lack of allied support for this position and the questionable strategic importance of these islands, the desirability of a review of China policy toward the offshore islands seems to be indicated."[72]

The reactions of Eisenhower and Dulles were very cold to those suggestions. Dismissing them as "unthinkable at the moment," the President firmly stated during a NSC meeting that although he was aware that neither the public nor the allies supported the administration's current position toward Beijing, as long as "I am in the White House, our China policy is not going to change." Dulles referred to the danger of possible leaks if studies of this type were to be made, and mentioned the serious implications it might have for the security of the regime in Taiwan. Concurring with Eisenhower that US-China policy should not change so far as recognition and admission into the UN was concerned, he further added that Washington had made a serious mistake in recognizing the USSR and that he would be much happier about a UN without Soviet membership.[73]

Consequently, despite an increasing call from the public for a review of US-China policy and dissent among the administration officials, no major change occurred in Sino-American relations in the last two years of Eisenhower's presidency. The President maintained his opposition to any relaxation toward the PRC even after Dulles' death in the spring of 1959. Only one major concession took place; upon his swearing in, new Secretary of State Christian Herter announced that following the increasing pressure from the media world, the State Department had validated the pass-

---

[71] Memorandum by Assistant Secretary of State for Policy Planning (Smith), October 1958, *FRUS*, IV, 1958–1960, 462–463.

[72] Memorandum from the regional Planning Adviser of Far Eastern Affairs (Green) to the Assistant Secretary of State for Far Eastern Affairs (Robertson), February 18, 1959, *FRUS*, IV, 1958–1960, 532–533.

[73] Dulles to Smith, December 15, 1958, JFD Papers, box 87, ML; 404 National Security Meeting, April 30, 1959, *FRUS*, IV, 1958–1960, 762.

ports of 33 journalists for travel to mainland China and anticipated that the Attorney General would waive restrictions on Communist Chinese newsmen who wished to enter the American territory.[74]

Two reasons explain the administration's' decision to pursue its hard line policy. First, Washington thought that the hard line policy was paying dividends as demonstrated by the latest Taiwan crisis where the Chinese Communists felt intimidated and insecure by the US line. A January 1959 memorandum prepared by Dulles and endorsed by Eisenhower described the firm US response to Beijing threats in the Straits as "effective" and the menace of nuclear weapons as "successful" in bringing the crisis to a conclusion. Second, for the same reason, many top administration figures, including Eisenhower, became convinced that America's Communist adversaries were experiencing serious differences which Washington could systematically manipulate.[75]

In October 1958, Allen Dulles reported to the Council of Foreign Relations that "all was not well" in the Communist world. The Soviet Union had been particularly disturbed by China's rise in prestige and power in Asia and saw that more as a challenge rather than a benefit for the Sino-Soviet bloc. In the words of the CIA Director:

> Many little indications convince me Moscow is nervous about the future relationship (Our Ambassador in Moscow shares this view). Interesting that so far as we know the Soviets have not given the Chinese nuclear weapons, for which we suspect Peiping has longed since asked. Also interesting, there is no evidence of new long term capital credits to Peiping. Not sure Moscow and Peiping always in full accord on foreign policy tactics, perhaps even in the Taiwan Straits. The Chinese may be more brash than the Soviets, less concerned over nuclear devastation…these things are difficult to judge, but I am inclined to see the Soviets as the more cautious partner, not anxious to see the Chicom strength grow too rapidly, but yielding (where essential to maintain amity) to importunities of their ally.[76]

The CIA report confirmed for Eisenhower and Dulles that they were correct in insisting on a hard line policy to drive a wedge between the

---

[74] "State Department to Authorise 33 Newspapermen to Travel to Red China," The *New York Times*, May 7, 1959, 1.

[75] Dulles to Eisenhower, January 13, 1958, *FRUS*, IV, 1958–1960, 593–595.

[76] Dulles, Allen, "An Intelligence Review of the Communist Bloc," October 28, 1958, Allen Dulles Papers, box 229, DDEL.

Soviets and the PRC. The document signaled a brief period of détente between Moscow and Washington. In the summer of 1958 the Russians accepted going ahead with control inspections, then Eisenhower announced that the US would suspend nuclear testing for a year. One year later, President Eisenhower invited Nikita Khrushchev to visit the US to discuss outstanding problematic issues.[77]

Those developments in US-Soviet relations which seemed to open the possibility for a genuine détente in the Cold War, combined with the opportunity of exacerbating Sino-Soviet ties, prevailed on the administration's thinking and shaped its rhetorical strategy throughout 1959–1960. A State Department memorandum drafted by Herter in June 1959 clearly stated that because of "possible improvements in Soviet-US relations" and "reports of difficulties between Moscow and Beijing," Washington should adopt a stance of "partial responsibility" in presenting the enemies to the public. Without overpraising the Russian leaders' attempts at relaxing East-West tensions, Herter argued that the administration should make a clear public distinction between Soviet Communists and Chinese Communists. Public utterances should present Moscow as a less dangerous threat to US national security than Beijing and should also state that the Soviet Union was not responsible for the aggressive record of the PRC. In other words, the PRC had to be portrayed as the main enemy of the US.[78]

The public relations strategy had come a long way. Upon taking office in 1953, Eisenhower and Dulles had agreed that presenting a monolithic view of Communism to the public was the best way to sell the administration's policies. Now, seven years later, in approving Herter's memorandum, the President reverted that decision. From June 1959 onward, sentences like "Peiping seeks world domination more than Moscow" or "Mao and his comrades are more dangerous than any Soviet leaders" became the main standards of Washington's rhetoric. At the same time, the administration's public support for Jiang Jieshi increased and culminated with Eisenhower's visit to Taipei as part of his Far East 1960 tour.[79]

---

[77] Robert Divine, *Foreign Policy and US Presidential Elections, 1952–1960* (New York: New Viewpoints, 1974), 183–188; Gordon Chang, *Friends and Enemies, The United States, China and the Soviet Union, 1948–1972* (Stanford: Stanford University press, 1982), 203–208.

[78] Herter to Eisenhower, June 17, 1959, DDE Papers, Herter Series, box 27, DDEL.

[79] *DSB*, June 1959–December 1960.

Sino-Soviet specialist Donald Zagoria has argued that "Washington's indiscriminate hostility certainly exacerbated frictions" between Beijing and Moscow, therefore, from a public relations point of view, the strategy was flawed. By portraying the PRC as the more dangerous enemy, the administration only fueled concern among popular opinion, which in turn further increased calls for a revision of China policy. By the end of 1960, the SDBPA reported that "70 percent of the press and general public favors a review of US-China policy" and that "73 percent of public opinion favored a neutralization of Taiwan through the UN." As throughout his Presidency, Eisenhower had given priority to national security and geopolitical interests rather than popular feelings in approving Herter's memorandum. His determination to protect American borders had prevailed over the public's demands for a reassessment of China policy.[80]

References

Bachrack, Stanley. *The Committee of One Million, "China Lobby" Politics.* New York: Columbia University Press, 1976.

Chang, Gordon. *Friends and Enemies, The United States, China and the Soviet Union, 1948–1972.* Stanford: Stanford University press, 1982.

Divine, Robert. *Foreign Policy and US Presidential Elections, 1952–1960.* New York: New Viewpoints, 1974.

Eisenhower, Dwight D. *The White House Years: Waging Peace.* London: William Heinemann LTD, 1965.

Eliades, George C. "Once More Unto the Breach: Eisenhower, Dulles, and Public Opinion During the Offshore Islands Crisis of 1958." *Journal of American-East Asian Relations* 4 (1993): 68–87.

Funigiello, Philip. *American-Soviet Trade in the Cold War.* Chapel Hill: University of North Carolina Press, 1988.

Kusnitz, Leonard. *Public Opinion and Foreign Policy: America's China Policy, 1949–1979.* Westport: Greenwood Press, 1984.

Soman, Appu K. "Who's Daddy in the Taiwan Straits? The Offshore Islands Crisis of 1958." *The Journal of American East-Asian Relations* 3 (1994): 373–398.

Zhang, Shu Guang. *Economic Cold War, America's Embargo Against China and the Sino-Soviet Alliance, 1949–1963.* Stanford: Stanford University Press, 2001.

---

[80] Gordon, Chang, *Friends and Enemies*, 205–207; "End of the Year Review of Public Opinion on Foreign Policy," December 1960, DOS, AI569J, box 1, NAII.

CHAPTER 8

Conclusions

On Monday, February 21st, 1972, President Richard M. Nixon landed in Beijing (Peiping) to begin a historic one-week visit of Communist China. As he disembarked Air Force One, he offered his right hand to Premier Zhou En-lai (Chou En-lai) who immediately reciprocated. The two shook hands for a long time to make sure that cameras and photographers from all over the world captured the moment. It was a symbolic and meaningful gesture that Nixon hoped would make up for John Foster Dulles's rude refusal to acknowledge Zhou's presence at the Geneva Conference in 1954.[1]

It also represented a complete U-turn of US-China policy of the last twenty years. During the 1960 presidential campaign, John F. Kennedy had accused the Eisenhower administration of having put US national security at risk by committing to the defense of Jinmen (Quemoy) and Matzu (Matsu). However, once in the White House, he continued to carry out his predecessor's hard line strategy toward the People's Republic of China (PRC), as did President Lyndon B. Johnson when he succeeded Kennedy after his tragic death. Indeed, Nixon himself had campaigned, and lost, on the basis that appeasement of any form, was not an option when dealing with the Chinese Communists. All Presidents and candidates, regardless of their political affiliation, ignored the increasing public demands for a revision

---

[1] Margaret MacMillan, *Nixon and Mao: The Week that Changed the World* (New York: Random House, 2007), 21.

© The Author(s) 2018
M. Oliva, *Eisenhower and American Public Opinion on China*,
https://doi.org/10.1007/978-3-319-76195-4_8

213

of China policy in favor of projecting an image of a tough and reliable US throughout Southeast Asia in the 1960s.[2]

However, the international scene changed drastically in the early 1970s. The US was bogged down in an unwinnable war in Vietnam. China was wrecked by the failed experiment of the Cultural Revolution and its relationship with its oldest ally, the Soviet Union, was at an all-time low. Both countries realized that they could benefit from a new friendship. As Nixon's national security advisor, Henry Kissinger, put it: "for both sides necessity dictated that rapprochement occur, and the attempt had to be made no matter who governed in either country." Therefore, in February 1972, Nixon embarked on "a journey for peace."[3]

The trip proved immensely popular among the American public. Although much work went into ensuring that Nixon's week in China would be fully reported by US and world networks and the press, and most of all, that it would be reported in a favorable light, the President did not face any of the public relations challenges that Eisenhower had to manage. Quite the contrary, the public was hungry for information about a country they had known little about for over twenty years. It was also hoped that this new development would finally bring much-needed relaxation in international tensions and possibly a way out of Vietnam.

This concluding chapter evaluates the findings of the analysis of the relationship between American public opinion and the Eisenhower administration's foreign policy toward the PRC. This study suggests that the traditional debate between realists and Wilsonian liberals regarding the influence of public opinion on the foreign policy making process is too simplistic. The impact of popular feelings cannot be dismissed as irrelevant or described as one of the key issues determining national security decisions. Its influence is far more subtle and complicated. President Eisenhower and Secretary of State John Foster Dulles, in line with their realist beliefs about public opinion, did not let popular feelings shape their national security agenda but used them only as warning signs to determine whether opposition was building against a policy. Consequently, public opinion did not influence the administration's hard line policy toward Beijing as previously assumed by historians and political scientists. The

[2] Robert Divine, *Foreign Policy and US Presidential Elections, 1952–1960* (New York: New View Points, 1974).
[3] Quoted in Margaret MacMillan, *Nixon and Mao*, 7.

decision to not relax tensions with Communist China remained solely with the President and the Secretary of State, yet public attitudes still had a significant effect on the implementation of that strategy.

Both Eisenhower and Dulles tailored their views and rhetoric during the 1952 presidential campaign to meet the public's favor; once in the White House however, they were determined not to let popular feelings shape their agenda. They believed that public opinion lacked sufficient knowledge and understanding to make a valuable contribution to the formulation of foreign policy, therefore, it was the government's duty to make the right decision. Considering, however, that public support for a certain policy was necessary for it to be successful, particularly in the case of military conflict, they made several efforts to educate and shape mass attitudes.

To keep a constant eye on popular mood, they regularly consulted opinion polls and reviews of Congressional opinion, checked four to five daily newspapers as well as a variety of media surveys prepared by the State Department and the White House, and often paid attention to the mail-bag. The information about public opinion that those channels conveyed did not serve as a source of policy innovation or direction. The administration used that information to formulate propaganda programs to persuade the public to support its policy approach rather than to implement what the people wanted. That indicates that public opinion affected policy more often in later, rather than in the earlier stages of decisions.

The information also disputes political scientist Douglas C. Foyle's argument that both the President and the Secretary of State were willing to modify their policies to appease the public. They were certainly keen on rallying popular support once a decision had been made in the field of foreign policy but they would never have compromised US national security. They made only two concessions: first, agreeing to sit down with Chinese Communist representatives in Geneva, and second, allowing the relatives of those American prisoners still held by the PRC to travel to Beijing, followed in 1960 by American newspapermen. Neither decision would have jeopardized US national security.[4]

However, the administration was not always successful in devising its public information campaign though. Despite Eisenhower's and Dulles's confidence in their ability to sway the public, they never managed to recover the loss of support for their hard line China policy after the war

[4] Douglass C. Foyle, *Counting the Public In: Presidents, Public Opinion, and Foreign Policy* (New York: Columbia University Press, 1999).

scare that was triggered by the first Taiwan crisis. Although Washington
was in a powerful position to shape the reporting about China thanks to
the routine of the press of the 1950s and the US traveling ban to the PRC,
its efforts to mold public opinion failed.

While the public had initially favored a policy of total hostility against
Beijing and supported the Nationalist government on Taiwan, the administration's aggressive rhetoric and fear that a nuclear war may break out
over a state of no importance forced a change in popular feelings and
resulted in an increase in calls for a reassessment of US-Sino relations. By
the end of 1960, the State Department Bureau of Public Affairs reported
that according to a National Opinion Research Center poll, 56% of those
interviewed believed that opposition to establishing diplomatic relations
with the PRC and its seating in the United Nations (UN) had reached an
all-time low. The same poll revealed that only 10% of respondents favored
US withdrawal from the UN in the event of admission of the PRC, and
62% favored trading with Beijing.[5]

In that sense, historians Kenneth Osgood, Martin Medhurst, and Ira
Charnus are correct when they argue that President Eisenhower's rhetoric
created a paradox. Eisenhower claimed to want peace but needed to wage
war rhetorically to create national unity and support for his foreign policy.
By doing so, he exacerbated the already hostile popular feelings toward
the enemy and increased public fear, hence making peace more difficult.[6]

Yet, despite the lack of popular support, the administration pursued its
policy of unrelenting pressure toward Beijing. National security interests
were the main reasons behind that decision. Both Eisenhower and Dulles
believed that a hostile stance toward the PRC would make it easier to drive
a wedge between Moscow and Beijing. They also feared that relaxing tensions with the Chinese Communists would project an image of American
weakness in the Far East, therefore, opening the door to a Communist
conquest of the rest of Asia.

[5] "Special Public Survey of US Public Opinion on PRC," December 1960, DOS, AI568N, box 33, NAII.

[6] Kenneth Osgood, *Total Cold War: Eisenhower's Secret Propaganda Battle at Home and Abroad* (Lawrence: University Press of Kansas, 2006); Ira Chernus, *Eisenhower's Atoms for Peace* (College Station: Texas A&M University Press, 2002); Chris Tudda, "Re-Enacting the Story of Tantalus: Eisenhower, Dulles and the Failed Rhetoric of Liberation," *Journal of Cold War Studies* 7 (2005): 3–35; and *The Truth Is Our Weapon: The Rhetorical Diplomacy of Dwight D. Eisenhower and John Foster Dulles* (Baton Rouge: Louisiana State University Press, 2006).

The traditional assumption that American public hostility toward the PRC forced the Eisenhower administration to abandon any plans of relaxing tensions with Beijing is therefore wrong. The argument put forward by David Mayers and Nancy Bernkopf Tucker that Eisenhower's fear of losing support from the Republican right wing in Congress shaped his China policy is not correct either. While the GOP old guard might have been a problem in the early years of the administration, by 1957, its influence had diminished considerably, leaving the Committee of One Million against the Admission of Communist China in the United Nations as the only significant source of opposition to any form of contact with the PRC. That combined with the death of Senator Joseph McCarthy (R-WS) and the fear of nuclear war allowed a freer debate on US-China policy to emerge. With the Democratic Party in full control of Congress after the 1958 elections, had Eisenhower wanted to make a change, he would have certainly not been restrained by his own party.

Finally, the argument by traditionalist scholars that John Foster Dulles was "the indisputably conceptual fount, as well as, the prime mover," of US foreign policy during those years is also incorrect. Had Eisenhower been dominated by his Secretary of State, he could have pushed for a new direction in US-China policy after Dulles' death in the spring of 1959. Instead, the President fully shared Dulles' view of the enemy and how to handle the situation. In that sense, the two were "a team," as Richard Immerman had written.[7]

REFERENCES

Chernus, Ira. *Eisenhower's Atoms for Peace*. College Station: Texas A&M University Press, 2002.

Divine, Robert. *Foreign Policy and US Presidential Elections, 1952–1960*. New York: New View Points, 1974.

Foyle, Douglass C. *Counting the Public In: Presidents, Public Opinion, and Foreign Policy*. New York: Columbia University Press, 1999.

Immerman, Richard, ed. *John Foster Dulles and the Diplomacy of Cold War*. Princeton: Princeton University Press, 1990.

MacMillan, Margaret. *Nixon and Mao: The Week that Changed the World*. New York: Random House, 2007.

---

[7] Richard Immerman, ed. *John Foster Dulles and the Diplomacy of Cold War* (Princeton: Princeton University Press, 1990), p. xxi.

Osgood, Kenneth. *Total Cold War: Eisenhower's Secret Propaganda Battle at Home and Abroad*. Lawrence: University Press of Kansas, 2006.

Tudda, Chris. "Re-Enacting the Story of Tantalus: Eisenhower, Dulles and the Failed Rhetoric of Liberation." *Journal of Cold War Studies* 7 (2005): 3–35.

———. *The Truth Is Our Weapon: The Rhetorical Diplomacy of Dwight D. Eisenhower and John Foster Dulles*. Baton Rouge: Louisiana State University Press, 2006.

Index[1]

[1] Note: Page numbers followed by 'n' refer to notes.

© The Author(s) 2018   219
M. Oliva, *Eisenhower and American Public Opinion on China*,
https://doi.org/10.1007/978-3-319-76195-4

Committee of One Million against the
  Admission of the People's
  Republic of China in the United
  Nations (Committee of One
  Million), 4, 184–185
Committee to Defend America by
  Aiding Anti-Communist China, 23
Communism, 2, 12, 17, 22, 25, 28,
  30, 31, 34, 35, 42, 44, 45, 49,
  59, 66, 77, 85, 87, 89, 92, 105,
  123, 144, 168, 175, 210
Communists, 1–6, 9–11, 15, 16,
  19–21, 23–32, 35, 38–40, 42–45,
  49–51, 59, 62–82, 86, 87, 117,
  183, 213
Congress, 3, 4, 8, 11, 18, 19, 22,
  34, 35, 50, 53, 55, 56, 61,
  68, 69, 79, 85, 86, 91, 94–96,
  99, 102–106, 108, 114, 117,
  118, 123–128, 130, 133, 134,
  136–139, 141, 143, 146, 150,
  151, 155, 157, 158, 168, 178,
  179, 184, 186n6, 193, 196,
  203, 217
Conlon Report, 205, 205n60,
  205n63, 206
Council of Foreign Relations, 3, 209

D
Dechen Islands, 64
Dienbienphu, 10, 85
Dulles, Allen, 72, 93, 191, 192, 209,
  209n76
Dulles, John Foster, 3, 3n5, 5, 7n13,
  8–10, 12, 34, 35, 35n49, 35n50,
  35n51, 43, 50, 52, 53n8, 54–56,
  54n12, 58–60, 63–66, 64n38,
  71, 74, 76, 77, 80–82, 85–88,
  95–109, 95n23, 98n30, 98n32,
  100n36, 101n37, 102n39,
  102n40, 103n41, 103n42,

107n51, 107n53, 108n55,
  111–115, 113n66, 118, 118n2,
  120–122, 120n6, 121n8, 122n9,
  124–131, 128n25, 133, 133n41,
  134, 135n45, 136–139, 136n49,
  141–147, 143n70, 147n82,
  150–152, 155, 158–163,
  159n10, 160n11, 163n23,
  163n24, 165, 168, 169,
  171–174, 176–179, 176n68,
  177n69, 178n75, 184, 187–189,
  191, 192, 195–197, 197n35,
  197n36, 198n38, 199–203,
  202n51, 203n52, 207–210,
  208n73, 209n75, 213–217,
  216n6

E
Eden, Anthony, 107, 107n53, 122, 142
Eisenhower administration, 4, 7–11,
  50, 70, 85, 87, 90, 117, 119,
  149, 152, 155, 156, 183, 184,
  194, 198, 213, 214, 217
Eisenhower, Dwight D., 2, 32, 49, 85,
  155, 183, 214

G
Generalissimo Jiang Jieshi, 1
Geneva Conference, 6, 85–115, 213
Geneva Negotiations, 63, 111, 156–169
Government of the Republic of China
  (ROC), 24n24, 63, 119, 121,
  130, 132

H
Hearst, 18, 22, 41, 67, 184
Ho Chi Minh, 86
House Committee of Un-American
  Activities, 36

Printed by Printforce, the Netherlands